JOSE GARCES
The Latin Road Home

JOSE GARCES
The Latin Road Home

Savoring the Foods of Ecuador, Spain, Cuba, Mexico, and Peru

photography by Jason Varney

Lake Isle Press
New York

Published by:
Lake Isle Press, Inc.
2095 Broadway, Suite 301
New York, NY 10023
(212) 273-0796
E-mail: lakeisle@earthlink.net

Distributed to the trade by:
National Book Network, Inc.
4501 Forbes Boulevard, Suite 200
Lanham, MD 20706
1(800) 462-6420
www.nbnbooks.com

Library of Congress Control Number: 2012939770
ISBN-13: 978-1-891105-49-4
ISBN-10: 1-891105-49-3

Book and cover design: Ellen Swandiak
Editors: Stephanie White, Jennifer Sit
Prop styling: Heather Chontos

This book is available at special sales discounts for bulk purchases as
premiums or special editions, including customized covers. For more
information, contact the publisher at (212) 273-0796 or by e-mail,
lakeisle@earthlink.net.

First edition
Printed in China
10 9 8 7 6 5 4 3 2

Cover photo: Hacienda Zuleta, Ecuador
www.haciendazuleta.com

Also by Jose Garces:
Latin Evolution (Lake Isle Press, 2008)

To my son, Andres.
This book will show you where you come from,
and I hope it inspires you to travel everywhere you
can—to love, to live, and to cook!

CONTENTS

ECUADOR

SPAIN

20

100

CUBA

164

MEXICO

218

PERU

292

ACKNOWLEDGMENTS

Miriam Backes—Thanks for capturing the crucial moments that have been near and dear to me and for bringing them back to life in the present. Frequently, we stumbled upon food memories that were largely gone, and you somehow managed to coax them out of my mind and bring them back, vividly. Many thanks for your patience with my hectic schedule. Your wealth of experience in the cookbook process added much needed efficiency to this entire project.

Andrew Sabin—It was a pleasure to work with you on this book. You were absolutely instrumental in bringing it all together. I still remember the day a few years back when we sat in the private dining room at Amada to take the very first steps. Then, and throughout, you were a terrific sounding board to think through the whole concept for the book, as well as to begin to pluck out some of the traditional recipes and menus. Thanks for your diligence through the testing process and the photo shoot. Your cooking experience and knowledge have truly been assets, and the dedication you showed to this project was tremendous.

Brooke Everett—My "Iron Assistant," you are the binding agent that holds the many disparate pieces of my life together and keeps them moving forward at a pace that astounds even me. Thank you,

Andrew Sabin, Brooke Everett, Jessica Mogardo, and Keith Raimondi

as ever, for your patience, your loyalty, your tremendous enthusiasm for what we do, and for always bringing your knowledge and talent to play when I need it most, especially in the creation of this book.

Jessica Mogardo—Thank you for lending your expertise in pastry and confections, and for being such an invaluable contributor to the photo shoot. Pastry is not my normal cup of tea, and your creations consistently—and deliciously—complement my vision.

Keith Raimondi—The tastings for your cocktail recipes were always my favorite tastings! You are truly a master of spirits. Thank you for rounding out the party menus with the perfect amount of party.

Jason Varney—Working with you during the photo shoot was a blast, despite spending several days in the back dining room of JG Domestic during construction! I've grown to appreciate and to love the shots, thanks to your vision and your eye for using natural light in photography. My family and I loved spending time with you in Ecuador as well. Traveling together and getting to know you was one of the best parts of making this book. You've really captured the essence of who I am, along with what this food means to me.

Clare Pelino—This book would not have happened without your support. Thanks for being so many critical things in my life: friend, advisor, publicist, literary agent, and now TV agent. It's been a great ride for the past ten years. Looking forward to the next ten, and beyond!

Hiroko Kiiffner —Your faith in this project was, in many ways, what got the job done. You've been one of my most powerful supporters from the very beginning, and your belief in me and in what I do is the pulse that drove this book forward to completion. I am grateful for your confidence, your capability, and your guidance.

Ellen Swandiak—You are a talented designer who really captured the spirit of the book and of each country on every page. Thank you.

Stephanie White & Jennifer Sit—You are an exceptional team, and your input, your effort, and your vision made this book a reality and made my thoughts, stories, and recipes jump off the page. Thanks for bringing your patience and your talents to this book.

To my family: Mamita Amada; my mom, Maggie; Beatriz; Olivia and Andres—I'd like to thank you all for your support and your love. Without it, many of my accomplishments, in my career and in my life, would never have come to be. You've all been my motivation all along, and every day, you inspire me to dig deeper and reach higher.

Garces Group—What a ride it's been! I couldn't have done any of this without the great team that surrounds me. I'd like to thank Melissa Scully, Terry Poyser, Julio Sanchez, Jon Friedman, Michael Fiorello, and all of the chefs and managers who keep the train rolling while I spend time on big projects like this one. Thank you for being consummate, exemplary professionals and for consistently excelling in the culinary and hospitality fields. Knowing I can depend on you pushes me to do more, and to do it better.

José Andrés—Thank you for your words, both in the foreword to this book and in our many interactions over the years. Your work has long been an inspiration to me, and I will continue to look to you for years to come as a true pioneer of our art.

Morimoto—Your brilliance on Iron Chef America never fails to astonish me. Your great understanding of flavor and technique has informed my cooking throughout the years, and I look forward to many more inspiring moments, on set and off.

Douglas Rodriguez, my good friend and mentor—You certainly have many cameos in this story! You played a key role in my development as a chef, as well as an adventurer. Thank you for your guidance and for your enthusiasm, as well as your generosity in sharing your gifts with me, then and now.

Hacienda Zuleta—I'd like to thank the Plaza family for opening up their farm to me and my family during our stay in Ecuador. It was truly an unforgettable experience!

In the long history of Spain, with the many cultures that have passed through, settled in, and come into contact with the Iberian Peninsula, you could easily argue that none is of greater importance to Spain than the Americas. Not the Romans nor the Visigoths, not the Muslims nor the Jewish people have had a greater or longer lasting impact on Spain. The Spanish Golden Age was ushered in by the discovery of the Americas and the Americas provided most of the wealth that fueled Spain's expansion and its cultural flowering. Everything—literature, art, music—benefitted from this relationship. Even the kitchen.

In fact, most of what we think of today as Spanish food, the iconic dishes of the Iberian peninsula, reflect the centuries-long exchange between Old World and New. *Tortilla de patatas*, *pisto Manchego*, *gambas al ajillo*, *gallina en pepitoria*, *arroz con leche*, even *chocolate con churros*, none of these classic Spanish dishes would exist if not for the potatoes, tomatoes, bell peppers, squash, chiles, vanilla, and cacao of the New World. Certainly versions of these recipes may have existed before the discovery of America but it was the addition of these new ingredients from the other side of the world that made them into what they are today. Imagine for a moment a Spain without the smokiness of pimenton. Or the Russian roulette of *pimientos de Padrón*, the little green sometimes spicy peppers that make an ideal tapa when fried in olive oil. Or the *pipas*, sunflower seeds, that so many Spanish snack on at sporting matches. Or gazpacho, the emblematic chilled tomato soup of southern Spain and its thicker, sauce-like cousin *salmorejo*. It is a Spain I would not want to live in!

The exchange between countries also went in the other direction. One needs only look at a Latin American cookbook to find techniques and recipes of Spanish origin. Terms like *sofrito*, *escabeche*, empanadas, chorizo, adobo, and more pepper the Latin American cooking lexicon. You even find versions of paella and Spanish rice throughout the region. Today, cooks in Latin America prepare dishes of chicken, pork, and beef, livestock that came over with the Spanish invaders and colonists. I personally cannot imagine a Mexico without *carnitas* made from pork or an Argentina without a *parillada* of beef. Those ingredients have been so thoroughly incorporated into the local cuisine that we tend to forget that there were no pigs, chickens, or cows in the Americas before contact with Spain. And it was not just livestock. Spaniards brought with them rice and sugar cane among other crops without which there would be no *arroz con gandules*, *gallo pinto*, *moros y cristianos*, rum, *piloncillo,* or *dulce de leche* cake.

To me this is what is most interesting about Jose Garces: as a cook and a person, he is a living embodiment of that exchange. Here you have an American, Chicago born and raised, with roots in Ecuador, who stayed in Spain soaking up all the flavors of my home country, studied and learned the Caribbean flavors of Cuba, the complex cooking of Mexico, and now Peru. Jose has opened restaurants that reflect all of who he is as a cook and a person, where he has been, and who he has dined with and worked for. His whole story is on the plate before you, a story full of love and passion for travel, cooking, and good food. With this book, home cooks can join Jose, one of America's most exciting chefs, on his journey back and forth across the Atlantic, cooking some of the best dishes from the Old World and New.

¡BUEN PROVECHO!
JOSÉ ANDRÉS

Mamita Amada is frying up a big batch of *empanadas de verde*, as she does whenever company comes. She's the matriarch of the Garces clan, my father's mother, and at ninety-one years old isn't getting any less particular about how things are done in her kitchen.

She peels and boils the bunch of green plantains herself, rices and kneads the starchy mush into a supple dough, rolls that out into small rounds, dollops those with *queso de Chone*, and forms them into dozens of tidy half-moons that she deep-fries in small batches in a big aluminum pot—all with remarkable speed and next to no mess. Meanwhile, culinary credentials notwithstanding, I stand by waiting, much as I always did as a child—watching my grandma work, savoring the toasty aroma of plantain dough sizzling in hot oil, and looking forward to that first bite of warm pastry, delicate and crispy on the outside, dense and gooey on the inside.

Yesterday was the big family reunion, a day of many relatives, eloquent speeches, and warm embraces. I'd invited some forty people from both sides of the family, four and five generations deep, to come together at a restaurant in Quito so that I could reconnect with them after having been gone for so long (fifteen years!)—and because I'd brought my wife, Beatriz, and our children, Olivia and Andres, to Ecuador to meet everyone. There was a celebratory meal and lots of gregarious fun, and between impromptu toasts (Tío Victor Hugo's words of congratulation and pride, welcome, and thankfulness were especially moving) and heartfelt welcomes from everyone, we felt honored and truly brought into the fold.

Now I'm here in Mamita Amada's kitchen thinking about yesterday and waiting for empanadas—my favorite. She finally gives me a job: holding a big ceramic serving platter. She piles it high with the finished pastries, golden brown and piping hot. Before we head into the dining room, she sets eight china cups on an old silver tray, pulls a pitcher out of the fridge, and pours into each cup about an inch of super-concentrated tar-black coffee, slow-brewed over the course of

the previous day. Then she tops up each cup with hot water from the kettle simmering on the stove, hoists the tray, and gives me the go-ahead, "¡Vamos, Josecito!"

We walk into the dining room and come upon a lively scene I'd never have pictured last time I was here. Seated around the long gleaming table, as they were way back then, are my dad's five sisters, their faces considerably softer and more deeply creased but beaming with joy, because now Beatriz, Olivia, and Andres are there, too.

Bea has been after me about this trip for years. I never disagreed with the idea in principle—of course I should bring her to Quito to meet my whole extended family and see where I spent a year living with my grandparents and going to school when I was seven years old; and naturally, now that we have two kids, there's all the more reason for a pilgrimage to the old country. The prospect had just made me a little uneasy.

My last visit, at age twenty-two, had been occasioned by sad circumstances: my maternal grandmother's passing. My older brother and I traveled from Chicago with my mom to see Abuelita in her final days, attend the funeral (at which Jorge and I were pallbearers), and be with my mom and her brothers and sisters and their kids through this time of mourning. We stayed for about a month, and of course grief is never easy, but I found the week in Quito after the funeral hard to get through. It was an endless circuit of family visits, trooping from one relative's home to the next, where round after round of coffee was sipped, the same stories were told and retold, and everybody just sat. Chalk it up to social awkwardness and emotional immaturity, or just being twenty-two and restless, but it drove me nuts. I had been reluctant to go back ever since.

But now here I am, a family man rather than a single guy, and a chef and restaurateur rather than a first-year culinary school student. The events of the previous day are sinking in more fully after a night's rest: I'd set out to throw a reunion and my relatives had transformed it into a real homecoming. I pull up a chair at the table next to Mamita Amada and she gives me a pat on the cheek and hands me one of the steaming cups of coffee. Across the table from us, Bea and Tía Magdalena are deep in conversation about her family's emigration from Cuba to the United States, while Olivia gives Tías Marta and Eulalia an animated account of her first-grade singing career, and four-year-old Andres works his charms on Tías Yolanda and Anna. Mamita Amada doles out the empanadas, putting a couple of pastries on each little plate and passing a dish of *encurtido* (pickled onion relish), the classic Ecuadorian accompaniment for cheese empanadas. Coffee is sipped, stories are told, and I just sit. How sweet it is.

And how beautiful Quito is—much more so than I'd remembered. Occupying a bowl-like valley high in the Andes, the metropolis creeps high up the valley's steep slopes before giving way to velvety green agriculture. Tucked into the city's miles and miles of modern South American sprawl is the Centro Historico (Old Town), a dense pocket of Spanish grandeur. Throughout the city, cosmopolitan Quiteños and indigenous folk from the countryside hustle and bustle along in the daily business of life. And behind them, what a skyline: eight cloud-piercing Andean peaks in sharp silhouette against a backdrop of celestial blue.

Then there are the food markets, which are fantastic. I especially enjoy the Mercado Santa Clara, where I spend an entire morning wandering the aisles, ogling the gorgeous produce, spices and dry goods, poultry, meat, and seafood. I stop and order a *jugo de tomate de árbol*—tree tomato juice. Tree tomatoes, as the name implies, grow on tall woody plants; the fruits range in color from yellowish to orange to purplish red and are shaped like small plum tomatoes with pointy tips. Peeled and puréed in a blender with water and sugar, *tomates de árbol* become a reddish orange beverage the consistency of pulpy orange juice. The first sip is a tangy, citrusy jolt that floods me with memories from way, way back when I was seven and my family lived with my mother's parents here in Quito and every day began with a little cup of fresh juice. Sometimes it was *tomate de árbol*, other times green juice from tiny orange *naranjillas*

or deep purple *jugo de mora* (Andean blackberries). I step back up to the counter. "Uno jugo de naranjilla y uno de mora"—for old time's sake.

Our week in Quito is a busy jumble of family gatherings and sightseeing, with one very special combination of the two, when Tío Pablo and Tía Liliana take us to El Panecillo, a high lookout point topped with a towering white statue of a winged Virgen de Quito. Tío Pablo is my mother's older brother and close confidant; she talks to him daily, long distance from Philadelphia. It's amazing to be here with him, taking in the 360-degree view of the city on this cloudless day, with massive Cotopaxi looming on the horizon in all its glacier-clad and volcanic glory. Below us is the city, above, a skyful of kites, and the wind and Andean panpipe music whistle all around us.

A few days later, I'm at an even higher altitude (10,000-plus feet above sea level) and the volcanoes are even closer. I'm sitting on horseback in a lush tranquil valley surrounded by cloud forest, and—as if it all weren't strange enough already—there is an Andean condor gliding soundlessly through the air overhead, its vast black wings spread impossibly wide. I'm staring up at the sky, utterly dumbstruck. Exactly why the condor has always fascinated me, I do not know—probably something to do with its mythic proportions, its iconic status in Ecuador, and the old folk tales my grandmas used to whisper to me at bedtime. These magnificent birds are increasingly rare, and to see one wheeling through the Andean stratosphere, here in this faraway place at the top of the world, feels like a vision—cosmic and unforgettable.

The condor refuge is part of an expansive estate where Bea and the kids and I are spending a serene several days not visiting relatives. A family-owned colonial-era ranch in the northern Sierra, Hacienda Zuleta is about two and a half hours up rough, twisty, mostly unmarked roads from Quito. And the spot we're in right now, watching the condor, is even more remote, about an hour's horseback ride away from the hacienda's verdant, sustainably managed farmland, across grassy plains, up past its mountainside trout hatcheries, and into a hidden valley.

Dinner that night at the hacienda is a bountiful spread of traditional Sierra dishes made with Zuleta-grown ingredients, and it is some of the finest Ecuadorian food I've ever had. The components are deeply familiar to me from my mother's and grandmothers' tables—quinoa and corn, potatoes and avocado, cream and cheese, chile and achiote—but here in the highlands, where these foods have been grown and cooked and savored for millennia, it all tastes more elemental, somehow.

I heave a happy sigh and look around the table at my family, all three of them digging in with great gusto. My heart swells with thankfulness and a long series of memories spools through my mind, a flickering reel of a great many other Latin meals I've savored at a great many other tables. Delicious.

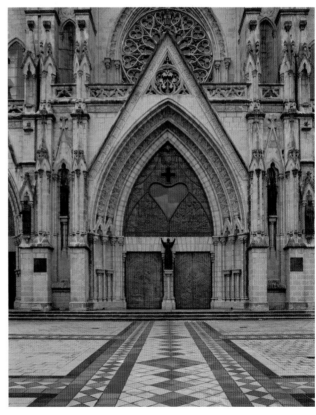

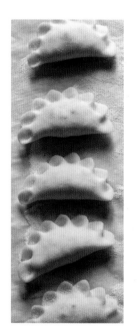

Five Latin food traditions have greatly influenced the course of my life, and this cookbook devotes a chapter to each one.

The starting point, naturally, is Ecuador, my ancestral homeland. Then there's Spain, where I spent a formative year right after culinary school. Next comes Cuba and the fortuitous intersection of my professional and personal paths. After that is Mexico, inspiration for the first restaurant concept I created. And, having recently been to Peru and had the pleasure of verifying its status as a gastronomic capital, I'm winding things up there—for now.

Each chapter offers four complete dinner menus, highlighting traditional dishes I'm fond of preparing and enjoying at home with friends and family. The last menu in each chapter is a more extensive spread, scaled for eight people (rather than four), and includes a cocktail and multiple courses as well as dessert—ideal for the kind of evening where the cooking is part of the party. I've shared numerous other favorite recipes in sidebars throughout the book.

My hope is that you will take pleasure in the entire process of making these meals: from reading the backstory to venturing into a Latin grocery for provisions; from tackling practicalities like planning and organizing to taking time out of your routine to prep components in advance; and from relishing the cooking itself to stepping back to admire the finished dishes on the table. And when you do sit down and dig in, I hope that you and your dining companions will partake not only of mighty fine food, but also a little *gastroturismo* right there at your table, savoring something of the places where I've found these dishes— the *fritada* from a sidewalk pushcart in Quito, *banderillas* at a *pintxo* bar in the Basque Country, *enchilado de langosta* at a Cuban family's *paladar* in Cienfuegos, *esquites* from a street vendor in Mexico City, *tiradito* in a beachfront *cevichería* in Lima, and so on. *¡Buen provecho y buen viaje!* Enjoy the meals and the journey!

ECUADOR

MENU 1

QUITO

Ceviche de Camarones | SHRIMP CEVICHE

Fritada | FRIED PORK

Las Cosas Finas | WARM HOMINY SALAD

MENU 2

SALINAS

Ceviche de Conchas | CLAM AND SEA BASS CEVICHE

Aguado de Gallina | CHICKEN AND RICE SOUP WITH ACHIOTE

Ensalada de Aguacate | AVOCADO SALAD

MENU 3

PORTOVIEJO

Ceviche de Atún | TUNA CEVICHE

Encocado de Pescado | CITRUS-MARINATED HALIBUT AND CALAMARI IN COCONUT BROTH

Ensalada de Habas | FAVA BEAN SALAD

MENU 4

CUENCA

Ceviche de Cangrejo | CRAB CEVICHE

Fanesca | SALT COD AND LEGUME CHOWDER

Llapingachos | GRIDDLED POTATO CAKES WITH QUESO FRESCO

Hongos con Ají | AJÍ MUSHROOMS WITH GINGER AND SAFFRON

Higos en Almíbar de Miel | FIGS IN HONEY SYRUP WITH GOAT CHEESE

ESSENTIALS | Ají PG 31 | Crunchy Things PG 44 | Empanadas PG 60 | Pan de Yuca PG 78
Crema de Quinoa PG 96

Raising three boys in mixed but mostly Irish and Polish neighborhoods on the northwest side of Chicago, my Ecuadorian-born parents did their level best to keep the family firmly rooted in our ethnic heritage. This became a real challenge once Jorge, Christian, and I were in grade school. Speaking Spanish at home fell by the wayside and we got on my mom's case about getting a better handle on English. As children of immigrants so often do, we grew intent on just being regular American kids.

To some extent, Ecuador stayed with us—literally: in any given year there would be extended visits from either of my grandmothers, one of my mom's sisters, and a steady stream of cousins passing through. Our connection to Ecuador as the family's homeland was also strongly reinforced by a yearlong stint living in Quito with Abuelita, Mom's mom, when I was about seven years old. But I didn't make the trip back again until about fifteen years later.

I realize now that the main way we stayed grounded in our culture was through food. The traditional dishes my mom mastered (with help from the visiting grandmas and aunts) and served up on a daily basis, ran the full gamut of Ecuadorian staples: *pan de almidón* and arepas, *locros* and *fritadas*, *humitas* and *quimbolitos* and empanadas, and, of course, *ceviche de camarones*.

When my dad's mom, Mamita Amada, came to stay, she would pretty much take over the kitchen. She has always been (and to my mind still is) the most serious cook in the family, and I'm sure Mom was happy to get a break from having to make all the meals in addition to working at a job outside our home. In any case, my grandma would really crank things up a notch, turning out a full Ecuadorian spread for every meal and plenty of baked goodies in between (I got to be a pretty chunky little kid). To this day, Mamita Amada is a force to be reckoned with. Now in her nineties, she still comes to visit, and she still holds sway in the kitchen. Her intensity and energy and sheer expertise are undeniable. She has been a great inspiration to me as a cook, and though I think I was always drawn to the frenetic environment of a busy kitchen, I was quite a bit older before I had the nerve to step up and help her out with any cooking.

When I was in third grade, I started giving my mom a hand in the kitchen. I'd get home from school at three-thirty in the afternoon and had about an hour to unwind before Mom walked in the door. From that point forward, it was a mad rush to get dinner on the table inside of an hour. My father would be home at five-thirty, so Mom was pressed for time to have the family meal happen right away—afterward she would need time to clean up the kitchen, get us kids ready for bed, and do all the other things that parents do in the evening to prepare for the next day.

"Okay, Josecito," she'd say, and that was my cue to get to work peeling potatoes and carrots, picking cilantro leaves off the stems, prepping whatever ingredients were involved in that night's meal. Four or five days out of most any week, our dinner was white rice accompanied by some sort of stew and *encurtido* (pickled onions). A favorite of mine was *carnitas con papas*: stew with tomatoes, onions, peppers, potatoes, and cubes of braised beef, finished with lots of cilantro. Sometimes we would make the sauce while the meat quick-cooked in a pressure cooker. (Today, I can be midbattle in Kitchen Stadium and the whistling sound of a pressure cooker still takes me back to the Chicago kitchen of my childhood.)

And that's how I first got to know my way around a kitchen. I would be on the far side of adolescence and a couple of years into community college before it occurred to me that cooking professionally was a sensible avenue to explore. I happened to notice that Kendall College's School of Culinary Arts was (at that time) just north of Foster Avenue Beach on Lake Michigan, where I was lifeguarding my way through a summer of major soul-searching. So on a bit of a lark I checked out the campus. As it turned out, everything about the place appealed to me, and I was very fortunate that the college took my interest seriously, accepting my application and providing a financial aid package that enabled me to enroll full time.

So I embarked on a career in cooking, but even then it was a few more years before I took a professional interest in the food I grew up eating. It would take another bout of soul searching, this one prompted by professional struggles, for me to find my way home, so to speak, and focus on Latin cuisine.

Through all the jobs I worked during and after culinary school, I amassed experience in a broad range of cuisines and styles, from Southwest American at Star Canyon in Texas to traditional Spanish at La Taberna del Alabardero in Andalucía; and once I moved to New York City, there was Greek at Molyvos, Hudson Valley cuisine at the Rainbow Room, and American regional at the Four Seasons. Then came Bolivar, a restaurant in midtown Manhattan where I got my first shot not only at an executive chef position, but also, since the menu was South American, at specializing in Latin cuisine. Unfortunately, it was an overly ambitious move—as grateful as I was for the opportunity, I was just not yet equipped to take the helm. Within six months business flagged and I was tactfully dismissed.

Facing this setback made me take a good hard look at my aspirations, and I emerged from these ruminations with a renewed commitment to forging a career in the restaurant business. I also resolved that from that point forward, I would have a specialty: Latin cuisine. It meant going back to square one and working my way up again from line cook, but that's exactly what I did. As luck would have it, that lowly rebound job was for chef-restaurateur Douglas Rodriguez, leader of the emerging *Nuevo Latino* cuisine. Between the courage of my convictions and a big helping of good fortune, I'd found my way straight to my mentor. Douglas put me firmly on the path toward success—first as his protégé, later as his collaborator, and ultimately on my own.

On the domestic front, getting married and starting a family has paved my way back to the dishes I loved as a kid. From the get-go, my wife Beatriz and I have enjoyed cooking together, especially on weekends, and we keep a lot of classic Ecuadorian food in the mix along with plenty of the Cuban dishes Beatriz grew up on. And in a turn of events that's been truly great for all of us, my mom has moved to Philadelphia and plays a major part in our home life, spending a lot of time with the kids—and she cooks!

And here we all are, sitting down together to enjoy the same dishes I grew up on. The Ecuadorian foods of my childhood will be part of my own children's experience—in a much bigger way than would have been possible day to day with the professions Bea and I are in. So we are at least one example that Ecuadorian traditions are being carried on, after all—in yet another big American city, with yet another Garces generation. Having my mom in our lives this way, having this beautiful continuity unfold, is something I am grateful for beyond words.

This chapter brings together some of my all-time favorite Ecuadorian dishes. I hope you will enjoy sharing these meals with your loved ones as I do with mine.

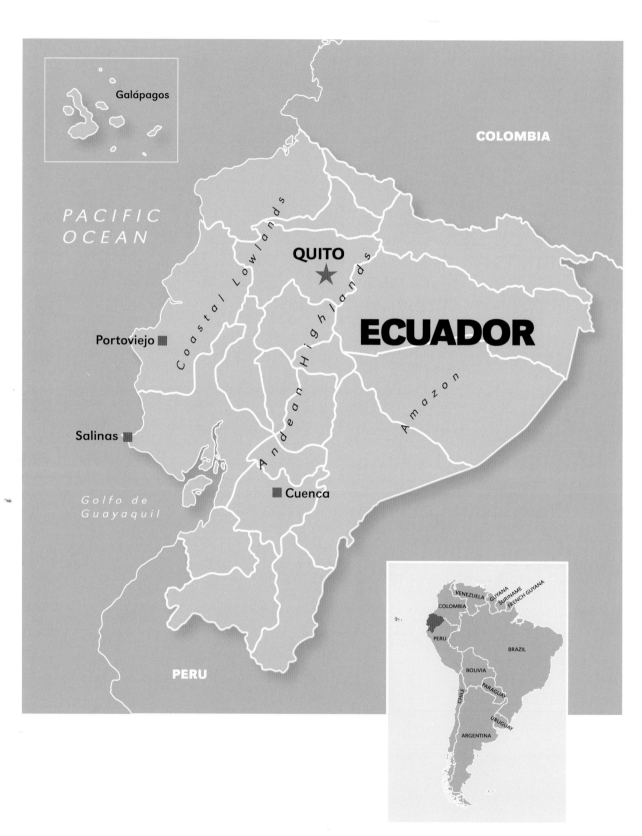

Galápagos

COLOMBIA

PACIFIC
OCEAN

Coastal Lowlands

QUITO
★

Andean Highlands

ECUADOR

Amazon

Portoviejo ■

Salinas ■

*Golfo de
Guayaquil*

Cuenca ■

PERU

VENEZUELA GUYANA SURINAME FRENCH GUYANA
COLOMBIA
PERU
BRAZIL
BOLIVIA
CHILE PARAGUAY
URUGUAY
ARGENTINA

QUICK INFO

LAND

• Located on the west coast of South America, straddling the earth's equator (*ecuador* in Spanish)

• One of the world's most biodiverse countries, encompassing coastal lowlands, Andean highlands, and Amazonian rainforest, as well as the Galápagos Islands (off the coast in the Pacific Ocean)

• Climate varies from tropical to subtropical, equatorial, and temperate, depending upon altitude, ocean currents, and other factors

PEOPLE

• Current population is approximately 14 million

• Ethnic groups include mestizo (mixed indigenous and white), indigenous Amerindian (40-plus different nations, including Quichua), *criollos* (Spanish and other European), Afro-Ecuadorian, and Asian

FOOD

• Generally hearty and starchy, especially in the highlands (*sierra*), where soups and stews frequently feature staples like potato, corn, cheese, and avocado; proteins include pork and cuy (guinea pig)

• Ceviche is common throughout the country; along the coast (*costa*) are a wider variety of dishes involving fresh fish and seafood, especially shrimp

• Other staple ingredients include plantains, yuca, and rice

• From the country's subtropical and tropical areas come various fruits such as bananas, mangos, and coconuts; peanuts are indigenous to the southern rainforest

---

500 CE
Diverse pre-Inca ancient cultures settle the region as early as 500 CE.

15TH CENTURY CE
The Incan empire expands northward into the region and rules for shortly over a century.

1532 CE
Spanish conquistador Francisco Pizarro arrives, defeating an Incan empire already weakened by civil war and begins a colonial period that lasts until the 1820s.

18TH CENTURY CE
Under colonial rule, indigenous people (and those of mixed Spanish and indigenous descent, the mestizos) are subjected to forced labor. Owners of cocoa and sugar plantations in the northwest import African slaves.

1830 CE
Ecuador becomes a fully independent nation.

AJÍ

In Ecuador, paired dishes of *ají*—one green (mild), one red (spicy)—are mealtime fixtures, as essential and ubiquitous as shakers of salt and pepper are here in the States.

Ají (which translates simply as "chile" but is used as a catchall term both for the peppers and the sauce made from them) functions more like a seasoning than a condiment, with little spoons perched in the small bowls, always at the ready to deliver *ajícito*, "a little something chile," to the plate. Foods are generally not particularly spicy, and *ají* is each diner's means of adding only as much heat as they like, along with a touch of acid and herbs. Rarely does any plate go un-*ají'd*—from ceviches to soups, breads to main courses, and, most important, all those starchy sides: potatoes, rice, plantains, bread. I love the way that *ajícito* wakes things up, heightening every flavor in its path.

Ají is typically made fresh, from serrano-like chiles: mild unripe green ones for the mellower sauce; ripe and red and thus hotter ones for the *picante*. Here in the States, green serranos and milder jalapeños are pretty easy to come by, but ripe red serranos are not. Red Fresno chiles, widely available in Latin grocers, make a good substitute. *(Recipe follows.)*

AJÍ COSTEÑO
ECUADORIAN HOT SAUCE

Here is a recipe for a spicy red *ají* in the light style of those typically made on the coast (*la costeña*). To turn up the heat, use the whole red Fresno chile. Note that it's important to chop the vegetables finely even though they're going into a food processor; otherwise your sauce will be too watery. Store it in a sealed container in the refrigerator, and it will keep for weeks. MAKES 1 CUP

4	red Fresno chiles, seeds and ribs removed, finely diced
1/2	plum tomato, finely diced
1/4	Spanish onion, finely diced
2	scallions (white and green parts), finely chopped
2 Tbsp	minced fresh flat-leaf parsley
2 Tbsp	minced fresh cilantro
2 Tbsp	distilled white vinegar
2 Tbsp	freshly squeezed lime juice
1 Tbsp	extra virgin olive oil
1/2 tsp	agave nectar (see page 72)
	Kosher salt

Combine all the ingredients in a bowl except for the salt and mix well. Remove half of the vegetables and set aside in a separate bowl. Pulse the remaining half in a food processor only until the vegetables are finely chopped; it should not be a smooth sauce. Fold in the reserved vegetables. Season the sauce to taste with salt. Chill before using.

QUITO

Ceviche de Camarones | SHRIMP CEVICHE

Fritada | FRIED PORK

Las Cosas Finas | WARM HOMINY SALAD

It seems only fitting that the first menu in this book should feature two of my top candidates for national dish of Ecuador: shrimp ceviche and *fritada* (fried pork with hominy). Both are mainstays of home cooking and popular street foods, and both rank high on my list of all-time favorite things to eat.

Though naturally at its very best and most abundant along the coast, fresh shrimp is also in steady supply in metropolitan areas (even at high elevations like Quito, nearly two miles above sea level), so *ceviche de camarones* is enjoyed much more widely than you might expect. (I do tend to steer clear of it in more remote areas, where freshness can become pretty questionable.) Whatever the altitude, and whether it's being served on a dinner table or sold at a street stand, the shrimp in Ecuador is traditionally boiled then marinated in lime juice (not just marinated raw, as is customary elsewhere). The typical sauce is a distinctly Ecuadorian combination of ketchup, citrus juices, chiles, cilantro, and salt. Then there are the assorted garnishes—my beloved crunchy things (pages 44 to 51), from popcorn to corn nuts to toasted favas —which are also uniquely Ecuadorian and always on hand alongside the ever-present *ají* chile sauce (page 31).

My mom, like most Ecuadorian cooks, has always served *ceviche de camarones* at family gatherings and celebrations. Throughout my childhood in Chicago, there wasn't a Garces summer barbecue that didn't start with shrimp ceviche. But my fondest memories of eating shrimp ceviche are from more ordinary occasions. My dad and I did the food shopping on Saturday mornings, and the neighborhood fishmonger was the last stop on our route. Mom would mix up some ceviche sauce while Dad and I were out, and minutes after we walked in the door the fresh shrimp we'd just bought would be transformed into shrimp ceviche. Some Ecuadorian cooks marinate their shrimp for an hour or even all day long, but I learned from my mom that what really makes the freshness and the flavors sing is to be quick about poaching and dressing the shrimp. There we'd sit at the kitchen table, my dad and mom and my two brothers and I, grocery bags all around us, eating the most refreshing midday snack imaginable. It was a taste of the ocean and of Ecuador there in the American Midwest, and it was delicious.

By contrast, and more in keeping with the general character of Ecuadorian cooking, *fritada* (Andean-style fried pork) is rich and hearty and fortifying. A classic dish with creole roots going back to the conquistadors, *fritada* (also known as *chicharrón* in some areas) is a savory home-cooked specialty served with a variety of tasty trimmings. It's also sold from stands, carts, and roadside shacks throughout much of Ecuador. My mom has always paired *fritada* with a hominy salad that she calls *las cosas finas*, "the fine things." I recently found out that this rather poetic turn of phrase is a common term Ecuadorians use to refer collectively to the various accompaniments for *fritada*, which can include potatoes and yuca.

Street vendors call the whole *fritada*-and-hominy combo *mote*, which means hominy but communicates much more than that—a warm little packet containing a mix of hominy, carrots, peas, cilantro, maybe some chickpeas, all topped with luscious *fritada*. The very thought of *mote* takes me back to the year my family spent in Quito when I was a young boy of about seven. We lived with my maternal grandmother, Abuelita, and her house was across the street from a city park where my brothers and I would spend afternoons playing soccer, shooting marbles, and generally running wild with the neighborhood kids. Safety wasn't a concern, and having the freedom to be on our own for hours on end was exhilarating. I even had a little pocket money for buying snacks and drinks from street vendors and various stands in the park. My favorite was the roving "*mote* lady," and we could always hear her coming from a ways off: "¡MOTE! MOTE! MOTE!" she'd holler at the top of her lungs, and we kids would all come running. We'd hand over a few coins apiece, the *mote* lady would hand us each a plastic bag that was wrapped in a piece of parchment and had a plastic spoon sticking out, and we'd gobble up the *mote* then and there on the dusty street, maybe with a little *ají*. When we'd scooped every last savory morsel out of the little bag we'd take off, dashing back to resume our adventures.

I enjoyed a fantastic helping of *mote* at the Santa Clara market in Quito last time I was there. It was supremely satisfying to find that it remains virtually identical to what I remember from when I was a little kid.

Stateside, I still adore my mom's *fritada con las cosas finas*, which she continues to make for me and my family now and then. The recipe I'm sharing with you here I only recently learned from her, and it involves a one-pot braising-frying method of cooking the pork that is traditional and downright brilliant. One pot, tons of flavor.

P. 38 Ceviche de Camarones

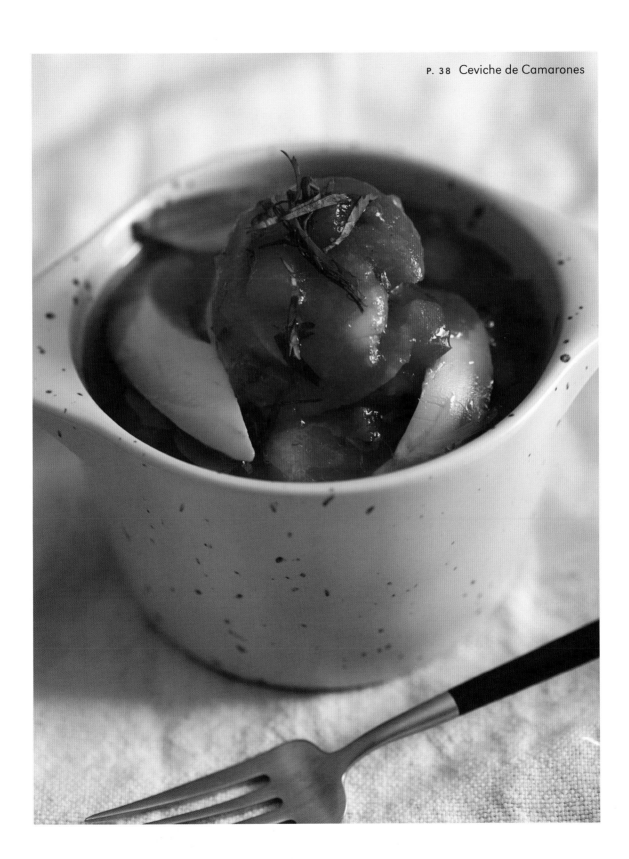

CEVICHE DE CAMARONES

SHRIMP CEVICHE

Freshness is essential for all of the ingredients in this quickly poached and briefly marinated ceviche—first and foremost the shrimp (don't bother with frozen; they just don't have the right flavor and texture), but also the ingredients for the sauce and the garnish. Only if all are pristinely fresh will your ceviche really sing. If you like, you can butterfly the shrimp (split them lengthwise down the back) to create more surface area to cover with the delicious sauce. (See photo, page 37) SERVES 4

POACHED SHRIMP

1 gallon	water
3 Tbsp	freshly squeezed lemon juice
2	cloves garlic, crushed
3 Tbsp	kosher salt
1 lb	fresh large peeled and deveined shrimp, tails removed

ECUADORIAN CEVICHE SAUCE

2	plum tomatoes, blanched and peeled
1/2	red Fresno chile, blanched and peeled, seeds and ribs removed
1/2 cup	freshly squeezed orange juice
2 Tbsp	freshly squeezed lime juice
2 Tbsp	tomato juice
1 Tbsp	ketchup
1 Tbsp	chopped fresh cilantro
1 Tbsp	honey
2 Tbsp	extra virgin olive oil
	Kosher salt

TO SERVE

1	plum tomato, diced small
1/4	red onion, finely diced
1	small jalapeño chile, finely diced
3	scallions (green tops only), thinly sliced on the diagonal
2 Tbsp	minced fresh cilantro, plus more for garnish
	Kosher salt
1	avocado, sliced
	Ají Costeño (page 33)
	Spicy Popcorn (page 46)

Prepare an ice bath in a large bowl. Line a baking sheet with several layers of paper towels.

TO POACH THE SHRIMP, combine the water, lemon juice, garlic, and salt in a saucepan and bring to a boil over high heat. Add the shrimp and cook until just firm, about 90 seconds. Use a slotted spoon to transfer the shrimp to the ice bath to chill thoroughly, about 1 minute. Drain the shrimp and spread them on the paper towels to dry. Refrigerate in an airtight container until needed, up to 2 days.

TO MAKE THE SAUCE, combine the tomatoes, chile, orange, lime, and tomato juices, ketchup, cilantro, and honey in a blender and purée on high speed until very smooth. With the machine running, slowly add the oil in a thin stream and continue to purée until the sauce is emulsified. Season to taste with salt.

TO SERVE THE CEVICHE, combine the chilled shrimp with the ceviche sauce in a bowl and let the shrimp marinate for 5 minutes. Add the diced tomato, red onion, jalapeño, scallions, and cilantro. Mix well and season to taste with salt. Divide the ceviche among four glasses or small bowls, garnish with the avocado slices and additional cilantro, and serve immediately with ají and popcorn on the side.

FRITADA

FRIED PORK

Straight from my mom, this ingenious preparation starts out a braise and ends up a fry. Cooking the pork in a mixture of stock and oil gets the meat tender and juicy throughout. Then, when all the stock that hasn't absorbed into the meat eventually evaporates, all that's left in the pot is the oil (which is now infused with porky flavor and all the seasonings from the rub) so the meat crisps up on the outside and the final result is succulent and tasty. SERVES 4

1/4 cup	kosher salt
2 Tbsp	freshly ground black pepper
2 Tbsp	ground cumin
2 Tbsp	garlic powder
1 1/2 lb	boneless pork shoulder, cut into about 12 (2 by 3-inch) chunks
1 lb	pork belly, cut into bite-size (1/2 by 1/2-inch) chunks
2 cups + 2 Tbsp	vegetable oil
1	Spanish onion, chopped
4	cloves garlic, chopped
2 cups	Chicken Stock (page 362)
	Kosher salt and freshly ground black pepper
	Warm Hominy Salad (recipe follows), for serving
	Ají Costeño (page 33), for serving

Combine the salt, black pepper, cumin, and garlic powder, mix well, and rub the mixture all over the pork shoulder and pork belly, coating evenly. In a large, straight-sided skillet, heat 2 tablespoons of the oil over medium-high heat and sear the pork until it is well browned, 3 to 5 minutes per side. Lift the pork out of the pan and set aside.

Add the onion and garlic to the oil and cook until translucent, about 10 minutes.

Pour in the stock and the remaining 2 cups oil, return the pork to the pan, and bring the mixture to a boil. Lower the heat to medium-low and simmer until the stock has evaporated and the pork is tender (simmering only in the oil), about 2 hours.

Lift the pork out of the oil and set it aside. Strain the oil into a clean sauté pan, heat it over medium-high heat, and fry the pork until crispy, 2 to 3 minutes per side. Lift the pork out of the oil and chop it coarsely. Mix the chopped pork with the hominy salad and serve with ají on the side.

LAS COSAS FINAS

WARM HOMINY SALAD

When my mom makes this dish in the springtime, she uses fresh garbanzo and fava beans as well as the English peas. If you spy either or both of them at your local farmers' market or Latin grocery, snap them up and add them to the mix; shucking, blanching, and peeling favas is a bit of a hassle, but they are fine things (*cosas finas*), for sure. English peas are often available in supermarkets year-round; note that when peas are in season, the pea pods tend to produce more peas per pod and the peas themselves are often larger, so you may not need to buy the full 2 pounds called for. Canned hominy is stocked in most supermarkets. SERVES 4

	Kosher salt
2 lb	fresh English peas, shelled
2 cups	canned hominy, drained and rinsed (see Sources)
1	jumbo carrot, peeled and finely diced
1/2	red onion, finely diced
1 Tbsp	minced fresh cilantro
2 or 3	cloves garlic, minced
6 Tbsp	extra virgin olive oil
2 Tbsp	freshly squeezed lime juice (about 2 limes)

TO PREPARE THE PEAS, bring a saucepan of generously salted water to a boil and prepare an ice bath in a large bowl. Cook the peas in the boiling water just until tender, 2 to 3 minutes. Drain and immediately transfer them to the ice bath to cool. Drain and set aside.

Combine the peas, hominy, carrot, onion, and cilantro in a large bowl and mix well. Stir in the garlic, oil, and lime juice and season to taste with salt.

CRUNCHY THINGS

If there is one thing Ecuadorian cuisine is famous for, it is the tradition of serving popcorn with shrimp ceviche. Less well known are the numerous other crunchy things, as I like to call them, that Ecuadorians pair with all sorts of ceviche and also enjoy as snacks.

I harbor a passion for crunchy things, so the amazing selection displayed at Quito's Mercado Santa Clara was cause for some real excitement. In addition to fruits and vegetables, seafood, and plenty of ceviche, this metropolitan market has stall after stall devoted to toasted dried fava beans (*habas*), plantain chips (*chifles*), toasted corn nuts (*tostaditos*), and all manner of other crunchy things. Clearly, Quiteños eat a lot of crunchy things. This stands to reason since high altitude notwithstanding, many of these folks consume ceviche on a daily basis.

The affinity for crunchy things with ceviche, and especially the practice of mixing them together in the same dish, is not necessarily shared or even respected elsewhere in South America. (Peruvians have been known to scoff.) My less-than-impartial take on the pairing is this: the fish or shellfish in a ceviche is fairly soft and the proteins are further broken down by the acidity of the marinade; introducing the crunchy, salty element provides a textural counterpoint to both the fleshiness of the seafood and the acidity of the marinade, and this creates a deliciously harmonious balance of textures and flavors. *(Recipes follow.)*

CANGUIL

SPICY POPCORN

It is distinctly Ecuadorian to serve popcorn with ceviche (especially shrimp ceviche); it's also often used as a garnish for soups. As with other "crunchy things," *canguil* **makes a terrific cocktail snack, especially with cold beer.** SERVES 4 AS GARNISH

1 cup	unsalted freshly popped popcorn, kept warm
1/4 tsp	kosher salt
1/4 tsp	granulated sugar
1/4 tsp	cayenne pepper
	Grated zest of 1/2 lime
2 Tbsp	unsalted butter, melted
	Ají Costeño (page 33), for serving

Combine the popcorn in a bowl with the salt, sugar, cayenne, lime zest, and butter and toss to coat. Keep the popcorn in an airtight container until needed, up to 1 day. Serve with any ceviche with ají on the side.

CHIFLES

PLANTAIN CHIPS

Sliced green plantains oxidize and turn brown very quickly, so you need to get them right into the oil. If you don't quite have the nerve to slice them directly into the hot oil, you can slice them (using a mandoline) onto a plate and immediately transfer the slices to the oil with a slotted spoon. MAKES ABOUT 50 CHIPS

8 cups	vegetable oil, for frying
1	green plantain, peeled (see page 67)
	Kosher salt
	Ají Costeño (page 33), for serving

Heat the oil to 375°F in a stockpot, using a candy or deep-fry thermometer to monitor the temperature. Line a baking sheet with parchment paper.

Use a Japanese mandoline to slice the plantain into thin rounds (about 1/16-inch-thick) directly into the hot oil.

Carefully stir the plantains in the hot oil with a slotted spoon to ensure even cooking.

Fry the chips until they are golden and crispy, 3 to 4 minutes. Use a slotted spoon to carefully transfer the chifles from the oil to the paper-lined baking sheet and season them to taste with salt. Serve with ají. Once cooled, the chips can be stored in an airtight container for 4 to 5 days.

TOSTADITOS

TOASTED CORN NUTS AND FAVA BEANS

Corn nuts (oil-roasted or deep-fried kernels of various types of South American corn) are crunchy on the outside and dry and almost cracker-like on the inside. Dried favas are crispy, nutty, and very savory; they come already toasted and their flavor deepens when you gently retoast them. I've added thyme to the mix, which adds a nice herbal note. Leftover *tostaditos* keep well for up to 3 days in an airtight container lined with paper towels. SERVES 4

2 Tbsp	unsalted butter
1 tsp	minced garlic (1 clove)
1 cup	unsalted corn nuts (see Sources)
1 cup	split and dried fava beans (see Sources)
2 tsp	minced fresh thyme
	Kosher salt

Melt the butter in a large stainless-steel sauté pan over medium heat. Add the garlic, corn nuts, and fava beans and cook, stirring often, until the garlic is very lightly toasted, 2 to 3 minutes. Transfer the toasted kernels and beans to a bowl, toss with fresh thyme, and season to taste with salt before serving.

SALINAS

Ceviche de Conchas | CLAM AND SEA BASS CEVICHE

Aguado de Gallina | CHICKEN AND RICE SOUP WITH ACHIOTE

Ensalada de Aguacate | AVOCADO SALAD

When I was twenty-two, my older brother, Jorge, and I went back to Ecuador for an extended visit. We traveled around the country with our paternal grandmother, Mamita Amada, visiting relatives by bus. Up and down through Andean terrain, giant rickety coaches lurched through miles of hairpin switchbacks. I'll never forget the sensation of the bus tilting out over the towering cliffs, treating us to views of sheer drops that were both gorgeous and terrifying. Mamita Amada and the other locals were unfazed by the wild ride. They also seemed not to notice as we sped past more than one overturned bus.

Although getting from place to place was a little harrowing, the visits in between were great. And the time we spent at my Tía Yolanda and Tío Carlos's house in Salinas, on the coast, was flat-out awesome. Salinas is a major surfing town, with big Pacific waves that really pack a wallop. Jorge and my uncle and I rolled out of our beds and straight down to the beach every morning for hours of swimming and body surfing. Once we'd finally had enough good rides and punishing wipeouts, we'd head to the beachfront seafood shack for a few helpings of Tío Carlos's favorite morning snack: black clam ceviche.

A *concha negra* connoisseur to his dying day (literally, but that's another story), my uncle turned me on to the glory of black clams on our first day in Salinas, and I got right away what he loved about them. Black clams are very tender, with an incredibly full flavor and a sweet, rich earthiness unlike any other shellfish. I've heard that this extraordinary flavor, along with the murky tinge to their liquor, is a sort of terroir, embodying the mangrove swamps where the clams are harvested.

My uncle would wash the clams down with a bottle or two of Pilsener (see page 82), the national brew of Ecuador. For me and Jorge, it was a little early in the day for beer, but Tío Carlos had the combo right for sure. Ceviche and beer is one of the world's best food and beverage pairings.

As good as it is for breakfast (in coastal areas of Latin America, ceviche of all kinds is standard breakfast fare), in this menu *ceviche de conchas* makes a great starter. Cooked middlenecks and some diced sea bass stand in for the black clam ceviche I remember; an approximation of the flavors and textures of the "real thing," which is nearly impossible to recreate so far from the Ecuadorian coast. The clean, fresh flavors are a nice prelude to the hearty chicken-and-rice soup that's a lot like the ones my mom would make on many a weeknight when I was growing up. Complementing both the ceviche and the *aguado* is a simple avocado salad, some form of which is almost always on the Ecuadorian dinner table.

CEVICHE DE CONCHAS

CLAM AND SEA BASS CEVICHE

Here the clams are lightly steamed, just long enough to make them pop open, so you are freed of the laborious task of shucking. I've been happy to find that good-quality fresh black clams have recently become more widely available here in the States, so it's worth checking to see if your fishmonger has a good source. They come from Ecuador, Peru (where they're also a national favorite), and sometimes Chile. SERVES 4

40	fresh clams (preferably middlenecks), scrubbed
1	fresh bay leaf
1 cup	dry white wine
1/2 lb	fresh boneless, skinless sea bass fillet, diced
1/2	red onion, finely diced
2 Tbsp	extra virgin olive oil
1/4 cup	bottled clam juice
	Grated zest of 2 limes
	Juice of 4 limes
1	jalapeño chile, minced
	Kosher salt
1	plum tomato, finely diced
2 Tbsp	chopped fresh cilantro
2 Tbsp	minced chives
	Plantain chips (page 48), for garnish
	Ají Costeño (page 33), for serving

Combine the clams, bay leaf, and white wine in a large saucepan and set over high heat. Cover the pan and steam the clams until they open, 3 to 5 minutes. Take the pan off of the heat and allow the clams to cool briefly. Discard any that don't open.

Remove the clam meat from the shells and transfer it to a bowl. Add the sea bass, onion, oil, clam juice, and the lime zest and juice. Add a little jalapeño, season lightly with salt, mix well, and set the ceviche in the refrigerator to marinate for 30 minutes.

Fold in the tomato, cilantro, and chives. Season again to taste with more jalapeño and salt. Divide the ceviche among four glasses, garnish each with plantain chips, and serve immediately with ají on the side.

AGUADO DE GALLINA

CHICKEN AND RICE SOUP WITH ACHIOTE

This kind of chicken and rice dish is typical in Latin home cooking, though the name *aguado* **(meaning "watery") usually implies something soupier than this particular version, which is more of a hearty stew. Made from achiote (***annatto***) seeds, achiote paste is a deep reddish-brown and often comes in large blocks; it lends robust color and flavor to many Ecuadorian dishes.** SERVES 4

3 lb	bone-in, skin-on chicken pieces (preferably legs and thighs)
	Kosher salt and freshly ground black pepper
2 Tbsp	vegetable oil
1	Spanish onion, chopped
2 Tbsp	minced garlic (4 to 6 cloves)
1	red bell pepper, diced
2 Tbsp	whole cumin seeds, toasted (see page 368) and ground
2 Tbsp	achiote paste (see Sources)
1 tsp	Spanish smoked hot paprika
2 Tbsp	tomato paste
1 1/2 qts	Chicken Stock (page 362)
2	fresh bay leaves
3	large plum tomatoes, diced
1 cup	long-grain white rice
2 lb	russet potatoes, peeled and diced small (4 cups)
1	large carrot, peeled and diced small
1 lb	fresh English peas, shelled and blanched (1 cup)
1 Tbsp	minced fresh oregano, or 1/2 tsp dried oregano
2 Tbsp	minced fresh flat-leaf parsley
2 Tbsp	minced fresh cilantro
	Ají Costeño (page 33), for serving

Generously season the chicken with salt and pepper. Heat the oil in a large cast-iron skillet or Dutch oven over high heat and sear the chicken in batches until skin is crispy and golden brown, about 2 minutes per side. Transfer the chicken to a plate.

Lower the heat to medium, add the onion, garlic, and bell pepper to the skillet and cook, stirring often, until the vegetables are translucent, about 10 minutes. Add the cumin, achiote paste, paprika, and tomato paste and cook, stirring constantly, for 3 to 5 minutes. Return the chicken to the pan, add the stock and bay leaves, and bring to a low boil over medium-high heat. Stir in the tomatoes and cook about 5 minutes.

Add the rice, potatoes, and carrot and return to a simmer. Cook, covered, until the chicken is tender and falling off the bone and the rice is fully cooked, about 40 minutes.

Stir in the peas, oregano, parsley, and cilantro and season to taste with salt and pepper. Serve immediately with ají.

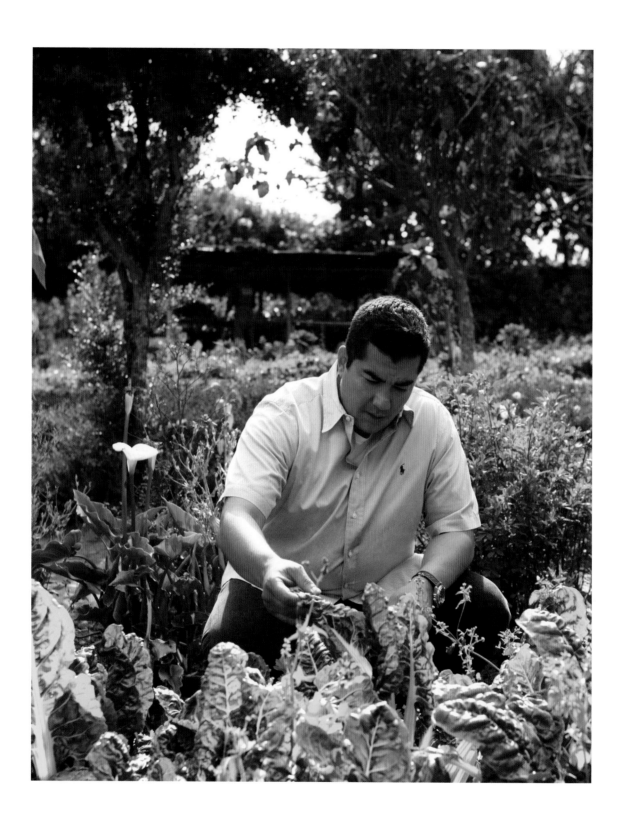

ENSALADA DE AGUACATE

AVOCADO SALAD

Avocado is a frequent accompaniment in Ecuadorian cooking, and it's especially common as a garnish for soups. On this menu, it's incorporated into a crisp, refreshing salad that complements the sparkling flavors and delicate textures of the ceviche and counterbalances the decidedly substantial stew. SERVES 4

1	romaine lettuce heart, sliced crosswise into thin ribbons
2	plum tomatoes, diced small
1	jalapeño chile, seeds and ribs removed, minced
2 Tbsp	minced fresh flat-leaf parsley
2 Tbsp	minced fresh cilantro
1/4 cup	freshly squeezed lemon juice (about 2 lemons)
1/4 cup	extra virgin olive oil
	Kosher salt and freshly ground black pepper
2	large hard-boiled eggs, peeled and quartered
4	avocados, sliced lengthwise into thin wedges
	Ají Costeño (page 33), for serving

Combine the romaine, tomatoes, jalapeño, parsley, and cilantro in a bowl. In a separate bowl, gently mix together the lemon juice and oil. Add it to the salad and toss to lightly dress. Season to taste with salt and pepper. Divide the salad among four plates, top each with egg and avocado wedges, and serve immediately with ají on the side.

EMPANADAS

Empanadas (from the Spanish *empanar*, "to fill") are an expansive food category unto themselves, with various forms and fillings throughout and beyond Latin countries and cultures. Within Ecuador, there are a number of different types of traditional empanadas—a wide assortment of doughs enveloping an even wider range of fillings, mostly savory.

For me, empanadas, maybe more than any other food, are all about family. This is an easy thing to say, cliché even, I know. But it's something I say in dead earnest. Food's a big thing in my family, and there is no food that we are more ritualistically devoted to than empanadas—two kinds in particular: Mom's *empanadas de viento* and Mamita Amada's *empanadas de verde*.

My mom has always made fantastic *empanadas de viento*, fried empanadas with a flour-based dough and cheese filling. The shell gets all bubbly and crispy on the outside when it fries, then it gets sprinkled with sugar, which makes it an even more heavenly vehicle for the savory, gooey cheese filling. Back when I was a kid, Mom would always make them on weekends, when she had more time to spend mixing up the dough and letting it rest. When she'd get to the frying step, the smell that filled the place was beyond appetizing. Typically, my brothers and my dad and I would be in the other room watching a Cubs or Bears game. Some of my fondest, if somewhat guilty, memories are of the four of us guys yelling at the TV between mouthfuls of freshly fried *empanadas de viento*.

My grandma's specialty is *empanadas de verde*. She may be on the far side of ninety, but no one can turn out green plantain empanadas like Mamita Amada can. Not only that, but she takes her show on the road: when she comes to call, this is a lady who arrives at your door with a tray of empanadas, ready to fry. Why? Because there can be no sitting and chatting without empanadas and coffee. It's a strict social code. Say she's staying with her sister in Peekskill and

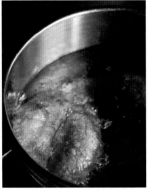

the two of them come down to Philly for the day to see me , Beatriz, and the kids: *empanadas de verde* for everyone. Or maybe, like one recent summer, there's a huge family gathering at my aunt's house in Ecuador: *empanadas de verde* for the whole gang. All crispy, fried outside and oozy cheese (or savory chicken or beef) inside, her empanadas are always a huge hit, and she always serves them with *encurtido de cebolla*, a delicious pickled onion condiment. I have been known to take down as many as four or five *empanadas de verde* in a single sitting. (Do not try this at home, kids: the eating part is bliss; the bellyache and catatonic stupor that soon follow, not so much).

I'm always amazed to watch Mamita Amada work, cranking out twenty or thirty of these beauties at a clip. There's a trick to getting the dough right, and even though I'd seen and even helped her make them countless times growing up, it eluded me for years. Finally, once when she was visiting us in Philly, I brought her into the kitchen at Alma de Cuba, where I was working on several different types of empanadas. She showed me, step by step, the techniques for boiling the plantains, ricing them, and then deliberately overworking the riced plantains to put their natural starches to work, cohering into a soft, malleable, elastic dough. No flour, no butter, no shortenings. Just boiled green plantains and a little salt. How beautiful is that? On the scale of big revelations in my cooking career, it's way up there. Amada's Empanada is a permanent item on the menu at Amada (my first restaurant—named for my grandma, of course); it's one small way I pay homage to the undisputed master of *empanadas de verde*.

Here are three of my favorite recipes for fried empanadas: one based on my mom's *de viento*, another adapted from my grandma's *de verde*, and a third using a traditional *arepa* (corn flour) dough. Feel free to mix and match the various fillings. Only the empanadas with the flour-based dough and cheese filling freeze well: the others are best eaten the day they're made. *(Recipes follow.)*

P. 64 Empanadas de Viento

P. 66 Empanadas de Verde con Pollo

P. 68 Empanadas de Morocho con Picadillo

EMPANADAS DE VIENTO

EMPANADAS WITH QUESO FRESCO

The dough must rest properly and has to be rolled out thinly to be workable, but once you get it down, this is an easy dough to handle. When forming the empanadas, make sure the edges are well sealed so they don't leak while frying. You can roll and crimp the edges a few times to help ensure that they're closed up tightly. Fully formed *empanadas de viento* can be frozen, wrapped tightly in plastic and foil, for up to 2 months; thaw in the refrigerator before frying. The dough can be refrigerated for up to 1 day. MAKES 12 EMPANADAS

DOUGH

2 cups	all-purpose flour, sifted
1 tsp	kosher salt
2 Tbsp	granulated sugar
1/2 cup	vegetable shortening
1	large egg yolk
1/2 cup	cold water

EMPANADAS

1/4 lb	queso fresco, grated (2 cups)
2 quarts	vegetable oil, for frying
1/4 cup	granulated sugar, for sprinkling
	Pickled Onions (recipe follows), for serving
	Ají Costeño (page 33), for serving

TO MAKE THE DOUGH, sift the flour, salt, and sugar together in a bowl. Use a pastry blender to cut the vegetable shortening into the dry ingredients until it is fully incorporated. Add the egg yolk and mix well. Adding 2 or 3 tablespoons at a time, knead in the water with your hands until a smooth dough forms. Pat the dough into a round, flat disk and wrap it tightly in plastic wrap. Refrigerate it for at least 1 hour or up to 1 day before making the empanadas.

TO ASSEMBLE THE EMPANADAS, divide the chilled dough into a dozen 1-inch balls. Using a manual tortilla press, a rolling pin, or the heel of your hand, press each dough ball into a circle about 1/8-inch thick and about 6 inches in diameter. Mound about 2 tablespoons of cheese in the center of each round and fold the dough over to form a half-moon. Use a dinner fork to crimp the outer edge. Alternatively, use a plastic empanada press from a Latin market.

TO COOK THE EMPANADAS, heat the oil to 350°F in a stockpot, using a candy or deep-fry thermometer to monitor the temperature. Line a baking sheet with parchment paper.

Fry the empanadas in batches until they are golden brown and crispy, 3 to 4 minutes each, turning once in the oil. Drain them on the baking sheet and sprinkle with sugar before serving with pickled onions and ají on the side.

CEBOLLAS ENCURTIDAS
PICKLED ONIONS

Mamita Amada's pickled onions are a wonderful condiment to serve with empanadas. They also make a nice addition to sandwiches and a tasty garnish for grilled meats and vegetables. The onions should have a nice al dente texture—it is essential to cool the pickling liquid before adding the onions, and to marinate them in the refrigerator. ABOUT 2 CUPS

2 cups	cold water
1 cup	white wine vinegar
1/2 cup	granulated sugar
1 tsp	kosher salt
2 sprigs	thyme
6	coriander seeds
1/4 tsp	crushed red pepper
2	large Spanish onions, very thinly sliced

Combine the water, vinegar, sugar, salt, thyme, coriander seeds, and red pepper in a saucepan and bring to a boil. Decrease the heat to low and simmer for 10 minutes.

Remove from the heat and strain the liquid through a fine-mesh sieve into a nonreactive container. Allow the pickling liquid to cool completely.

Add the sliced onions, cover the container, and leave to marinate for at least 1 hour in the refrigerator. Serve chilled.

EMPANADAS DE VERDE CON POLLO

GREEN PLANTAIN EMPANADAS WITH BRAISED CHICKEN

The plantains must be squeezed through a ricer twice to create a smooth dough and develop the starches. The small dough rounds can be refrigerated for a few hours if covered tightly with plastic wrap; same goes for the formed empanadas. But don't push the timing—the dough will begin to dry out and crack after 3 hours. Any leftover chicken filling is excellent in tacos or on a salad. MAKES 12 EMPANADAS

PLANTAIN DOUGH

2	green plantains (about 1 lb)
	Kosher salt

CHICKEN FILLING

2 Tbsp	unsalted butter
1 Tbsp	extra virgin olive oil
1/4 lb	boneless, skinless chicken thighs, coarsely cut into 1/2-inch pieces
1/4 lb	boneless, skinless chicken breast, coarsely cut into 1/2-inch pieces
1/2	Spanish onion, diced small
1 Tbsp	minced garlic (3 to 4 cloves)
1 tsp	Spanish smoked sweet paprika
1 Tbsp	achiote paste (see Sources)
2 Tbsp	tomato paste

1 tsp	whole cumin seeds, toasted (see page 368) and ground
1 cup	Chicken Stock (page 362)
1	small Yukon gold potato, peeled, diced small, and blanched
1/2 lb	fresh English peas, shelled and blanched
1/4 cup	minced fresh cilantro
2 Tbsp	minced fresh flat-leaf parsley
2	scallions (white and green parts), minced
	Kosher salt and freshly ground black pepper

1 1/2 qts	vegetable oil, for frying
	Kosher salt

	Ají Costeño (page 33), for serving

TO PEEL THE PLANTAINS, split the skins lengthwise with a sharp knife and soak the plantains in warm water until the skins are easily removed, about 30 minutes.

TO MAKE THE DOUGH, bring a large saucepan of lightly salted water to a boil and cook the plantains until they are soft, about 30 minutes. Remove from the heat and allow the plantains to rest in the water until they are cool to the touch.

Pass the cooked plantains through a ricer into a bowl. Rice the plantains a second time. Knead the resulting dough until it is very smooth, about 5 minutes. Allow the dough to rest at room temperature, covered with a damp towel, for 1 hour before making the empanadas.

TO MAKE THE FILLING, heat the butter and olive oil in a cast-iron skillet over medium-high heat. Add the chicken, onion, and garlic and cook until lightly browned, 8 to 10 minutes. Add the paprika, achiote paste, tomato paste, and cumin and cook for 2 to 3 minutes more. Add the stock, potato, peas, cilantro, parsley, and scallions and season to taste with salt and pepper. Let the mixture cool to room temperature. Lift out the chicken meat, shred it, and mix it back into the filling.

TO ASSEMBLE THE EMPANADAS, divide the dough into a dozen 1-inch balls. Using a manual tortilla press, a rolling pin, or the heel of your hand, press each dough ball into a circle about 6 inches in diameter. Mound 2 tablespoons of the filling in the center of each round and fold over to form a half-moon shape. Use a dinner fork to crimp the outer edge. Alternatively, use a plastic empanada press from a Latin market.

TO COOK THE EMPANADAS, heat the vegetable oil to 350°F in a stockpot, using a candy or deep-fry thermometer to monitor the temperature. Line a baking sheet with parchment paper.

Fry the empanadas in batches until golden brown and crispy, 3 to 4 minutes each, turning once in the oil. Drain them on the baking sheet. Season to taste with salt before serving with ají.

EMPANADAS DE MOROCHO CON PICADILLO

CORN EMPANADAS WITH SPICED GROUND BEEF

Made with *arepa* flour (instant white corn flour), this is a somewhat richer dough that will overpower mild fillings, so it's best suited to picadillo and other savory, highly flavorful mixtures. Take care getting the temperature of the frying oil right, otherwise the absorbent dough will take on excess oil. Any leftover picadillo makes killer tacos. MAKES 12 EMPANADAS

WHITE AREPA DOUGH

1 cup	Doñarepa brand white arepa flour (see Sources)
1/2 cup	all-purpose flour
1 Tbsp	kosher salt
1 tsp	granulated sugar
1 cup	hot water
1 Tbsp	vegetable oil

BEEF PICADILLO FILLING

2 Tbsp + 1 Tbsp	unsalted butter
1/2 lb	ground beef
1	Spanish onion, minced
1 Tbsp	minced garlic (3 to 4 cloves)
2 Tbsp	Spanish smoked sweet paprika
2 tsp	whole cumin seeds, toasted (see page 368) and ground
1 tsp	cayenne pepper
2/3 cup	Beef Stock (page 363)
2	large eggs, hard-boiled, peeled, and diced small
6 to 8	large green olives, pitted and finely chopped
2	scallions (white and green parts), thinly sliced on the diagonal
1 Tbsp	minced fresh oregano
1 Tbsp	minced fresh flat-leaf parsley
2 Tbsp	dried currants
	Kosher salt and freshly ground black pepper
1 1/2 qts	vegetable oil, for frying
	Kosher salt
	Ají Costeño (page 33), for serving

TO MAKE THE DOUGH, sift together the flours, salt, and sugar into a bowl. Add the hot water and oil and knead the mixture until it forms a soft, smooth dough. Cover the bowl with plastic wrap and set the dough aside to rest at room temperature for 1 hour before making the empanadas. (At this point the dough can be wrapped tightly in plastic wrap and refrigerated for up to 2 days.)

TO MAKE THE PICADILLO FILLING, melt 2 tablespoons of the butter in a large cast-iron skillet over medium heat. Add the beef, onion, and garlic and cook, stirring often, until the meat is browned and the onion and garlic are translucent, about 10 minutes. Add the paprika, cumin, cayenne, and stock and cook for 3 minutes more. Remove from the heat and use a ladle to remove any excess fat. Stir in the eggs, olives, scallions, oregano, parsley, currants, and remaining 1 tablespoon butter. Season to taste with salt and pepper. Let cool to room temperature. (This will allow some of the liquid to be absorbed and some to evaporate.)

TO ASSEMBLE THE EMPANADAS, divide the dough into a dozen 1-inch balls. Using a manual tortilla press, a rolling pin, or the heel of your hand, press each dough ball into a 6-inch round, about 1/8-inch thick. Mound 2 tablespoons of picadillo in the center of each dough round and fold over to form a half-moon. Use a dinner fork. or a plastic empanada press from a Latin market to crimp the outer edge.

TO COOK THE EMPANADAS, heat the oil to 350°F in a stockpot, using a candy or deep-fry thermometer to monitor the temperature. Line a baking sheet with parchment paper.

Fry the empanadas in batches until golden brown and crispy, 3 to 4 minutes each, turning them once in the oil. Lift them out of the oil with a slotted spoon and set them on the baking sheet to drain. Season to taste with salt before serving with ají.

PORTOVIEJO

Ceviche de Atún | TUNA CEVICHE

Encocado de Pescado | CITRUS-MARINATED HALIBUT AND CALAMARI IN COCONUT BROTH

Ensalada de Habas | FAVA BEAN SALAD

Encocado de pescado, "coconutted fish," is a specialty along the Ecuadorian *costa*, where coconut and other tropical fruits are plentiful. The fish and shellfish are soaked in a marinade of fresh citrus juices, garlic, and aromatic spices, then lightly stewed in a fragrant sauce made with fresh young green coconut—often both the meat and the water (the copious juice at the heart of the fruit). *Encocado* is served over white rice, and heat is added to taste at the table via the ever-present *ají* chile sauce (see page 31).

To me a good *encocado* has an Asian feel, reminiscent of a mild Thai curry—lightly sweet, creamy without being too rich, and incredibly fresh-tasting. I especially like the subtle layering of flavors that comes across in the citrus-infused seafood. I also really enjoy how distinct this dish is in every way from the bolder and bulkier stews more typical inland.

In fact, *encocado* is one of the only Ecuadorian dishes in this book that is not drawn directly from my mom's repertoire: she's from mountainous Quito, but learned coastal creole cooking from her mother, who was from Manabí. But when I set about developing an *encocado* for this book, I got to thinking about my very first taste of fresh young green coconut.

At some point during the year my family lived in Ecuador, back when I was about seven years old, we visited my Tía Eulalia on her farm, or *finca*, in Portoviejo, a fertile valley in the Pacific lowlands of western Ecuador. A Chicago kid, I'd never spent time on a farm before, so the *finca* with its lush groves of tropical fruit trees was just amazing to me. I remember big juicy mangoes that we picked and immediately peeled and ate, sweet and syrupy, right off the trees. From the tamarind trees we pulled down dangling, fuzzy, brown pods, stripping away the hard shell to get at the pulpy fruit, which my grandma cooked up into a paste that she used to make a sweet-and-sour drink.

Everything seemed exotic and tasted delicious, but best of all were the coconuts. I remember trooping around under my aunt's towering coconut palms with my brothers and cousins, all of us brandishing big, long bamboo poles that we poked up into the trees, aiming for the coconuts clustered way up at the top of the trunks, which were straight and tall as telephone poles. Whenever we managed to shake one loose, we'd all shriek and run for cover as our prize came bombing down. Someone—an obliging grownup or older kid—must have used a machete or a cleaver to carve off the outer layer of the coconut and cut an opening in the top for each of us. All I remember is sticking in a straw and slurping out the luscious and thirst-quenching coconut water. There was lots of watery, faintly sweet liquid in there. Once everyone drained their coconut, we scooped out the meat, which was sweet and rich and delectably gummy. (The flesh of a young coconut has a gelatinous consistency. The more familiar hard coconut meat comes from mature fruits that have ripened to the point of falling to the ground. They dry out as they ripen, going from green to brown on the outside and drier and firmer on the inside.)

To make an *encocado* that's easy to prepare as part of a quick seafood-centric weeknight menu, I've combined canned coconut milk and fish stock to capture the right balance of flavor and richness. The starter here is a tuna ceviche that, with its citrus marinade and Thai basil, sets just the right tone for the main dish. On the side is a lightly dressed salad of fresh fava beans, which are abundant in springtime and rank among my favorite green things—nutty and buttery and a perfect complement to the other two dishes on the menu.

CEVICHE DE ATÚN

TUNA CEVICHE

Be sure to use the freshest but most sustainable tuna option available (good information is available at the Seafood Watch section of the Monterey Bay Aquarium website, seafoodwatch.org).The combination of oranges and freshly squeezed lime juice is the secret to making this ceviche "pop." Agave nectar lends a touch of sweetness; it's sold in health food stores and can also often be found in supermarkets, either with the honey and syrups or in the natural foods section. SERVES 4

SAUCE

1	navel orange, peel, pith, and membranes removed, segments cut into chunks
1	lime, zest grated, pith and membranes removed, segments halved crosswise
1/4	red onion, finely diced
1	jalapeño chile, seeds and ribs removed, cut into thin strips
1	habanero chile, seeds and ribs removed, minced
1 Tbsp	minced fresh chives
1 Tbsp	finely chopped fresh cilantro
4	fresh Thai basil leaves, finely shredded
1 Tbsp	extra virgin olive oil
2 Tbsp	avocado oil (see Sources)
2 Tbsp	freshly squeezed lime juice
1 Tbsp	agave nectar
	Kosher salt

TUNA

3 Tbsp	Arbequina olive oil (see Sources)
1/2 lb	fresh sushi-grade sustainable tuna, diced
	Kosher salt
	Crunchy Things (pages 46–51), for serving

TO MAKE THE SAUCE, combine the orange segments with the lime zest and segments in a nonreactive bowl and add the onion, chiles, and herbs. Add the extra virgin olive oil, avocado oil, lime juice, and agave nectar and mix well. Season to taste with salt.

TO DRESS THE FISH, combine the tuna and Arbequina olive oil and season with kosher salt.

Divide the sauce among four chilled plates and top with the tuna. Serve immediately, accompanied by your choice of crunchy things.

P. 76 Ensalada de Habas

P. 72 Ceviche de Atun

P. 74 Encocado de Pescado

ENCOCADO DE PESCADO

CITRUS-MARINATED HALIBUT AND CALAMARI IN COCONUT BROTH

Halibut is delicious in an *encocado*, but any fresh firm-fleshed, flaky white fish will work well. If you find fresh young coconut and its water in the refrigerated section of your Latin grocery, you can substitute an equal mix of the two for the canned coconut milk (see photo, page 73). SERVES 4

MARINATED SEAFOOD

1 Tbsp	minced garlic (3 to 4 cloves)
1/4 cup	freshly squeezed lime juice
1/4 cup	freshly squeezed orange juice
2 tsp	whole cumin seeds, toasted (see page 368) and ground
2 tsp	Spanish smoked sweet paprika
2 Tbsp	extra virgin olive oil
2 lb	fresh boneless, skinless Alaskan halibut or any firm-fleshed white fish, cut into 1-inch chunks
1/2 lb	fresh calamari, tentacles and tubes cut into rings

COCONUT BROTH

1 Tbsp	extra virgin olive oil
1 Tbsp	minced garlic (3 to 4 cloves)
1	Spanish onion, diced
1	red bell pepper, diced
1	green bell pepper, diced
4	plum tomatoes, diced
2	(13.5- to 14-oz) cans coconut milk, well shaken
1 cup	Fish Stock (page 365)
	Kosher salt

TO SERVE

	White Rice (page 367)
2 Tbsp	chopped fresh cilantro
	Ají Costeño (page 33)

TO MARINATE THE SEAFOOD, whisk together the garlic, citrus juices, cumin, paprika, and oil in a bowl. Pour half the mixture into a second bowl. Add the halibut to one bowl and the calamari to the other bowl, tossing each to coat. Cover the bowls and marinate the seafood in the refrigerator for about 1 hour.

TO MAKE THE BROTH, heat the oil in a saucepan. Add the garlic, onion, and bell pepper and cook over medium heat, stirring occasionally, until just translucent, about 10 minutes. Stir in the tomatoes and continue to cook until all of the liquid has evaporated, about 5 minutes. Add the coconut milk and stock, bring to a boil, then lower the heat to a simmer. Season the broth to taste with salt.

Drain the halibut and calamari, discarding the marinade. Add the halibut to the broth and cook for 2 to 3 minutes. Add the calamari and cook for 2 minutes more. Both the fish and the calamari should be opaque and feel firm to the touch.

TO SERVE, portion the rice into four soup bowls and top with a ladle of the stew. Garnish with the cilantro and serve hot with ají on the side.

ENSALADA DE HABAS

FAVA BEAN SALAD

Fava beans are one of my absolute favorite foods. While English peas are widely available in supermarkets, especially in spring and summer, fresh favas are often limited to local farmers' markets and Latin grocers. Unless they are very young and still quite small, favas have a fibrous skin on each bean that needs to be removed. The skins will loosen a bit when you blanch the beans. Getting them all off can be a little tedious but it's well worth the effort—these tender gems are really something special. Here they make for a lovely salad with peas and watercress, also nutty and sweet. Parsley, shallots, and radishes perk up the whole mix (see photo, page 73). SERVES 4

	Kosher salt
1 lb	fresh fava beans, shelled
2 lb	fresh English peas, shelled
1	bunch watercress, stemmed (2 cups, loosely packed)
2	shallots, thinly sliced
2	radishes, cut into matchsticks
2 Tbsp	minced fresh flat-leaf parsley
2 Tbsp	extra virgin olive oil
2 Tbsp	freshly squeezed lemon juice
	Freshly ground black pepper
	Ají Costeño (page 33), for serving

Bring a large saucepan of heavily salted water to a rolling boil. Prepare an ice bath. In small batches, boil the favas until tender, about 3 minutes, using a sieve or skimmer to transfer each batch from the boiling water to the ice bath.

Repeat with the peas, cooking for about 4 minutes and cooling in the ice bath. Drain the favas and peas. Peel off and discard the outer skins of the favas.

Combine the favas, peas, watercress, shallots, radishes, and parsley. Add the oil and lemon juice and toss to lightly dress. Season to taste with salt and freshly ground black pepper before serving with ají on the side.

PAN DE YUCA

The distinctive aroma of *pan de yuca* floats forth from kitchens, bakeries, and pushcarts all over South America. These little round loaves are made of an ingenious combination of yuca flour and *queso fresco* that makes for a bread like no other. The crust is crisp and tasty in a way that always reminds me of pork cracklings. Inside, the rolls are uniformly soft and spongy when they're pulled from the oven, but little air pockets form as they begin to cool. It is impossible to say which is better, hot or warm. My solution is to always have both.

Pan de yuca is simple fare, made in more or less the same way wherever you find it. And yet one quick whiff is all I need to tell my mom's *pan de almidón* (as it's also called in Ecuador) from my grandma's. Having been in the United States for the better part of forty years now, Mom's long accustomed to using the standard *queso fresco* available in Latin grocers. I am a big fan of her *pan de yuca*, and I am man enough to allow her to continue to make it for me on a regular basis—there's no better midmorning pick-me-up than a *pan de yuca*, warm from the oven.

But for Mamita Amada, the cheese must be *queso de Chone*, which is made only in a particular rural area in the coastal lowlands of Ecuador. I think it's an unpasteurized peasant-style cheese, and may be *guajada*, which is the first fermented cheese-like product of the curdled milk. All I know is that every time my grandma visits, she wants to make *pan de yuca* for our family, and despite valiant efforts on my part to lay before her a worthy substitute for her cherished *Chone*, I have never once managed to do so. Not even close. And this does not please her. "No. It is not right. This is terrible cheese. Wrong flavor. I cannot use this cheese of the United States. I cannot make the bread this way. No." And so

on. (I revere Mamita Amada. She is very dear to me and has cherished me my whole life long. She is also very, very stubborn.)

When I was younger, back in the days when a person could still get on an airplane with a pound of stinky cheese curds in their carry-on, Mamita Amada went BYO with the *queso*, so she could make her *pan de yuca* whenever she came to stay with my family in Chicago. The whole place would be swathed in a certain fragrant funk emanating from the *queso de Chone*, and the bread was incredibly delicious. Nowadays, though, I have to go see Mamita Amada on her home turf to have her *pan de yuca*—at least until I find a match for that damn *queso de Chone*. (*Recipes follow.*)

PAN DE YUCA
YUCA BREAD WITH QUESO FRESCO

The ratio of flour to cheese seems crazy, but it works. Serve the bread hot (for a spongy texture) or warm (for a denser interior with the dough settling more and forming air pockets).

MAKES ABOUT 20 LITTLE ROLLS

1 cup	yuca flour (see Sources)
1 lb	queso fresco, finely grated (about 4 cups)
1	large egg, beaten
1 tsp	baking powder
2 Tbsp	whole milk
1 Tbsp	unsalted butter, melted
1 tsp	kosher salt
1 tsp	granulated sugar
	Guava-Chile Butter (recipe follows; optional)

Preheat the oven to 375°F. Lightly grease a baking sheet or line it with parchment paper.

Combine the flour, cheese, egg, baking powder, milk, butter, salt, and sugar in a bowl and knead them together until thoroughly mixed and fairly smooth. Form the dough into about 20 round balls. Bake the rolls on the baking sheet for 20 minutes or until golden brown. Serve warm. To reheat, cover the bread loosely with aluminum foil and heat for 6 to 8 minutes in a 200°F oven.

MANTEQUILLA DE GUAYABA Y CHILE
GUAVA-CHILE BUTTER

At Chifa, my Peruvian-Asian restaurant, the *pan de yuca* with this delicious sweet-spicy-salty spread is a hit among our customers. It would also be tasty on crusty bread, toast, or savory scones. MAKES 4 CUPS

1	(21-oz) can guava paste
1/4 cup	Chinese black vinegar
1/4 cup	sriracha sauce
2 Tbsp	salted butter, at room temperature

In the bowl of a stand mixer, using the paddle attachment, beat the guava paste until it is smooth and has lightened in color. Scrape down the sides of the bowl with a rubber spatula several times. Slowly drizzle in the vinegar while mixing on low speed and scrape the bowl down again. Add the sriracha and continue mixing on low. Scrape down the sides of the bowl, then beat in the butter. Mix just to combine thoroughly.

Store the butter in the refrigerator in an airtight container for up to 1 week.

CUENCA

Ceviche de Cangrejo | CRAB CEVICHE

Fanesca | SALT COD AND LEGUME CHOWDER

Llapingachos | GRIDDLED POTATO CAKES WITH QUESO FRESCO

Hongos con Ají | AJÍ MUSHROOMS WITH GINGER AND SAFFRON

Higos en Almíbar de Miel | FIGS IN HONEY SYRUP WITH GOAT CHEESE

The headliner for this festive menu is my take on *fanesca*, an extraordinary soup that Ecuadorian home cooks make but once a year, in celebration of Good Friday. Even at restaurants and markets, *fanesca* is available only during Holy Week: signs announce ¡HOY FANESCA! ("*fanesca* today!") in the windows of establishments serving this singular specialty. Once you taste a classic *fanesca*, you understand what all the fuss is about. There's simply nothing like it: a thick, rich, and astonishingly complex concoction of milk-soaked salt cod, squash, all manner of beans and grains, herbs, and a variety of garnishes that can include slices of boiled egg, fried plantains, slices of *queso fresco*, chiles, and even tiny empanadas.

Once Holy Week is over, that's it. This seems to be an absolute rule, and I see two clear reasons for it. First there's the religious significance of Holy Week (the soup traditionally includes twelve types of beans and grains, one for each apostle). Can't argue with that. Second is the extensive preparation (a dozen different beans and grains, each cooked separately before being combined!). Having been involved in two full-on *fanesca* makings as a kid, one in Ecuador and one in Chicago, I can attest to the labor intensiveness of the process. We—and by that I mean my aunts, uncles, cousins, brothers, parents, and grandparents— were soaking and shucking and shelling and peeling and blanching for days. The fact that the whole family gets involved is part of what makes this dish so special. There's a third good reason to keep my intake of traditional *fanesca* strictly annual: for me, this wonderful stuff is a direct route to a major nap. Do not pass go, do not collect $200. Lights out. End of story.

So I've come up with a lighter, brothier *fanesca* that tempers the heft of the original while still feeling and looking pretty extravagant. Retaining key elements, like the milk-soaked cod, the squash, and a modest range of dried and fresh legumes and grains that are easy to obtain in the States, this rendition evokes the traditional *fanesca* without putting you in a coma.

To start the meal, the crab ceviche is a nice, light opener for the lushness of both the fanesca and potato cakes that follow.

For the other celebratory menus in this book, I've proposed a mixed drink to open or accompany the meal. But here, there's no doubt that a lighter beer (wheat beer, lager, or a pilsener with nice citrus notes) is the beverage of choice because it pairs beautifully with seafood and also cuts the richness. The carbonation in beer actually cleanses your palate with each sip, lightening the effect of heavier foods.

CEVICHE DE CANGREJO

CRAB CEVICHE

What I love most about the way ceviche is prepared in Ecuador is how all of the various notes sing out distinctly—the bright flavors and acidity of the citrus fruits and tomato, the heat and crunch of the jalapeño and onion, the smooth savor of the olive oil, the tender sweetness of the crabmeat, the pungent leafiness of the cilantro, and the gentle spike of the salt all fall into perfect harmony. SERVES 8

1/2	red onion, finely diced
2	small plum tomatoes, finely diced
2	small jalapeño chiles, seeds and ribs removed, minced
	Grated zest of 2 oranges
1/4 cup	freshly squeezed orange juice
	Grated zest of 2 limes
1/4 cup	freshly squeezed lime juice
1/4 cup	extra virgin olive oil
2 tsp	agave nectar (see page 72)
2 lb	shelled, cooked peekytoe crabmeat
1 lb	shelled, cooked stone crab claws
1/4 cup	minced fresh cilantro
	Kosher salt and freshly ground black pepper
	Crunchy Things (pages 46 to 51), for serving
	Lime wedges, for serving
	Ají Costeño (page 33), for serving

Combine the onion, tomato, jalapeño, orange and lime zests and juices, oil, and agave nectar. Mix well. Gently fold in the crab and cilantro and season to taste with salt and pepper. Divide the ceviche among eight small bowls, garnish with your choice of crunchy things, and serve immediately with lime and ají.

FANESCA

SALT COD AND LEGUME CHOWDER

Fanesca is, by definition, springtime fare. It is at that time of year when fresh favas and English peas are available at Latin grocers, farm markets, even in good supermarkets. Peeled wedges of butternut squash are pretty commonplace and make sense for this recipe since you don't need very much; just be sure they are nice and fresh. This recipe is a very simplified version of the traditional *fanesca*, but you can streamline the work further by doing your shopping early in the week and taking care of some of the prep work a few days in advance: Soak the dried beans overnight, then rinse them and store in the refrigerator covered with fresh water and sealed in airtight containers. Once the *bacalao* (salt cod) has been soaked in the milk, it too can be rinsed thoroughly, immersed in water, covered, and refrigerated for a few days, but the water must be changed daily. Both the beans and the cod need to be rinsed once again before using. SERVES 8

(continued)

FISH SOAK

1 lb	boneless, skinless salt cod fillet (see page 132)
	Whole milk, for soaking

BEAN SOAK

1/2 cup	dried baby lima beans
1/2 cup	dried kidney beans
1/2 cup	dried cannellini beans

STEW

4 Tbsp	unsalted butter
2	Spanish onions, diced (2 cups)
1/4 cup	minced garlic (12 to 16 cloves)
1 Tbsp	achiote paste (see Sources)
2 tsp	whole cumin seeds, toasted (see page 368) and ground
2 tsp	dried oregano
5 qts	Vegetable Stock (page 364)
5 cups	whole milk
1/2 cup	green lentils
1/2 cup	long-grain white rice
1	small zucchini, diced
1/2	butternut squash, peeled, halved, seeded, and diced small (about 1 cup)
2 Tbsp	creamy, unsweetened peanut butter
	Kosher salt and freshly ground black pepper
1 lb	boneless, skinless black cod, cut into 1-inch cubes
1 lb	fresh fava beans, shelled, blanched, and peeled
1 lb	fresh English peas, shelled and blanched
	Kernels cut from 2 ears fresh white sweet corn (1/2 cup) or 1/2 cup thawed and drained frozen white corn kernels

TO SERVE

1/2	head green cabbage, finely shredded
1/4 cup	minced fresh flat-leaf parsley
1/4 cup	minced fresh cilantro
4	jalapeño chiles, sliced crosswise into thin rounds
	Fried Sweet Plantains (page 175)
4	large hard-boiled eggs, peeled and quartered
2	ripe avocados, sliced
1/4 cup	extra virgin olive oil
	Ají Costeño (page 33)

TO SOAK THE SALT COD, set the fish in a deep dish or a bowl, pour in enough milk to completely immerse the fish, cover tightly with plastic wrap, and soak in the refrigerator for 24 hours. Drain and rinse the fish, then flake it with a fork or your fingers.

TO SOAK THE BEANS, combine the lima, kidney, and cannellini beans in a large pot or bowl, cover with cold water by at least 2 to 3 inches and leave to soak overnight at room temperature. Drain when you're ready to make the stew.

TO MAKE THE STEW, melt the butter in a stockpot over medium heat and add the onion. Cook until translucent, about 10 minutes. Add the garlic and cook for 2 to 3 minutes more. Stir in the achiote paste, cumin, and oregano and cook, stirring frequently, until very fragrant, about 5 minutes. Add the stock, milk, and lima, kidney, and cannellini beans and simmer, uncovered, until the beans are just tender, 1 1/2 to 2 hours.

Stir in the lentils, rice, zucchini, butternut squash, peanut butter, and salt cod and cook the stew for 20 minutes more.

Season to taste with salt and pepper. Add the black cod, fava beans, peas, and corn and cook just until the black cod is cooked through (firm and opaque), 3 to 5 minutes.

TO SERVE, ladle the fanesca into eight bowls and garnish each with a little cabbage, parsley, and cilantro, a few jalapeños and fried plantains, a wedge or two of hard-boiled egg, and a few slices of avocado. Drizzle each with olive oil. Alternatively, offer all of the garnishes in little bowls to be added to taste at the table, along with the ají.

LLAPINGACHOS

GRIDDLED POTATO CAKES WITH QUESO FRESCO

This Ecuadorian specialty, a side dish of mashed potato patties stuffed with cheese and cooked on a griddle or *plancha*, originated in the highlands and then spread to the coast and eastern lands. It is typically served with a peanut sauce, but to me that makes the dish too rich. I reinterpreted the dish, lightening it up and adding a topping of *ají* mushrooms. Note that the formed *llapingachos* can be made up to two days in advance, then cooked just before serving. SERVES 8

5	large russet potatoes (about 5 lb)
1/4 cup + 2 Tbsp	vegetable oil
1	large Spanish onion, diced
2 tsp	achiote paste (see Sources)
	Kosher salt and freshly ground black pepper
3/4 lb	queso fresco, grated
1	bunch scallions (green tops only), minced
4	egg whites, beaten
	Ají Mushrooms with Ginger and Saffron (recipe follows)
	Ají Costeño (page 33), for serving

Preheat the oven to 350°F. Bake the potatoes for 45 minutes. Let cool just enough to handle. Remove and discard the skins and pass the potatoes through a ricer or food mill into a large bowl while still hot.

Heat 1/4 cup vegetable oil in a large skillet over medium-low heat and cook the onion gently until softened but not browned, 8 to 10 minutes. Stir in the achiote paste and cook for 2 to 3 minutes more, stirring frequently.

Take the pan off of heat, add the potatoes, and mash together until smooth. Season to taste with salt and pepper. Transfer to a bowl, cover, and refrigerate until chilled, at least an hour. (A cold batter is much easier to form into cakes.)

To prepare the filling, combine the queso fresco and scallions in a bowl.

To form the cakes, use your hands to shape the potatoes into 1 1/2-inch patties. Press a generous pinch of filling into the center of each patty, fold it over to enclose the filling, and re-press into a thick patty. Brush patties on both sides with the beaten egg whites.

Heat the remaining 2 Tbsp oil in a cast-iron skillet over medium-high heat and fry the patties until golden brown, 2 to 3 minutes per side. Serve warm with the mushrooms and ají.

HONGOS CON AJÍ

AJÍ MUSHROOMS WITH GINGER AND SAFFRON

You can use any variety of mushrooms you like, but don't bother with expensive varieties such as chanterelles or morels—their delicate flavor would be overpowered by the potent, spicy sauce. SERVES 8

1/3 cup	vegetable oil
2 Tbsp	unsalted butter
1 lb	cremini mushrooms, sliced
1 lb	shiitake mushrooms, stemmed and sliced
1 lb	royal trumpet mushrooms, sliced or oyster mushrooms, stemmed and sliced
1/2	Spanish onion, diced
2	red bell peppers, diced
2	jalapeño chiles, finely diced
1 tsp	minced garlic (1 clove)
1 tsp	minced peeled fresh ginger
2 cups	Mushroom Stock or Vegetable Stock (page 364)
	Pinch of saffron threads
1/2 cup	heavy cream
2 Tbsp	ají amarillo paste (see Sources)
1/4 cup	minced fresh cilantro
2 Tbsp	minced fresh flat-leaf parsley
	Kosher salt and freshly ground black pepper

Heat the oil and butter in a large sauté pan over high heat. Add all the mushrooms and sauté until browned, 7 to 10 minutes. Transfer the mushrooms to a plate.

Decrease the heat under the pan to medium-low and add the onion, bell peppers, jalapeños, garlic, and ginger and cook until translucent, about 10 minutes. Add the stock and saffron and continue cooking to reduce the liquid by half, about 7 minutes. Add the cream and cook to reduce the liquid by one-third, another 5 minutes.

Stir in the ají amarillo paste and cooked mushrooms. Cook just to heat through. Fold in the cilantro and parsley and season to taste with salt and pepper.

HIGOS EN ALMÍBAR DE MIEL

FIGS IN HONEY SYRUP WITH GOAT CHEESE

Fresh figs are just amazing when they are in season. Here, a honey syrup enhances their subtle sweetness, and the gentle dry tanginess of the goat cheese brings the whole confection into balance. The recipe comes together in a series of simple steps over the course of three days, with two overnight soaks for the fruit. SERVES 8

24	firm fresh Black Mission figs
3 qts	water
	Pinch of baking soda
3 1/2 cups	firmly packed dark brown sugar
1 1/2 cups	honey
4	cinnamon sticks
	Grated zest of 2 lemons
12 oz	soft mild goat cheese
2 Tbsp	heavy cream
	Pinch of kosher salt

Cut a small "X" in the bottom of each fig, combine the fruit with the water, cover, and leave to soak overnight at room temperature.

The next day, transfer the figs and water to a large saucepan and add the baking soda. Bring to a boil, lower the heat, and simmer the figs gently for 15 minutes. Remove from the heat, transfer the figs and water to a nonreactive container, cover, and leave to soak at room temperature a second night.

On the third day, lift the figs out of the water and set them aside. Transfer the fig soaking water to a large saucepan. Add the sugar, honey, cinnamon sticks, and lemon zest and bring to a boil. Lower the heat and simmer to reduce the syrup by half, about 2 hours.

Turn the heat to very low, add the figs to the syrup, and lightly poach for 1 hour.

Whip the goat cheese with the heavy cream and salt just to combine.

Divide the goat cheese among eight dessert plates and serve with the figs and syrup.

ZULETA

CREMA DE QUINOA

The first time I took my wife and kids to Ecuador, the four of us spent several days at Hacienda Zuleta, about two hours north of Quito, resting up from traveling around the country visiting various relatives.

High in the Andes amid fertile valleys, evergreen slopes, and volcanic peaks, Zuleta is an amazing place. You stay in the original hacienda building that dates back to the 1690s and enjoy the gorgeous setting and gracious hospitality, which includes three square meals daily, all prepared by Ecuadorian cooks using ingredients produced on Zuleta's working farm. The Zuleta operation is an impressive model of sustainable agriculture that includes extensive gardens and orchards as well as dairy production and a cheese factory, vegetable farm, and trout farm.

Throughout our stay we enjoyed lots of delicious meals featuring classic Ecuadorian ingredients. One dish in particular had kind of a profound effect on me. It was a *crema de quinoa*, and it was quite something: a creamy stew reminiscent of a *locro*, a thick potato soup that's a staple of Ecuadorian home cooking. But here the main ingredient was quinoa, an indigenous grain. There was a rich, dairy-based broth and potatoes and achiote and corn, all Andean staples, plus avocado floating on top. To me, it was like Ecuador in a bowl, a heady combination of flavors and aromas that spoke to me—of ancient culinary traditions, home cooking, and my heritage. Looking around the table at Beatriz, Olivia, and Andres, all hunkering down over their bowls, I savored the moment—and every last spoonful of that phenomenal soup.

No doubt about it, I was inspired, and soon after we got back I set about the task of developing a quinoa soup that captured the essence and resonance of the Zuleta *crema*. When I take on a traditional dish, my goal is less to reproduce it than respond to it. So the outcome here, my own *crema de quinoa*, has a couple of twists, namely shoestring potatoes and crispy bacon. *(Recipe follows.)*

CREMA DE QUINOA DE ZULETA

QUINOA CHOWDER WITH SWEET CORN

Fresh corn is always the best choice, but may not be in season when you find yourself most in need of this kind of creamy, comforting sustenance—so frozen corn is fine in a pinch. SERVES 4

2 cups	vegetable oil, for frying
1	small russet potato, peeled and cut into matchsticks
	Kosher salt
2 Tbsp	unsalted butter
1 Tbsp	extra virgin olive oil
1/2	Spanish onion, finely chopped
2 Tbsp	minced garlic (4 to 6 cloves)
1 Tbsp	achiote paste (see Sources)
1 1/2 cups	quinoa (any color)
	Kernels cut from 2 ears fresh white sweet corn or 1 cup thawed and drained frozen white corn kernels
5 cups	Vegetable Stock (page 364)
1 cup	heavy cream
2 Tbsp	minced fresh flat-leaf parsley
2 Tbsp	minced fresh chives or cut into 1 1/2-inch strips
1/4 lb	smoked bacon, cut into strips, cooked until crisp, and drained
	Sliced avocado, for serving
	Ají Costeño (page 33), for serving

Line a baking sheet with parchment paper. Heat the vegetable oil to 375°F in a Dutch oven over medium heat, using a candy or deep-fry thermometer to monitor the temperature.

Fry the potatoes in batches, turning in the oil until golden brown and very crispy on all sides, 1 to 2 minutes per batch. Use a slotted spoon to transfer the fried potatoes to the baking sheet to drain and cool. Season to taste with salt.

Heat the butter and olive oil in a stockpot over medium heat. Cook the onion and garlic, stirring occasionally, until translucent, about 10 minutes. Stir in the achiote paste and cook for another 5 minutes. Stir in the quinoa and corn and cook, stirring often, until the grain is lightly toasted, about 5 minutes. Add the stock and cream and bring to a boil. Decrease the heat to medium-low and simmer the chowder uncovered until the quinoa is very tender and the liquid is reduced by one-quarter, about 45 minutes.

To serve, fold in the parsley, chives, bacon, and fried potatoes. Season to taste with salt. Garnish with avocado and serve ají on the side.

SPAIN

MENU 1
COSTA DEL SOL

Ajo Blanco | ALMOND GAZPACHO WITH SMOKED TROUT

Almendras Tostadas con Mantequilla | BUTTER-TOASTED MARCONA ALMONDS

Fedeua con Mariscos | SEAFOOD VERMICELLI PAELLA

Allioli de Piquillo | PIQUILLO PEPPER AÏOLI

MENU 2
SEVILLA

Ensalada Verde | GREEN SALAD WITH SHERRY-IDIAZÁBAL VINAIGRETTE

Merluza en Salsa Verde | HAKE FILLETS IN CLAM AND HERB SAUCE

Calçots con Salbitxada | GRILLED SPRING ONIONS WITH ALMOND SAUCE

MENU 3
BARCELONA

Pulpo Gallego | SPANISH OCTOPUS WITH POTATO CONFIT

Arroz a la Cazuela | BRAISED RABBIT, SHRIMP, AND LOBSTER RICE STEW

Allioli de Azafrán | SAFFRON AÏOLI

Alcachofas Asadas | ROASTED ARTICHOKES

MENU 4
SAN SEBASTIÁN

Sangría de Tinto | SPICED APPLE SANGRÍA

Banderillas | MELON SKEWERS WITH ANCHOVIES AND PICKLED PEPPERS

Montadito de Pato | CANAPÉS WITH DUCK CONFIT AND SERRANO HAM

Chanquetes Fritos con Romesco | FRIED LITTLE FISH WITH ROMESCO

Salmorejo | GAZPACHO WITH STRAWBERRIES, QUAIL EGGS, AND OLIVES

Entrecôte con Membrillo y Queso de Cabra | SIRLOIN STEAK WITH QUINCE PASTE AND GOAT CHEESE

Espinaca a la Catalana | CATALAN SPINACH

Espárragos con Trufas | WHITE ASPARAGUS WITH BLACK TRUFFLE AND EGG

Crema Catalana | CHOCOLATE CUSTARD WITH VANILLA BERRIES

PINTXO BAR

ESSENTIALS | Canned Spanish Seafood PG 117 | Bacalao PG 132

SECOND STOP:
SPAIN

When it comes to gastronomy, Spain is unsurpassed. I am by no means alone in this opinion—there has been a ton of great press about Spanish cuisine, especially over the past several years. For the record, though, I came to this conclusion independently, back when I was a wet-behind-the-ears culinary school hatchling.

It was 1996, within days of graduation, that I first set foot on Spanish soil. The next six months would be full of hard work and great food. As a junior cook at a celebrated restaurant on the Costa del Sol, I got a thorough introduction to the ingredients and techniques central to the fine cuisine of the southern region.

At the restaurant there was a Basque cook named Gorka who made the daily staff meal, and he always cooked up some form of "*Arrrrrrrooooozzz,*" as he called it—rolling out the word in deep Basque-inflected tones—meaning rice dish flavored with squid ink or saffron, fish fumet or duck stock, and invariably accompanied by a fresh homemade aïoli and slices of toasted baguette. Assisting Gorka in preparing these staff meals was how I first learned to cook proper Spanish rice dishes. To this day, whenever I say "*arroz*" (which in my line of work is pretty often) I say it Gorka's way and it brings those days right back to me.

I got to know classic home-style Spanish dishes better as I found my way to local eateries with cheap daily specials. I was delighted and relieved to discover the *menús del día*—full meals, complete with make-your-own sangría, that were affordable even on my minuscule stipend (I'd landed with about a thousand bucks in my pocket, but was counting on that lasting me a year). The *menús* often featured main courses that were soothing in both their wholesomeness and familiarity—soupy *cazuelas* in particular were recognizably related to Latin dishes my mom fed me when I was a kid—but at the same time they were altogether new. What set them apart, and really wowed me, was that each one seemed like a perfect synthesis of the best local ingredients. Even the humblest dish featuring the most commonplace staple—squid, for example (here at the seaside, the waters were thick with them), or hake (a fish in the cod family)—was rendered so deftly, with such reverence for the raw ingredients that it came off like a celebration.

I've now been to Spain a dozen times (and counting). For me, the allure is triple-decked. First, the ingredients are unparalleled—their quality is superb and their variety is dazzling. Second, the regional cuisines fascinate me—sharply distinct by virtue of geographical and cultural complexity, deeply steeped in tradition, and, here and there, on the cutting edge of innovation. And the third element is the clincher, the magic ingredient: unabashed pleasure in all things relating to food—components, preparation, consumption—a rare unifying thread that binds these decidedly autonomous cultures.

Spain is where you take a break from work in the middle of the day to go home for a big nap because dinner doesn't get going until 10:00 or 11:00 p.m. It's where pressing olive oil and curing ham are forms of high art. Spain is where you celebrate the harvest of spring onions with a ritual feast involving big fires made of grapevine cuttings. And it's where both great chefs and housewives select their night's menu from the same gorgeous produce, seafood, meat, poultry, and charcuterie at the central market. Spain is where food traditions like paella and gazpacho were created long ago, and where canned seafood is aged like fine wine.

It's taken numerous visits for me to get to know a few areas, mainly Andalucía and environs down south, the Basque Country up in the north (sharing a border with France), and Catalonia over in the northeast. Every trip is an immersion in local cuisines and a collecting expedition, gathering experiences, ideas, and ingredients to bring back and share, recreating what moves me.

As a chef, I want to take people there. While a meal at Amada or Tinto (my Spanish restaurants in Philadelphia) or Mercat a la Planxa (in Chicago) would be all about transporting you to a seaside *chiringuito* on the Mediterranean, a Basque pintxo bar in San Sebastián, a stall at Barcelona's La Boquería market, or even a table at Arzak restaurant, in this chapter I've created menus that will take you to the home cook's side of the Spanish gastronomic experience. Procuring and preparing the ingredients, cooking these mostly traditional dishes, and enjoying them with friends and family should be a real pleasure. *¡Salud!*

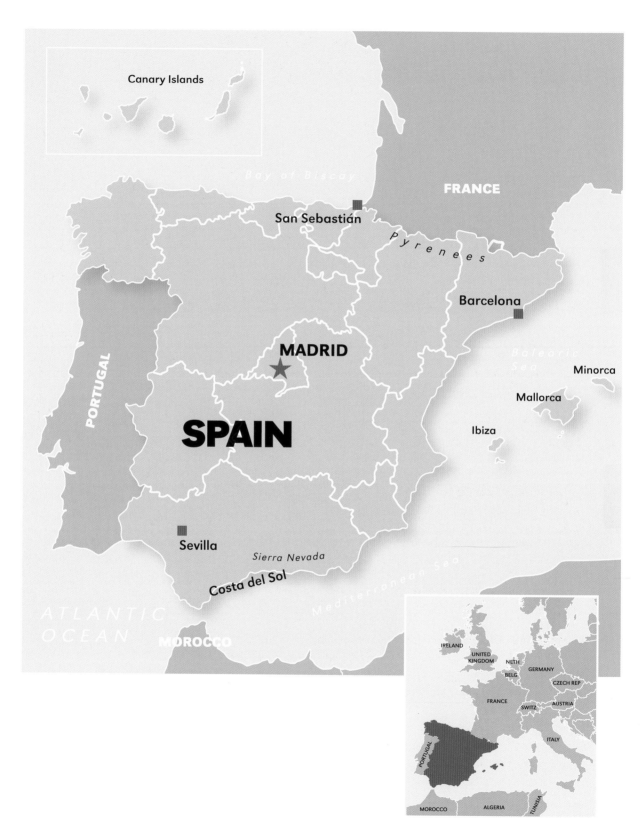

Canary Islands

Bay of Biscay

FRANCE

San Sebastián

Pyrenees

Barcelona

Balearic Sea

Minorca

MADRID

Mallorca

PORTUGAL

Ibiza

SPAIN

Sevilla

Sierra Nevada

Costa del Sol

ATLANTIC
OCEAN

Mediterranean Sea

MOROCCO

IRELAND

UNITED
KINGDOM

NETH

GERMANY

BELG

CZECH REP

FRANCE

SWITZ

AUSTRIA

PORTUGAL

ITALY

MOROCCO

ALGERIA

TUNISIA

QUICK INFO

LAND

• Landscape dominated by highland plateaus and the Pyrenee and Sierra Nevada mountain ranges, with alluvial plains along the coasts shaped by major rivers, including the Guadalquivir, the Tagus, and the Duero

• Climate variable by region from Mediterranean in the south to semiarid in the southeast; hot summers and cold winters in the high central plains; warm weather year round in Andalucía; ocean dictates temperature along coastline

PEOPLE

• Current population is approximately 46.5 million

• Country consists of seventeen administrative regions called *Communidades Autónomias* (autonomous communities)

• National identity is diverse and complex; traditional regional cultures include Basque, Catalan, Galician, and Castilian; also many distinct local identities

• Other ethnic groups include Gitano (Romani) and immigrants from Africa, South America, the Caribbean, and various parts of Asia and the Middle East as well as Eastern Europe

FOOD

• Cuisine reflects intersection of myriad cultures, peoples, and empires throughout the ages

• With Greeks came olive trees and grape vines; Muslims developed irrigation and introduced citrus, sugar cane, rice, and grain; from the New World, Spanish explorers brought tomatoes, potatoes, chiles, beans, squash, chocolate, and vanilla

• Distinct regional cuisines reflect diverse cultural identities and local traditions; "national" foods include ham and other pork products, paella, a wide range of seafood dishes, and various tapas

---

1 MILLION BCE–8TH CENTURY CE
Cultures and tribes inhabit the peninsula and nearby islands including the Greeks and Phoenicians, Iberians and Celts, Carthaginians, Romans, Visigoths, Arabs, and Berbers.

8TH CENTURY CE
Muslim conquest establishes Al-Andalus, the medieval Muslim state a.k.a Moorish Iberia, and endures for hundreds of years.

1492 CE
The fall of Granada marks the Christian reconquest of the north.

16TH–17TH CENTURY CE
The Spanish empire reaches its apex, at times encompassing most of Europe in addition to vast overseas colonies.

COSTA DEL SOL

Ajo Blanco | ALMOND GAZPACHO WITH SMOKED TROUT

Almendras Tostadas con Mantequilla | BUTTER-TOASTED MARCONA ALMONDS

Fedeua con Mariscos | SEAFOOD VERMICELLI PAELLA

Allioli de Piquillo | PIQUILLO PEPPER AÏOLI

I made a beeline for Spain straight out of Kendall College, armed with a culinary degree, an open-ended plane ticket, my entire savings, and the promise of a summer apprenticeship at La Taberna del Alabardero, a restaurant on the southern coast.

The chef, aka Capitán or Capi, ran a tight ship. The pace of prep and dinner service was fast, furious, and intense; the menu was extensive, and high end, and executing everything perfectly brought every cook in that kitchen together on a nightly basis.

The family meals we had prior to dinner service were my introduction to the traditional dishes of Spain. I must have had thirty different varieties of paella and rice dishes, all prepared by great Spanish cooks. On my occasional days off, I sought out other examples of classic fare, albeit on a shoestring. My monthly stipend was meager and, being a single, sociable young guy, I needed to keep a few of my *pesetas* in reserve for nightlife. (Puerto Banús was quite the hotspot.) So I was delighted to discover mom-and-pop joints around town and in nearby Marbella that offered a *menú del día*, or daily special, that included a pitcher of wine and a dish of fruit to make your own sangría, a basket of bread, a salad, and a fish of the day.

These *menú del día* meals were solitary respites—good cheap eats enjoyed on open-air patios. They gave me a chance to catch my breath, reflect on my adventures, and got me acquainted with aspects of Spanish cuisine that were new to me. One prime example: tomato-less gazpacho served in a drinking glass.

Then came that unsung cousin of paella—*fedeua*. A Valencian mainstay of short, toasted vermicelli-like pasta (*fideos*) with fresh fish or seafood and often some squid ink or saffron, *fedeua* (also called *fideuá*) was my greatest find. It often featured an inexpensive local catch, like squid, as a main ingredient, and it filled my belly and fed my soul, leaving me a happy guy, whether I was heading out for a night on the town or back to my bunk at the local hostel.

Everything on the menu here was directly inspired by those *menú del día* meals. The *ajo blanco* is much the same as the first white gazpacho I ever tasted; the *fedeua* has a wider variety of seafood than the ones I typically had in Marbella, but is otherwise true to the spirit of the original; and the aïoli harkens back to the Catalan-style *allioli*, a garlicky emulsion that was ubiquitous, especially when it came to seafood.

P. 110 Fedeuà con Mariscos

P. 111 Allioli de Piquillo

AJO BLANCO
ALMOND GAZPACHO WITH SMOKED TROUT

This *ajo blanco* is much like the first one I ever had, very light and flavorful, with a garlic aroma that's subtle, not overpowering, and served with assorted traditional garnishes that complement and contrast with the texture and flavor of the soup. Note that using blanched (skinless) almonds is essential to the creamy-white look of the final dish. In Spain the bread is always soaked in mineral water (still, not sparkling); we maintain that practice at Amada. SERVES 4

SOUP

4	slices white bread, without crust, torn into 1-inch pieces (2 cups)
2 cups + 3/4 cup	mineral water
1 1/4 cups	toasted blanched almonds (see page 368)
2	cloves garlic, crushed
1 1/4 cups	whole milk
2 Tbsp	sherry vinegar
1/4 cup	extra virgin olive oil
	Kosher salt

TO SERVE

1 cup	seedless green grapes, halved
1/4 lb	smoked trout, skinned, boned, and flaked (1/2 cup)
1/4 cup	chopped Butter-Toasted Marcona Almonds (recipe follows)
2 Tbsp	Arbequina olive oil (see Sources)

TO MAKE THE SOUP, in a small, shallow bowl, soak the bread in 2 cups of the mineral water until the bread is completely saturated (most of the water should be absorbed). Drain the bread but do not squeeze it dry.

Combine the bread with the almonds, garlic, milk, and vinegar in a blender and purée on high until very smooth. With the machine running, add the extra virgin olive oil in a thin stream until emulsified. Continue to blend until the soup thickens, 1 to 2 minutes more.

Strain the soup through a fine-mesh sieve into a bowl or container. Mix in the remaining 3/4 cup mineral water and season to taste with salt. Cover and refrigerate until chilled.

TO SERVE, pour the soup into four chilled bowls. Garnish with the grapes, smoked trout, toasted almonds, and Arbequina olive oil.

ALMENDRAS TOSTADAS CON MANTEQUILLA

BUTTER-TOASTED MARCONA ALMONDS

Once toasted, the almonds can be stored for weeks in a sealed container at room temperature. This toasting method can be used for other types of shelled nuts, such as pecans and peanuts; toasting time will vary with size. MAKES 1 CUP

2 Tbsp	unsalted butter
1 cup	raw Marcona almonds
	Kosher salt

Line a baking sheet with paper towels.

Melt the butter in a large stainless-steel sauté pan over medium heat. Once the bubbles begin to disappear (meaning the water in the butter has evaporated), add the almonds and season to taste with salt. Carefully stir the nuts every few minutes until the butter is lightly browned and the mixture is very fragrant, 6 to 8 minutes. Transfer the almonds to the baking sheet to cool.

FEDEUA CON MARISCOS

SEAFOOD VERMICELLI PAELLA

Spanish vermicelli or *fideos* can be found in specialty markets and online. You can also substitute thin spaghetti or angel hair pasta broken into 2-inch pieces (see photo, page 107). SERVES 4

6 Tbsp	extra virgin olive oil
1	Spanish onion, diced
2 Tbsp	minced garlic (4 to 6 cloves)
1	green or red bell pepper, diced
1 lb	Spanish vermicelli
4	piquillo peppers, drained, rinsed (if packed in brine or oil), seeded, and cut into thin strips
2	dried guindilla peppers (see Sources)
1 1/2 qts	Fish Stock (page 365)
	Pinch of Spanish saffron threads
1/2 lb	fresh boneless, skinless halibut, cut into 1-inch cubes
1/2 lb	fresh extra large shrimp, peeled and deveined
1/2 lb	fresh cleaned calamari tubes, cut crosswise into 1/2-inch rings
12	fresh clams (preferably Spanish cockles or littlenecks), scrubbed and rinsed under cold water
12	fresh mussels (preferably PEI Blue Bay), scrubbed, debearded, and rinsed under cold water
2 Tbsp	finely chopped fresh flat-leaf parsley
	Kosher salt

TO SERVE

8	slices baguette, toasted
1/4 cup	Piquillo Pepper Aïoli (recipe follows)
	Lime wedges (optional)

Place a rack in the middle position and preheat the oven to 375°F.

Heat the olive oil in a large oven-safe paella-style pan over medium heat. Add the onion, garlic, and bell peppers and cook the vegetables until translucent, about 10 minutes. Add the vermicelli, stirring to coat the pasta thoroughly with the oil. Cook for 5 minutes, stirring frequently, until the pasta is lightly toasted. Add the piquillo peppers, dried peppers, fish stock, and saffron. Bring to a simmer, stirring frequently to ensure that the pasta cooks evenly. Add the halibut, shrimp, calamari, clams, and mussels. Continue to stir until the pasta is al dente, the clams and mussels are open (discard any that do not open), and the halibut, shrimp, and calamari are opaque and firm, 2 to 3 minutes. Mix in the parsley and season the fedeua to taste with salt.

Transfer the pan to the oven and bake the fedeua for 5 minutes, or until the pasta is lightly browned at the edges.

TO SERVE, divide the fedeua among four wide, shallow soup bowls. Garnish with toasted baguette slices spread with piquillo aïoli. Offer lime wedges and provide an empty bowl for discarding the empty clam and mussel shells.

ALLIOLI DE PIQUILLO
PIQUILLO PEPPER AÏOLI

This *piquillo allioli* recipe makes more than you need for the *fedeua*, but it will keep in the refrigerator in an airtight container for up to 3 days—and you will have no trouble using up the leftovers as a dip or sandwich spread. MAKES ABOUT 2 CUPS

2	large egg yolks
1 Tbsp	sherry vinegar
	Juice of 1 lemon
1/4 tsp	cayenne pepper
2 or 3	piquillo peppers, drained, rinsed (if packed in brine or oil), and seeded
1 1/2 cups	vegetable oil
	Kosher salt

Combine the egg yolks, vinegar, lemon juice, cayenne, and piquillo peppers in a blender or food processor and purée until the mixture is very smooth and frothy, about 2 minutes. With the machine running, slowly add the oil in a thin stream. Scrape down the sides of the container and blend again to ensure that the allioli is uniformly emulsified. (The allioli should have the consistency of mayonnaise.) Season to taste with salt. Transfer to an airtight container and keep refrigerated for up to 3 days.

SEVILLA

Ensalada Verde | GREEN SALAD WITH SHERRY-IDIAZÁBAL VINAIGRETTE

Merluza en Salsa Verde | HAKE FILLETS IN CLAM AND HERB SAUCE

Calçots con Salbitxada | GRILLED SPRING ONIONS WITH ALMOND SAUCE

I learned to make *merluza en salsa verde* in the first few days of my apprenticeship in Spain, when I was fresh out of culinary school. Simple and speedy—really just fish fillets and a few clams with a white wine–butter pan sauce and a handful of herbs—this was the very first Spanish fish dish I was taught to make, there in the bustling kitchen at Taberna del Alabardero in the ritzy marina of Puerto Banús near Marbella on the Costa del Sol. I remember so clearly now, fifteen-plus years later, because that *merluza* was a real eye-opener for me.

First of all, when I tasted the finished dish, I was floored. After all my training in elaborate classical French cuisine, it just astounded me that something that took five minutes to cook could be so nuanced and perfectly balanced.

Then, as I learned more about Spanish cuisine and the specialties of Andalucía (capital, Sevilla), it dawned on me that *merluza en salsa verde* wasn't just a Taberna del Alabardero specialty, but a deeply traditional Spanish dish. And this brought what was for me a new insight about culinary tradition: there is, now and then, a simple but superb dish that comes down through the ages unchanged because it is so easy and so perfect that anyone who makes it once adopts it into their repertoire forever.

It was a full decade and a good many cooking jobs later, but when I began opening my own restaurants, I started with one focused on bringing traditional Andalucían food to Philadelphia. Amada (named for my ultimate culinary inspiration, my grandma) has been going strong since 2005, and we often feature *merluza en salsa verde* on the menu.

Accompanying the *merluza* here on this menu are two other greatest hits from Amada: to start, a salad that combines several of my favorite green things (arugula, asparagus, fava beans, avocado) all dressed in a creamy vinaigrette with *Idiazábal*, a smoky Basque sheep's-milk cheese. And for alongside the hake, a popular Amada tapa: grilled spring onions with a classic Spanish almond sauce.

P. 116 Calçots con Salbitxada

P. 115 Merluza en Salsa Verde

ENSALADA VERDE

GREEN SALAD WITH SHERRY-IDIAZÁBAL VINAIGRETTE

It might seem odd to combine fava beans, asparagus, and avocado, but the distinct flavors and textures are highly complementary—so much so that this has long been the bestselling salad at Amada. The dressing makes more than you will need for the salad, but it keeps well in a sealed jar in the fridge for up to 3 days and is delicious with any green salad or blanched green vegetable. SERVES 4

VINAIGRETTE

1	large egg yolk
3 Tbsp	sherry vinegar
	Juice of 1 small lemon (about 2 Tbsp)
	Kosher salt and freshly ground black pepper
1/2 cup	vegetable oil
2 oz	Idiazábal or Parmesan cheese, finely grated (about 1/2 cup)

SALAD

	Kosher salt and freshly ground black pepper
1/2 lb	fresh fava beans, shelled
1 lb	green asparagus, stalks trimmed and peeled
1	romaine lettuce heart, finely shredded
1	(6-oz) bunch watercress, coarsely chopped
2	heads frisée, coarsely chopped
4 oz	baby arugula
1	avocado, diced

TO MAKE THE VINAIGRETTE, combine the egg yolk, vinegar, lemon juice, and a little salt and pepper in a blender and purée until slightly frothy, about 2 minutes. With the machine running, slowly add the oil in a thin stream until the vinaigrette is completely emulsified. Add the cheese and continue running the machine to incorporate it. Season with additional salt and pepper to taste. Measure out 1/2 cup of the vinaigrette to use on the salad. (Store the remainder in the refrigerator for another use, up to 3 days.)

TO BLANCH THE FAVA BEANS, bring a large saucepan of heavily salted water to a rolling boil and prepare an ice bath. In small batches, boil the beans until tender, about 3 minutes. Remove them with a slotted spoon or skimmer and immerse them in the ice bath until cool. Peel off and discard the tough outer skins of the beans.

Repeat with the asparagus, boiling for 1 to 2 minutes and cooling in the ice bath. Cut the asparagus crosswise into 1-inch pieces.

TO FINISH THE SALAD, combine the romaine, watercress, frisée, and arugula in a bowl with the asparagus, fava beans, and avocado. Dress the salad with the vinaigrette, toss lightly, and season to taste with salt and pepper before serving.

MERLUZA EN SALSA VERDE

HAKE FILLETS IN CLAM AND HERB SAUCE

Hake is a member of the cod family. It has a light, slightly sweet flavor and an agreeably firm texture. Any firm-fleshed, flaky white fish can be substituted (see photo, page 113). SERVES 4

2 Tbsp + 2 Tbsp	vegetable oil
4	fresh boneless, skinless hake fillets (about 1/4 lb each)
4 Tbsp + 2 Tbsp	unsalted butter
1	medium shallot, finely diced
1 Tbsp	minced garlic (3 to 4 cloves)
20	fresh clams (preferably Spanish cockles or littlenecks), scrubbed and rinsed under cold water
1/4 cup	dry white wine
	Kosher salt
1/4 cup	finely chopped flat-leaf parsley

Place a rack in the middle position and preheat the oven to 400°F.

Heat 2 tablespoons of the oil in a large stainless-steel sauté pan over medium-high heat. Lightly season the fish with salt. When the oil begins to shimmer, carefully set the fillets in the pan and let them cook undisturbed for 1 minute. Transfer the pan to the hot oven to cook the fish for 3 minutes more, then return the pan to the stovetop over medium heat. Add 2 tablespoons of the butter to the pan and baste the fish for 1 minute, or until the edges flake easily and the center is firm to the touch. Use a flexible spatula to transfer the fillets to a serving dish or individual plates. Cover with aluminum foil to keep warm.

Heat the remaining 2 tablespoons oil in a sauté pan over medium heat. Cook the shallot and garlic, stirring often, until translucent, about 1 minute. Add the clams and white wine, cover the pan, and steam the clams until they open, 2 to 3 minutes. Discard any that don't open. Lift the clams out of the pan with tongs and continue cooking the liquid in the pan, uncovered, until it has reduced by half to about 1/4 cup. Add the remaining 4 tablespoons butter and whisk gently until the butter is melted and the sauce is emulsified, 1 to 2 minutes. Season with salt to taste and stir in the parsley.

Return the clams to the pan to get them a little saucy. Place them alongside the fish, lightly spoon sauce over all, and serve.

CALÇOTS CON SALBITXADA
GRILLED SPRING ONIONS WITH ALMOND SAUCE

This is my interpretation of the Catalan tradition of the *calçotada*, an end-of-winter ritual in which spring onions (*calçots*) are roasted over outdoor fires and eaten in mass quantities. It is simple to prepare, but I do have a few key bits of advice: First, remove the roots and wash the onions carefully; you are cooking them whole and they tend to contain a fair amount of grit. Second, you want the sauce to be white with nice green flecks, so be sure to chop the parsley and fold it in at the very end; otherwise it will turn the sauce an unappetizing shade of green. Third, the sauce needs time to chill, about two hours, so plan accordingly. Last, you will have about 1/2 cup of the *Salbitxada* sauce left over, but it keeps well for a few days in a sealed jar in the fridge; it's good with just about any vegetable (see photo, page 113). SERVES 4

SALBITXADA SAUCE

1	clove garlic, crushed
2	plum tomatoes, coarsely chopped
2 Tbsp	red wine vinegar
1/8 tsp	crushed red pepper
2 Tbsp	honey
1/2 cup	sliced blanched almonds, lightly toasted (see page 368)
1 cup	extra virgin olive oil
2 Tbsp	coarsely chopped flat-leaf parsley
	Kosher salt

CALÇOTS

3	bunches spring onions or scallions, trimmed and thoroughly rinsed (about 2 dozen onions)
3 Tbsp	extra virgin olive oil
	Coarse sea salt

TO MAKE THE SAUCE, combine the garlic, tomatos, vinegar, red pepper, and honey in a food processor and purée the mixture until smooth, periodically scraping down the sides of the bowl. Add the almonds and purée again until smooth. With the machine running, slowly add the oil in a thin stream and process until the sauce is emulsified. Stir in the chopped parsley and season to taste with salt. Refrigerate about 2 hours or until thoroughly chilled.

TO COOK THE ONIONS, heat a stovetop griddle or cast-iron skillet over medium-high heat. Brush the onions with some of the oil and season them lightly with sea salt. Cook the onions on the griddle, turning as needed to char them on all sides until nicely caramelized and tender, 3 to 4 minutes per side. Lightly drizzle the onions with more of the oil and season to taste with additional sea salt. Serve the onions immediately, with the chilled salbitxada sauce.

CANNED SPANISH SEAFOOD

Canned Spanish seafood is a delicacy unto itself. Tiny squid, razor clams, mussels, octopus, sardines, goose barnacles, Galician clams, baby eels, scallops, sea urchins, cockles, mackerel—if it's fished from the seas, chances are the Spanish have found a delicious way to preserve it in a can or jar.

On a trip to Barcelona, I visited Quimet i Quimet, a tiny bodega in the Poble Sec neighborhood that specializes in tapas made from an astonishing array of fine preserved foods from around Spain and all over the world. The crowd stood shoulder to shoulder, the walls were lined floor to ceiling with bottles of *cava* (sparkling wine) and other wine, beer, and spirits, and a brother-and-sister team (the place has been in the Quim family for nearly a century) served up ingenious tapas composed largely of food from cans and jars—including seafood. Some of the dishes were elegant and complex combinations of several exquisite products, but two of my favorites were very simple: both the *ventresca de bonito del norte* (tuna belly) and the *berberechos* (minuscule cockles) were served straight out of the tin, perched on a simple round of toast and embellished with just a sprinkling of coarse salt and a dribble of olive oil. The clams were delectably briny and tender, and the tuna was rich and velvety. See the Sources section (page 371) for where to buy them in the States. *(Recipe follows.)*

MAYONESA DE ATÚN

TUNA MAYO WITH CAPERS

One of my favorite varieties of canned seafood is *bonito del norte* tuna packed in oil. It's dense and flavorful and delightfully rich. At Amada, we do a version of tuna mayo with black olive oil (oven-dried kalamata olives puréed with olive oil) that's served alongside a house-baked garlic lavash (cracker bread). To me, it's such a great start to a meal that it's served compliments of the house. SERVES 4

1	can or jar bonito del norte (about 8 ounces), drained well
1/4 cup	mayonnaise
2 Tbsp	crème fraîche
3 Tbsp	capers, rinsed, drained, and chopped
2 Tbsp	freshly squeezed lemon juice
	Kosher salt
	Lavash or toasted baguette slices, for serving

In a mixing bowl, combine the tuna, mayonnaise, crème fraîche, capers, and lemon juice. Mix well and season to taste with salt. Serve chilled, with warm lavash or toasted baguette.

BARCELONA

Pulpo Gallego | SPANISH OCTOPUS WITH POTATO CONFIT

Arroz a la Cazuela | BRAISED RABBIT, SHRIMP, AND LOBSTER RICE STEW

Allioli de Azafrán | SAFFRON AÏOLI

Alcachofas Asadas | ROASTED ARTICHOKES

In Galicia, on Spain's Atlantic coast just north of Portugal, octopus is a delicacy and *pulperías* (market stands, portable carts, and octopus bars) cater to the voracious local appetite for platters piled high with boiled tentacles. More broadly appealing is the *pulpo gallego* or *pulpo a la gallega* (Galician-style octopus), in which octopus is paired with potatoes and dressed in olive oil, garlic, and smoky paprika. The dish is iconic, on a par with paella, and I don't think I'm exaggerating when I say that I've had it everywhere I've been in Spain, from the Basque Country to Catalonia, Andalucía to Valencia. Most recently, I finally visited landlocked Extremadura, famous for its decidedly terrestrial *pimentón* and *jamón ibérico de Bellota*, a sweet, rich ham made from bristly black pigs that range freely in oak forests, dining on acorns and herbs. In the first bar I walked into after a long day wandering through bucolic pasturelands, there it was: *pulpo gallego*, much the same as everywhere else and every bit as delicious.

In my experience, the only variables are the size and shape of the pieces of potatoes and octopus. Remarkably enough, the octopus is always tender, succulent, and buttery—I never knew octopus could be like this until I went to Spain. In Galicia, the old custom is to boil the octopus whole in a copper cauldron, then remove the head and leave the tentacles to sit in the hot water. Even if this is not still a common practice, solid prep methods are clearly being handed down. Over the years, I've developed my own foolproof technique (see page 123).

Pulpo gallego brings together sea and earth, and the main course on this menu is a fuller expression of that theme from Catalonia (capital city: Barcelona; which is situated on the Mediterranean Sea on the opposite side of the Iberian peninsula from Galicia), where the *mar y montaña* tradition is especially strong. *Arroz a la cazuela*, with its characteristically harmonious balance of rice, broth, and multiple proteins, is rich with rabbit, shrimp, chorizo, and lobster. Typically cooked in an earthenware pot (*cazuela*), this classic preparation has clear affinities with the soupy rice dishes common to all Latin cooking. The saffron *allioli* is a nice accent for the *arroz*, especially if you spread it on wedges of toast. And if some of the *allioli* finds its way onto the side dish of roasted artichokes, so much the better. *¡Buen provecho!*

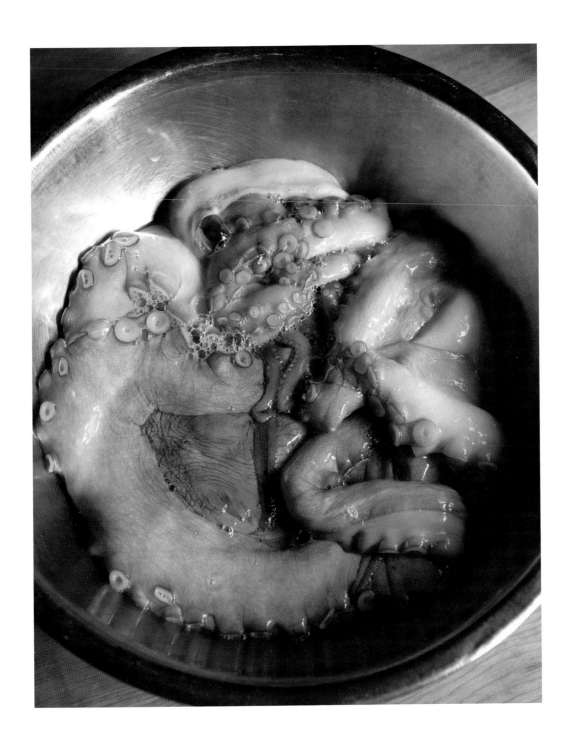

PULPO GALLEGO
SPANISH OCTOPUS WITH POTATO CONFIT

This recipe incorporates my tried-and-true method for poaching tender, succulent octopus. Cooking the octopus whole—head and all—helps keep the tentacles from curling up (a straight tentacle is easier to work with than one that's coiled into a spiral). Both the octopus and the potato confit can be prepared ahead of time, so all that's left to do on the day you want to serve the dish is the final sautéing step (here a stainless-steel pan is called for to ensure that everything browns nicely). The potato confit is versatile and addictive; it makes a great side dish for meat, poultry, and seafood. Store the confit oil for another use, such as roasting vegetables, or for making more potato confit: simply strain it through a fine-mesh sieve and store in an airtight container in the refrigerator for up to two weeks. SERVES 4

(continued)

OCTOPUS BOIL

1 Tbsp	yellow mustard seeds
1 Tbsp	coriander seeds
1 tsp	crushed red pepper
1 gallon	water
1/2 cup	red wine vinegar
1	lemon, halved
2	cloves garlic, crushed
1/4 cup	kosher salt
1	whole fresh or frozen Spanish or Mediterranean octopus (2 to 3 lb)

POTATO CONFIT

4	fingerling potatoes (about 1/3 lb), peeled and cut into 1/4-inch-thick coins
2/3 cup	vegetable oil
2/3 cup	extra virgin olive oil
1	sprig whole rosemary
2	cloves garlic
	Kosher salt and freshly ground black pepper

PULPO GALLEGO

2 Tbsp	vegetable oil
	Kosher salt and freshly ground black pepper
1 Tbsp	minced garlic (3 to 4 cloves)

TO SERVE

1 Tbsp	smoked sweet Spanish paprika
1 Tbsp	Arbequina olive oil (see Sources)
	Grated zest of 2 to 3 lemons
2 Tbsp	minced fresh flat-leaf parsley
	Lemon wedges

TO COOK THE OCTOPUS, combine the mustard seeds, coriander seeds, and red pepper in a square of cheesecloth and tie securely with kitchen twine to form a sachet. Combine the sachet, water, vinegar, lemon, garlic, and salt in a stockpot and bring to a boil. Add the octopus and cook at a full boil for about 30 minutes.

Check for tenderness: Use a pair of tongs to lift the octopus out of the boiling water. Use a very sharp knife to cut off one of the tentacles at its base and slice a 1/4-inch-thick coin from the thickest end; taste for doneness. If the octopus isn't yet tender, return the tentacle to the pot and continue cooking, testing again for doneness at 5- to 7-minute intervals.

Transfer the octopus to a baking sheet to cool. Discard the cooking liquid. Cover with plastic wrap and refrigerate until thoroughly chilled, about 1 hour or up to 2 days. When the octopus has thoroughly chilled, remove and discard the head; slice the tentacles crosswise into 1/4-inch-thick coins.

TO MAKE THE POTATO CONFIT, place a rack in the middle position and preheat the oven to 350°F. Combine the potatoes, vegetable oil, olive oil, rosemary, and garlic in a shallow nonreactive baking dish. Season with salt and pepper, cover tightly with foil, and bake until the potatoes are just fork-tender, 12 to 15 minutes. Use a slotted spoon to lift the potatoes out of the oil and set them on a dish in a single layer to cool. (The potatoes can sit at room temperature for up to 2 hours. If you're not going to use them within 2 hours, transfer the potatoes and the confit oil to an airtight container and store in the fridge for up to 3 or 4 days.)

TO FINISH THE PULPO GALLEGO, heat the vegetable oil in a large stainless-steel sauté pan over high heat. When the oil begins to shimmer, add the sliced octopus, season with salt and pepper, and cook on one side until lightly browned, 1 to 2 minutes. Turn the octopus, add the garlic and the potato confit to the pan, and sauté until the garlic is lightly toasted, about 1 minute. Transfer the pulpo gallego to a serving plate. Garnish with the paprika, Arbequina olive oil, lemon zest, parsley, and lemon wedges.

ARROZ A LA CAZUELA

BRAISED RABBIT, SHRIMP, AND LOBSTER RICE STEW

The braised rabbit can be made ahead of time and kept in an airtight container in the refrigerator for up to 3 days. If you need to poach the lobster in advance to make this dish happen, you can do so the day before, but it's best if done the same day, while the rice is cooking. SERVES 4

RABBIT

2 Tbsp	vegetable oil
2 lb	rabbit legs (see Sources)
	Kosher salt and freshly ground black pepper
2	Spanish onions, diced
6 to 8	cloves garlic, crushed
2 Tbsp	(4 to 6 cloves) Roasted Garlic (page 366)
1/4 cup	tomato paste
1 cup	dry white wine
4	dried guindilla peppers (see Sources)
2	sprigs thyme
2	fresh bay leaves
1 Tbsp	whole black peppercorns
4 qts	Roasted Chicken Stock (page 362)

RICE

2 Tbsp	extra virgin olive oil
1/2 lb	Spanish chorizo, peeled and finely diced
1 Tbsp	unsalted butter
1/2	Spanish onion, diced
1 Tbsp	minced garlic (3 to 4 cloves)
2 cups	Calasparra rice (see Sources)
1 tsp	saffron threads
1/4 cup	chopped Roasted Plum Tomatoes (see page 366)
	Kosher salt
16	large fresh rock shrimp, peeled and deveined
2 Tbsp	minced fresh flat-leaf parsley
2	scallions (white and green parts), thinly sliced on the diagonal

TO SERVE

	Poached and Seared Maine Lobster (recipe follows)
	Juice of 1/2 lemon
8	slices baguette or other bread, toasted
1/4 cup	Saffron Aïoli (page 130)

TO BRAISE THE RABBIT LEGS, heat the vegetable oil in a large Dutch oven over medium-high heat. Season the rabbit with salt and pepper and sear the legs on both sides until browned, 2 to 3 minutes per side. Lift the legs out of the pot and set them aside. Add the onion and the raw and roasted garlic to the pot and cook, stirring occasionally, until translucent and lightly caramelized, about 10 minutes. Stir in the tomato paste and cook for 5 minutes more. Pour in the white wine and simmer until the liquid has reduced by half, about 5 minutes. Add the guindilla peppers, thyme, bay leaves, peppercorns, and stock and bring to a boil. Season to taste with salt and pepper. Lower the heat and return the rabbit to the pot. Cover and simmer until the meat is tender, about 1 hour.

Lift the rabbit legs out of the braising liquid and set them aside to cool to room temperature. Strain the braising liquid through a fine-mesh sieve, pressing on the solids with the back of a wooden spoon. Set aside the braising liquid and discard the solids.

Shred the rabbit meat, discarding the bones. At this point, the meat and braising liquid can be stored in separate airtight containers in the refrigerator for up to 3 days.

TO MAKE THE RICE, heat the olive oil in a large Dutch oven over medium-high heat. Add the chorizo and cook, stirring occasionally, until the fat is rendered and the chorizo is browned, about 5 minutes. Add the butter, onion, and garlic and cook, stirring occasionally, until the onion is translucent, about 10 minutes more. Add the rice and cook, stirring often, until the grains are lightly toasted, about 5 minutes. Add the reserved braising liquid, saffron, and roasted tomatoes and bring to a boil. Season to taste with salt. Lower the heat and simmer, stirring often, until the rice is al dente, 18 to 20 minutes.

Fold in the rabbit meat and shrimp and continue simmering the mixture until the shrimp are opaque and firm and the rabbit meat is warmed through, 2 to 3 minutes. Add the parsley and scallions and mix well.

TO SERVE, garnish the rice with the lobster and toasted baguette slices, and squeeze lemon over the top. Spread the saffron aïoli on the toast or serve it on the side.

LANGOSTA HERVIDA

POACHED AND SEARED MAINE LOBSTER

Only the tails and claws are needed for the *Arroz a la Cazuela*. You can enjoy the knuckle meat in the usual way, with drawn butter, or you could combine it with leftover aïoli, chopped celery, and onion and tuck the mixture into a toasted bun for a delicious lobster roll. (The meat from the little legs is good too; the easiest way to extract it is to roll over the legs with a rolling pin, then squeeze the meat out of the crushed shell. The lobster bodies, on the other hand, don't have much to offer, unless you want to make lobster stock for another use.) MAKES ABOUT 2 CUPS LOBSTER MEAT

2	fresh Maine lobsters (1 1/2-lb ea), tails and claws only
2 qts	water
2 Tbsp	kosher salt, plus more for seasoning
2 Tbsp	olive oil
1 Tbsp	unsalted butter

Thread bamboo skewers through the lobster tails along the top of the shell, to prevent them from curling as they cook. Prepare a large ice bath.

Bring the water and salt to a rolling boil in a stockpot large enough to keep the lobster tails submerged. When the water comes to a boil, take it off of the heat, add the lobster tails, and let them sit, immersed in the hot water, for 2 minutes. Add the claws and keep everything immersed in the hot water for another 5 minutes.

Transfer the tails and claws to the ice bath and let them cool completely. Use kitchen shears to cut lengthwise along the top of the tails, then carefully open the shells and remove the meat in one whole piece. Discard the shells, remove the vein from the tail, and cut the tail meat crosswise with kitchen shears into coins 1/2-inch thick. Crack and shell the claws, setting aside the knuckle meat for another use.

Just before serving the finished rice dish, heat the oil and butter in a sauté pan over medium-high heat. Season the lobster slices with salt and sear them until lightly browned on all sides and warmed through, 2 to 3 minutes per side.

P. 126 Arroz a la Cazuela

P. 126 Arroz a la Cazuela

P. 131 Alcachofas Asadas

ALLIOLI DE AZAFRÁN

SAFFRON AÏOLI

The leftover aïoli will keep, refrigerated in an airtight container, for up to 3 days, and it's delicious on a sandwich or served with steamed vegetables or crudités. MAKES ABOUT 2 CUPS

	Pinch of saffron threads
1 Tbsp	hot water
2	large egg yolks
	Juice of 2 lemons (about 1/4 cup)
1	clove garlic, minced
1 1/2 cups	vegetable oil
	Kosher salt

Combine the saffron and hot water and steep until the water is bright red, about 5 minutes. Combine the saffron water with the egg yolks, lemon juice, and garlic in a blender or food processor and purée until the mixture is very smooth and frothy, about 2 minutes. With the machine running, slowly add the oil in a thin stream and blend until the aïoli is emulsified (it should have the consistency of mayonnaise). Season to taste with salt.

ALCACHOFAS ASADAS

ROASTED ARTICHOKES

Immersing the trimmed artichokes in acidulated water preserves the lovely pale green color of the inner leaves. If you don't get them right into the lemon water, exposure to the air will turn them an unappetizing brown. You will have plenty of lemon vinaigrette left over: it keeps well in the refrigerator for up to a week and is delicious on any salad or blanched fresh vegetable (see photo, page 129). SERVES 4

VINAIGRETTE

	Juice of 2 lemons (about 1/4 cup)
1/2 cup	extra virgin olive oil
1	shallot, minced
	Kosher salt

ARTICHOKES

4	lemons
2 qts	cold water
2	large globe artichokes, stems attached
1 cup	Vegetable Stock (page 364)
2 Tbsp	extra virgin olive oil
2	cloves garlic, crushed
1	sprig rosemary
1 Tbsp	kosher salt
1/4 cup	fresh flat-leaf parsley leaves
1/4 cup	celery leaves
2	scallions (white and green parts), thinly sliced on the diagonal

Place a rack in the middle position and preheat the oven to 375°F.

TO MAKE THE VINAIGRETTE, whisk together the lemon juice, oil, and shallot and season to taste with salt. Measure out 2 Tbsp of the dressing and store the remainder for another use. (Transfer to an airtight container and keep refrigerated for up to 1 week.)

TO PREPARE THE ARTICHOKES, cut 3 lemons in half and squeeze into the water in a large bowl and add the squeezed halves to the water as well. Remove and discard the toughest outer leaves of the artichokes. Quickly peel the stems, cut the artichokes in half lengthwise, and immerse them in the lemon water. Cut the remaining lemon into quarters.

Combine the stock, oil, garlic, lemon quarters, rosemary, and salt in a shallow baking dish. Remove the artichokes from the lemon water and add them to the baking dish. Cover tightly with aluminum foil and bake until the artichokes are tender when pierced with a fork, about 40 minutes. Allow the artichokes to rest in the baking dish for 10 minutes (lift the corners of the foil to allow some steam to vent so that the artichokes stay warm without overcooking).

Use a teaspoon to gently scrape out and discard the fibrous inner choke. Slice the roasted artichokes lengthwise on the diagonal about 1/4-inch thick and toss gently with the parsley leaves, celery leaves, scallions, and lemon vinaigrette. Season to taste with salt. Serve hot.

BACALAO

Bacalao **(salted dried cod, aka salt cod) is a prized ingredient in Spanish cooking that dates back several centuries. When I walked into the Mercado de la Bretxa, the subterranean central market in San Sebastián, I was reminded that it was Basque fishermen who introduced it to Spain (likely using cod they caught in the Bay of Biscay, which San Sebastián overlooks).**

I've seen some impressive displays of salt cod: a staple ingredient in most Latin cuisine, it's accorded prime real estate in many of the great markets I've visited, from Lima to Quito, Mexico City to Havana, Madrid to Barcelona. Still, the scale and scope of the *bacalao* selection at La Bretxa was staggering: fillets of all shapes and sizes, impeccably arrayed in layered stacks and elaborate fan formations, the largest pieces hung aloft like giant wings. This profusion of *bacalao* stood out even amid the dazzling abundance of pristine seafood that stretched from one end of the immaculate tiled marketplace to the other.

Even from a distance I could see pronounced differences in texture. The *bacalao* varied from moist and dense to almost crusty. Looking closer, I saw labels indicating each type's curing time—from as little as four hours to as long as six months—and it struck me that the different varieties were calibrated to a range of uses that might only exist here in the San Sebastián area. I can't prove this hypothesis (though I would enjoy an opportunity to go about doing so), but it seems clear enough to me that the culinary virtues of salt cod would be understood and experienced on a whole other level in these parts; the locals have earned an epic reputation as passionate gastronomes and *bacalao* is one of their cherished food traditions. A good *bacalao* dish brings you straight to the sweet briny sea as quickly as just-shucked oyster.

Simply put, cod that has been salted and dried is an amazing repository of ocean-fresh flavor, which is unlocked through a process of repeated soaking and rinsing. It can be taken in various directions depending on the cooking method—from the simplest spreads and salads to savory *vizcaina* and creamy *pil-pil* (both archetypal Basque dishes). Here we have *brandade*, traditional in French and Basque cuisines and something else altogether: rich yet delicate in flavor, lush yet light in texture, it's basically an emulsion of *bacalao* with garlic, potato, and milk, baked to lavish perfection. *(Recipe follows.)*

P. 136 Brandade

BRANDADE

BAKED SALT COD WITH HERBED BREADCRUMBS

Note that the salt cod needs to be soaked for 24 hours, with a change of water every 6 to 8 hours and a thorough rinsing at the end. You can continue to store the soaked cod for 2 to 3 more days in the refrigerator, so long as you keep it immersed in water and continue to change the water daily (see photo, page 135). SERVES 4

COD

1 1/2 lb	boneless, skinless salt cod

HERBED BREADCRUMBS

2 Tbsp	unsalted butter
1 cup	finely ground panko breadcrumbs (see headnote, page 184)
1 Tbsp	minced fresh flat-leaf parsley
1 tsp	minced fresh thyme
	Kosher salt

BRANDADE

1	large (12-oz) russet potato, peeled and diced small
2 cups	heavy cream
1	fresh bay leaf
1	sprig rosemary
1 cup	Caramelized Onions (page 366)
16	cloves Roasted Garlic (page 366)
	Sliced baguette, buttered or brushed with olive oil and toasted, for serving

TO PREPARE THE COD, soak it in a covered container in the refrigerator for 24 hours, changing the water at least once. Drain the fish, rinse thoroughly, drain again, and cut into large chunks.

TO MAKE THE BREADCRUMBS, melt the butter in a large sauté pan over medium heat and add the panko. Toast, stirring often, until the panko is golden brown and evenly toasted, 10 to 12 minutes. Stir in the parsley and thyme and season gently with salt. Allow the breadcrumbs to cool to room temperature. If necessary, store in an airtight container at room temperature for up to 2 weeks.

Place a rack in the middle position and preheat the oven to 375°F.

Boil the salt cod in water to cover in a saucepan until the chunks of fish are easy to flake into smaller pieces with a fork but remain somewhat firm, about 20 minutes. Drain.

TO MAKE THE BRANDADE, meanwhile, in a separate small saucepan, combine the potatoes, cream, bay leaf, and rosemary. Simmer over low heat until the potatoes are tender and the mixture has reduced in volume by about a third, 10 to 12 minutes. Remove the bay leaf and the rosemary stem (the leaves will have fallen off). Drain the potatoes over a bowl to catch the cream. While the potatoes are still warm, combine them in a food processor with the cod, onion, and garlic and purée the mixture, slowly adding the reserved cream, until it is very smooth.

Transfer the brandade to a shallow casserole and top with breadcrumbs. Bake the brandade until it is hot all the way through and the top is golden brown, 15 to 18 minutes. Serve with sliced baguette.

SAN SEBASTIÁN

Sangría de Tinto | SPICED APPLE SANGRÍA

Crema Catalana | CHOCOLATE CUSTARD WITH VANILLA BERRIES

The first time I walked into a Basque *pintxo* bar, it felt for a split second like a scene from one of those old Westerns I've always loved: Battered cowboy lurches into saloon. Place goes silent, tinkly piano stops. Everyone turns, casts stony glance. All resume boozing and brawling. Okay, so it was a figment of my jet-lagged imagination. The bar bore no resemblance whatsoever to a frontier watering hole—it was all dark wood, stained glass, and blue-and-white Talavera tile. But my trusty sidekick (good friend and fellow chef Chad Williams) and I were definitely looking bedraggled after our overnight flight from Philly and the seven-hour haul from Madrid to San Sebastián on a local train that stopped every half hour. Red-eyed, rumpled, and famished (no dining car!) to the point of giddy near-hysteria, we did turn some heads among the well-heeled clientele at Bar Bergara.

The Basque barkeep didn't bat an eye. With his cool twirly moustache and immaculate white dress shirt and bowtie, he manned that bar with panache, pouring *manzanilla*, serving *pintxos*, and attending to all his guests' needs, smooth as silk, more Old World than Old West.

Once Chad and I collected ourselves and made our way up to the bar, we found a smorgasbord of exquisite little canapés: toasts (*montaditos*), sandwiches (*bocadillos*), and skewers (*brochetas* and *banderillas*), all scaled to offer a delectable bite or two. These were *pintxos*, as tapas are known in these parts, and they were not to be believed.

Now, this particular corner of Spain, the Basque Country (bordered on the west by the sea and heading into the Pyrenees in the east) is renowned the world over for mind-blowingly sophisticated food, an idiosyncratic marriage of French and Spanish cuisine. It is the homeland of culinary heavy hitters like Juan Mari Arzak, Martín Berasategui, Andoni Luis Aduriz, and Pedro Subijana. And San Sebastián is the capital of Basque gastronomy, a small city that glitters with Michelin stars. The people here are really, really into food. *Txokos*, or private culinary societies, are a long-standing (and largely all-male) tradition. And the *tapeo*, or tapas bar pub crawl, known in these parts as a *poteo*, is an important social ritual: it's typical to head out for dinner via five or six *pintxo* bars.

At Bar Bergara that night, the *pintxos* included *montaditos* topped with foie gras terrine and mango glazed in a sherry reduction, warm tartlets filled with braised duck meat and Cabrales blue cheese, and miniature croissants layered with smoked salmon and egg salad, to name just a few. Chad and I pretty well ravaged the selection—I think our final count of *pintxos* consumed was twenty-nine. It was a legendary food experience for sure, and one that spawned the concept for my second restaurant venture. The following year, back in Philadelphia, along came Tinto, a place with the relaxed yet refined atmosphere and the delectable food of a Basque *pintxo* bar.

In this menu, some of my favorite *pintxos* kick things off on a savory and sophisticated Basque note, excellent with the festive spiced-apple Sangría de Tinto. Then comes a parade of elegant and mostly traditional Spanish dishes: *salmorejo*, a refined gazpacho based on the ones from Córdoba in Andalucía; steak with Catalan-style spinach; white asparagus with truffle oil, a specialty in northern Spain; and, finally, a Catalan crème brûlée.

SANGRÍA DE TINTO

SPICED APPLE SANGRÍA

Sangría is deeply rooted in Spanish tradition, dating back to Roman times when fruit was added to light, young red wines to boost their flavor. Nowadays sangrías are also often made with white wine. Keith Raimondi, one of my go-to guys when it comes to developing new cocktails, got the inspiration for this particular sangría one day when he was munching on an apple. The apple brandy and spiced apple simple syrup infuse the sangría with a pronounced apple flavor. When we were developing the recipe, we used a locally made apple brandy that imparted the flavors of the Mid-Atlantic region. Keep the leftover apple syrup in a sealed jar in the refrigerator, for future use—for another batch of sangría or drizzling over vanilla ice cream. SERVES 8

SPICED APPLE SYRUP

2	crisp organic apples
1 1/2 cups + 3 cups	water
	Juice from 2 lemons
1 cup	granulated sugar
2	cinnamon sticks
1 Tbsp	whole black peppercorns

MACERATED FRUIT

1	navel orange, peel on, finely diced
1	pear, cored and finely diced
6 Tbsp	(3 oz) orange liqueur
6 Tbsp	(3 oz) Simple Syrup (page 367)

SANGRÍA

1	(750 ml) bottle tempranillo or other full-bodied red wine
10 Tbsp	(5 oz) apple brandy
6 Tbsp	(3 oz) orange liqueur
6 Tbsp	freshly squeezed lemon juice, strained (about 1 1/2 lemons)

TO MAKE THE APPLE SYRUP, remove the peel and core from the apples and put the trimmings in a small saucepan. Set aside the flesh of 1 apple for the macerated fruit (to keep the apple from browning, cover it in a mixture of 3 cups water and the juice from 2 lemons); eat the other one or save it for another use. Add the 1 1/2 cups water, sugar, cinnamon sticks, and black peppercorns to the apple trimmings and bring to a boil. Lower the heat and simmer until the syrup thickens, about 15 minutes. Remove from the heat and allow the syrup to cool completely. Strain the syrup, discarding the trimmings, and measure out 1/2 cup. Refrigerate the remainder in an airtight jar for another use.

TO MAKE THE MACERATED FRUIT, cut the reserved apple into small dice, combine it in a bowl with the pear, orange, orange liqueur, and simple syrup and leave it to soak, refrigerated, for 30 minutes.

TO MAKE THE SANGRÍA, combine the wine, brandy, liqueur, lemon juice, and 1/2 cup apple syrup and stir vigorously. Serve the sangría over ice, with about 2 tablespoons of fruit in each serving.

BANDERILLAS

MELON SKEWERS WITH ANCHOVIES AND PICKLED PEPPERS

Banderillas are named for the resemblance of the little skewers to the dart-like *banderillas* wielded by the *banderilleros* in traditional bullfighting. Like other *pintxos* (Basque tapas), *banderillas* combine select ingredients—from simple to rarefied—for a delicious morsel. Here is one of my favorite examples, in which the brininess of the anchovies, the sweetness of the melon, and the acidity and heat of the pickled guindilla peppers come together for a perfectly balanced bite. Galia melon resembles a cantaloupe on the outside but has pale green flesh that looks like honeydew and has a luscious sweet flavor all its own. If it is not available, substitute conventional cantaloupe. SERVES 8 AS AN APPETIZER

24	(1-inch) cubes peeled Galia melon (about 2 melons)
24	marinated white anchovy fillets (see Sources), drained
24	pickled guindilla peppers (see Sources), drained, stemmed, and cut crosswise into 1/2-inch pieces
2 Tbsp	Arbequina olive oil (see Sources)
2 Tbsp	minced fresh flat-leaf parsley
	Coarse sea salt

Gently wrap each melon cube with an anchovy fillet and thread onto 24 (3-inch) bamboo skewers, along with a guindilla pepper (see photo). Serve chilled, garnished with a few drops of Arbequina olive oil (about 1/4 tsp each), a sprinkling of parsley, and sea salt to taste.

MONTADITO DE PATO
CANAPÉS WITH DUCK CONFIT AND SERRANO HAM

Montadito translates as "up in the saddle." The *pintxos* (Basque tapas) known as *montaditos* are open-faced mini sandwiches with tasty tidbits "mounted" on slices of bread—meats, cheeses, salmon, fried cod, anchovies, caviar, mayonnaise-based salads, anything that can go on bread, really. I'm happy to share my own take on a *montadito* here: duck wrapped in ham and seared crisp sits astride a spread made from blue-veined and buttery La Peral cheese. It's all topped off with a slightly sour black cherry conserve in rich syrup. You'll have enough cheese spread left over to incorporate into a sandwich or enjoy with bread, crackers, or figs the next day. SERVES 8 AS AN APPETIZER

CHEESE SPREAD

6 oz	La Peral (see Sources) or other blue-veined cheese, rind removed
2 Tbsp	crème fraîche

DUCK

2 Tbsp	vegetable oil
6	confit duck legs, each skinned, boned, and cut into 4 equal pieces (approximately 2 1/2 lb meat) (see Sources)
24	slices Serrano ham (about 6 oz)

TOAST

24	slices baguette
2 Tbsp	extra virgin olive oil

TO SERVE

24	Amarena black cherries in syrup (see Sources)
2 Tbsp	minced fresh flat-leaf parsley

TO MAKE THE CHEESE SPREAD, combine the cheese and crème fraîche in a small bowl and mix until very creamy. Measure out 1/4 cup and refrigerate the remainder in an airtight container for another use, up to 3 days.

TO COOK THE DUCK, heat a grill pan or nonstick sauté pan over medium heat and add the oil, swirling to thoroughly coat. Wrap each piece of the duck leg meat with a slice of ham. Sear on all sides until the ham is crispy and the duck is warmed through, about 6 minutes total.

TO MAKE THE TOAST, heat the broiler to medium-high. Brush the baguette slices with the olive oil and lightly toast, turning once to toast both sides.

TO SERVE, top each toast with a dab of the cheese spread, one piece of duck, and one cherry with syrup. Garnish the montaditos with parsley and serve warm.

CHANQUETES FRITOS CON ROMESCO

FRIED LITTLE FISH WITH ROMESCO

Young guy that I was back when I apprenticed at La Taberna del Alabardero in the beach resort of Puerto Banús, I made the happy discovery that the town was a real hub for nightlife—the bars and clubs stayed open all night long and into the morning. One time I was out until 8:00 a.m. and figured I'd be better off staying awake than going back to the hostel for the mere two hours before I was due for my shift. So at ten in the morning, there I stood outside the restaurant, just looking like hell, and when Capitán (the chef) arrived he could see right away the state I was in. He didn't miss a beat—just handed me a bucket of a couple thousand *chanquetes*, tiny fish about half the size of a pinky finger, and said "Okay, Joe, I want you to take all of these and clean them." The fish were very much alive and swimming around the bucket frantically, so it was all I could do even to get hold of one. I'd spent half the day getting maybe ten or twelve of them clean when Capi finally told me to go home. Of course there was no need to clean all those little fish—the head, tail, and bones all break down when they're fried, so you can simply pop the whole thing in your mouth. Spaniards love to eat them, and so do I, even if my first encounter with them was a bit of a cruel joke. SERVES 8

(continued)

ROMESCO

16 pieces	Roasted Plum Tomatoes (page 366)
1	jarred roasted red bell pepper, drained, rinsed (if packed in brine or oil), and seeded
1	clove garlic, crushed
1 tsp	honey
2 Tbsp	sherry vinegar
1/4 tsp	crushed red pepper
1/3 cup	sliced almonds, toasted (see page 368) and ground
1/2 cup	vegetable oil
	Kosher salt

FISH

4 cups	all-purpose flour
2 cups	cornstarch
2 Tbsp	Spanish smoked sweet paprika, plus more as needed
2 Tbsp	kosher salt
2 tsp	freshly ground black pepper
2 qts	vegetable oil
2 lb	fresh or thawed frozen baby whitebait or other small smelts or baby sardines (see Sources)

TO SERVE

	Coarse sea salt
	Spanish smoked sweet paprika
2 Tbsp	minced fresh flat-leaf parsley
	Fresh lemon wedges

TO MAKE THE SAUCE, combine the tomatoes, roasted pepper, garlic, honey, vinegar, and red pepper in a food processor and purée until smooth. Add the almonds and process a bit before slowly adding the oil in a thin stream with the machine running, until the sauce is emulsified. Season to taste with salt. Store, refrigerated, in a sealed container until needed, up to 3 days.

TO PREPARE THE FISH, combine the flour, cornstarch, paprika, salt, and pepper in a bowl and mix well. Pass through a sifter or fine-mesh sieve to break up any lumps. At this point, the seasoned flour can be stored in a sealed, dry container until needed.

Heat the oil to 375°F in a stockpot, using a candy or deep-fry thermometer to monitor the temperature. Line a baking sheet with parchment paper.

Put the seasoned flour in a large bowl and, working in small batches, gently toss the fish in the flour until completely coated. Shake off any excess flour and fry the fish in batches (only as many as will fit in a single layer) in the hot oil until golden brown and crispy, about 2 minutes. Drain on the paper-lined sheet and season to taste with sea salt and paprika.

SERVE HOT with the romesco sauce, parsley, and lemon wedges.

SALMOREJO

GAZPACHO WITH STRAWBERRIES, QUAIL EGGS, AND OLIVES

A very thorough purée is essential; you want the tomato seeds completely pulverized so that the base has a very smooth, uniform texture. For both the puréeing and the subsequent emulsifying step, you will need to work in batches, divvying up the ingredients proportionally according to the size of your blender and seasoning each to taste with salt and sugar and additional vinegar, if desired. Be sure that the batches are proportional (otherwise the texture of the finished soup will be off—grainy from too much bread in one batch, or overly viscous from excess olive oil in another batch.) But don't worry if the batches come out slightly different colors; the soup will blend into one uniform shade when you whisk the batches together. There are at least three good options for serving this traditional Catalan gazpacho and its various accompaniments: garnish each bowl with a little of each of the embellishments; pass all the extras at the table; or my favorite way (as pictured, page 153), arrange the garnishes in the bottom of each bowl and serve each portion of chilled *salmorejo* in a small crock alongside, to pour over all the goodies. SERVES 8

SOUP

2 1/2 lb	ripe beefsteak tomatoes
1	cucumber, peeled, seeded, and coarsely chopped
3	cloves garlic, crushed
1/2 cup	sherry vinegar, plus more to taste
1	small day-old baguette, crust on, torn into 1-inch pieces
1 cup	extra virgin olive oil
1/2 cup	Arbequina olive oil (see Sources)
	Kosher salt
1/2 tsp	granulated sugar (optional)

TO SERVE

16	ripe strawberries, stemmed and halved lengthwise
8	Boiled Quail Eggs (page 311), peeled and quartered, or 1 chicken egg, hard-boiled, peeled, and chopped
2 Tbsp	pitted, slivered kalamata olives
2	(4-oz) cans ventresca tuna packed in olive oil (see page 117), drained and flaked
	Minced fresh chives (optional)
	Garlic Chips (page 242; optional)

TO MAKE THE SOUP, combine the tomatoes, cucumber, garlic, vinegar, and baguette in a large bowl and mix thoroughly. Purée in small batches in a blender or food processor for 2 to 3 minutes per batch, until the mixture is very smooth and the tomato seeds are no longer visible. Continue puréeing the mixture while slowly adding the extra virgin olive oil in a thin stream and process until emulsified (try to add proportional amounts of oil to each batch, see headnote). Season to taste with salt. Strain through a fine-mesh sieve, pressing through the solids with the back of a wooden spoon.

Working in batches, return a portion of the purée to the blender. With the machine running, slowly add a proportional amount of the Arbequina olive oil in a thin stream, processing until the mixture is emulsified. Again season to taste with salt and (if necessary) sugar and/or additional vinegar. Repeat with the remaining portions of the tomato purée and Arbequina oil, then whisk the batches together. Taste and adjust seasoning with more salt and sugar.

Cover and refrigerate the soup until it is well chilled, at least 1 hour.

FOR THE GARNISH, first char the strawberries. Heat a cast-iron skillet over medium heat. Place the strawberries in the pan and quickly char on one side. Remove the berries from the skillet and keep warm.

Serve the salmorejo cold, garnished with the warm charred strawberries, quail eggs, olives, tuna, chives, and garlic chips.

ENTRECÔTE CON MEMBRILLO Y QUESO DE CABRA

SIRLOIN STEAK WITH QUINCE PASTE AND FRESH GOAT CHEESE

Membrillo, or quince paste, provides a touch of sweetness in contrast to all the savory elements in this dish. **Membrillo** is also a perfect accompaniment for Spanish and other cheeses. SERVES 8

MARINADE

24	cloves Roasted Garlic (page 366)
2 Tbsp	minced fresh rosemary
2 Tbsp	minced fresh thyme
1/2 cup	extra virgin olive oil

STEAKS

8	(6-oz) sirloin steaks
2 Tbsp	vegetable oil
	Kosher salt and freshly ground black pepper

TO SERVE

	Catalan Spinach (page 156)
2 Tbsp	membrillo (quince paste)
1/2 cup	soft mild goat cheese (about 1/4 lb)
1/3 cup	Rosemary Oil (recipe follows)

TO MAKE THE MARINADE, combine the roasted garlic, rosemary, thyme, and olive oil and mix well. If making the marinade ahead, store it in an airtight container in the refrigerator until needed, up to 3 days.

COMBINE THE STEAKS and marinade in a large zip-top bag and refrigerate at least 2 hours, ideally overnight.

Place a rack in the middle position and preheat the oven to 450°F.

Heat the vegetable oil in a large stainless-steel sauté pan over medium-high heat. Remove the steaks from the marinade and pat dry. Season generously with salt and pepper and gently set the steaks in the pan and sear until well browned on one side, about 2 minutes. Turn the steaks, transfer the pan to the oven, and cook to desired doneness, 6 to 7 minutes for medium-rare. Transfer the steaks to a cutting board and allow the meat to rest for 3 minutes before slicing.

TO SERVE, slice the steaks and season to taste with salt and pepper. Serve with the spinach, garnishing each plate with a little membrillo paste, goat cheese, and rosemary oil.

ACIETE DE ROMERO

ROSEMARY OIL

Store leftover oil in an airtight container at room temperature (out of direct sunlight) for up to 3 weeks; use on roasted vegetables and as a marinade for beef, chicken, pork, or game.

MAKES ABOUT 1/2 CUP

1/2 cup	extra virgin olive oil
	Leaves from 2 sprigs rosemary, stems discarded
1/4 cup	densley packed Italian parsley leaves

Combine the olive oil and rosemary in a small saucepan and heat over low heat until bubbles begin to form around the edges of the rosemary leaves, 2 to 3 minutes. Remove from the heat and allow the oil to cool to room temperature.

Combine the rosemary and oil with the parsley in a blender and purée until very smooth.

ESPINACA A LA CATALANA

CATALAN SPINACH

SERVES 8

2 Tbsp	extra virgin olive oil
2 Tbsp	minced garlic (6 to 8 cloves)
2	shallots, finely diced
2 lb	baby spinach
1	large Granny Smith apple, peeled, cored, and diced small
1/2 cup	dried black currants
1/2 cup	pine nuts, toasted (see page 368)
2 Tbsp	sherry vinegar
	Kosher salt

Heat the olive oil in a large stainless-steel sauté pan over medium-high heat. Cook the garlic and shallots until translucent, stirring often, about 2 minutes. Add the spinach, apple, currants, pine nuts, and vinegar and cook until the spinach is wilted, about 1 minute. Season the spinach to taste with salt.

ESPÁRRAGOS CON TRUFAS

WHITE ASPARAGUS WITH BLACK TRUFFLE AND EGG

White asparagus is elegant in appearance and delicate in flavor, and in Spain it is often served simply with olive oil, garlic, salt, and pepper. It is white rather than green because the stalks are kept covered with soil as they're growing, which prevents them from developing chlorophyll. The stalks are peeled prior to cooking to remove the tough, bitter outer layer. Any leftover Parmesan cream can be kept refrigerated in an airtight container for up to 2 days and enjoyed drizzled over steamed vegetables, pasta, or a simple omelet. SERVES 8

PARMESAN CREAM

1 qt	heavy cream
4	cloves Roasted Garlic (page 366)
1/2 lb	Parmesan cheese, finely grated (about 1 1/2 cups)
	Kosher salt

EGGS

8	large eggs
	Distilled white vinegar

ASPARAGUS

4	bunches fresh white asparagus (about 4 lbs), peeled, trimmed, and blanched
2 Tbsp	extra virgin olive oil
	Kosher salt

TO SERVE

2 Tbsp	Arbequina olive oil (see Sources)
	Freshly ground black pepper
1/2 oz	shaved fresh black truffles
2 Tbsp	cooked and drained, chopped thick-cut bacon (about 4 slices)
	Grated Parmesan cheese
2 Tbsp	minced fresh flat-leaf parsley

Place a rack in the middle position and preheat the oven to 450°F. Line a baking sheet with parchment paper.

TO MAKE THE PARMESAN CREAM, combine the heavy cream and roasted garlic in a small saucepan and simmer over medium heat, stirring occasionally, until reduced by half, 10 to 12 minutes (it will coat the back of a spoon). Slowly whisk in the Parmesan, stirring until the cheese is completely melted and the cream reduction thickens. Season to taste with salt, strain through a fine-mesh sieve into a clean saucepan, and keep warm until needed (or refrigerate in an airtight container for up to 2 days and gently rewarm before using).

TO POACH THE EGGS, crack an egg into a small cup or dish. Heat a few inches of water with a splash of vinegar in a saucepan. Line a large plate with paper towels. When the water is hot enough to form bubbles across the bottom of the pan but still shy of simmering, lower the heat to keep the water below the boiling point and swirl the water with a spoon to make a whirlpool. Gently slip the egg from its dish into the center of the whirlpool. Cook the egg until it is nearly set (it should barely jiggle in the center when nudged with a spoon), 3 to 4 minutes. Lift the egg out of the pan with a slotted spoon and set it on paper towels to drain. Repeat to cook the remaining 7 eggs.

TO ROAST THE ASPARAGUS, brush the spears with the extra virgin olive oil and season with salt. Roast the asparagus on the paper-lined baking sheet until the spears are warmed through and lightly caramelized, about 5 minutes.

TO REWARM THE POACHED EGGS just before serving, return them to the hot (but not boiling) water for 1 minute, remove them carefully with a slotted spoon, and dry again on paper towels.

TO SERVE, remove the asparagus from the oven, drizzle with Arbequina olive oil, and season with salt and pepper. Divide the asparagus among eight serving plates. Top with a warm poached egg and garnish with shaved black truffles, bacon, Parmesan cream, grated Parmesan, and parsley.

CREMA CATALANA
CHOCOLATE CUSTARD WITH VANILLA BERRIES

Crema catalana is a classic Spanish dessert similar to the French crème brûlée. Here the basic recipe gets a twist with the addition of chocolate and fresh berries. Note that you will need a culinary or crème brûlée torch to caramelize the sugared top of the custard. You can make the vanilla syrup up to two weeks in advance, but hold off macerating (soaking) the fruit until no more than 15 minutes before you are going to serve the custards. The custards need to chill for about four hours, but once caramelized, they shouldn't sit more than about 10 minutes: you want the tops brittle and the creamy custard beneath cold. SERVES 8

(continued)

CUSTARD

1 cup	cold whole milk
3 1/2 tsp	unflavored granulated gelatin
1 1/2 lb	good-quality dark chocolate, such as Valrhona or Scharffen Berger, grated (3 cups)
2 1/2 cups	cold heavy cream
1 cup	granulated sugar
18	large egg yolks, at room temperature
1/4 tsp	kosher salt

VANILLA-MACERATED BERRIES

1	Tahitian vanilla bean (see Sources)
2 cups	water
2 cups	granulated sugar
5 cups	mixed seasonal berries, such as strawberries, blackberries, and raspberries

BRÛLÉE

	Raw sugar (such as Demerara, sanding, or raw cane sugar), for sprinkling

TO SERVE

	Lemon zest, for garnish

TO MAKE THE CUSTARD, combine the milk and gelatin and let sit for 10 minutes or until the gelatin is completely dissolved.

Set a double boiler over medium heat with 2 inches water in the bottom and bring to a boil. Decrease the heat to low, place the chocolate in the top of the double boiler, and stir to melt the chocolate, taking care not to let it scorch.

Combine the cream and sugar in a saucepan and bring to a simmer over low heat, stirring occasionally, 3 to 5 minutes. Put the egg yolks in a large heatproof bowl. Pour half of the hot cream mixture in a steady stream into the egg yolks, stirring constantly. Add the tempered yolks back to the cream mixture in the saucepan and cook over low heat, stirring constantly, until the custard thickens to the point of coating the back of a spoon. Remove the custard from the heat. Add the gelatin mixture and melted chocolate and mix well to incorporate them. Stir in the salt.

Strain the custard through a fine-mesh sieve and pour it into eight shallow 6-ounce custard cups. Allow the custard to cool to room temperature. Refrigerate for at least 4 hours or up to 3 days, covered tightly with plastic wrap to keep the tops from drying out and to prevent refrigerator smells from permeating the custards.

TO MAKE THE VANILLA MACERATING SYRUP, split the vanilla bean lengthwise and combine it in a saucepan with the water and granulated sugar. Bring to a boil, then lower the heat and simmer for 15 minutes. Remove from the heat and allow it to cool to room temperature. Discard the vanilla bean and measure out 1/4 cup of the syrup, storing the remainder for another use. (It will keep in an airtight container in the refrigerator for up to 2 weeks.)

When you are ready to serve the custards, macerate the fruit: combine the berries in a bowl with the 1/2 cup vanilla simple syrup; they can be left to soak at room temperature for up to 15 minutes.

TO CARAMELIZE THE CHILLED CUSTARDS, just before serving, coat the tops with the raw sugar, gently tipping off any excess: it should be a fine, thin layer of sugar. Use a culinary or crème brûlée torch to caramelize the sugar evenly across the top of each custard. This should take about 1 minute per custard, but may happen more quickly: be watchful and use caution.

Garnish the custards with berries and lemon zest and serve immediately.

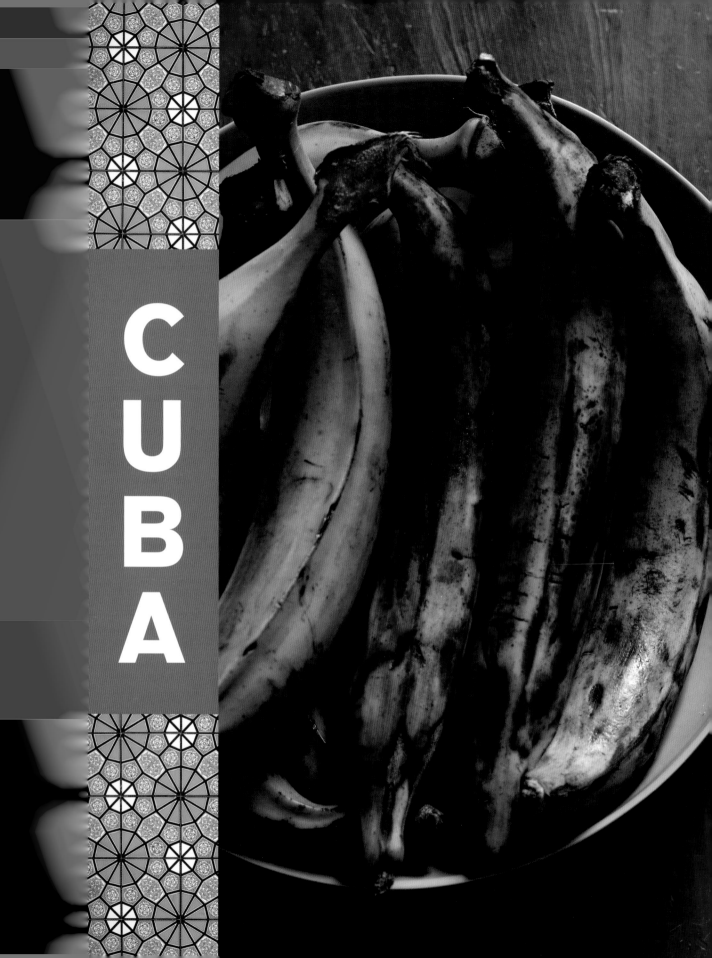

CUBA

MENU 1
HAVANA

Vieiras con Rabo Encendido y Tamal en Cazuela | SCALLOPS WITH BRAISED OXTAIL AND PORRIDGE

Plátanos Maduros | FRIED SWEET PLANTAINS

MENU 2
CIENFUEGOS

Enchilado de Langosta | LOBSTER IN SPICY TOMATO SAUCE

Cachuchas Fritas | FRIED STUFFED CHILES

Ensalada de Garbanzos | GARBANZO BEAN SALAD WITH LEMON-DIJON DRESSING

MENU 3
SANTIAGO DE CUBA

Ensalada de Palmito | HEARTS OF PALM WITH COCONUT VINAIGRETTE

Ropa Vieja con Frijoles Colorados | SHREDDED BEEF STEW WITH RED BEANS

MENU 4
MIAMI

La Tormenta | DARK AND STORMY MOJITO

Frituras de Malanga | MALANGA FRITTERS

Frituras de Bacalao | SALT COD FRITTERS

Sopa de Calabaza con Cangrejo | ROASTED SQUASH SOUP WITH CRAB AND ZUCCHINI

Lechón Asado | ACHIOTE- AND CITRUS-MARINATED ROAST SUCKLING PIG

Moros y Cristianos | BLACK BEANS AND RICE

Yuca con Mojo Criollo | YUCA WITH SOUR ORANGE MOJO

Tostones | CRISPY FRIED GREEN PLANTAINS

Pasteles de Guayaba | GUAVA AND CREAM CHEESE TURNOVERS

ESSENTIALS | Café Cubano PG 176 | Cubano PG 186

THIRD STOP:
CUBA

Cuba—Cuban food, Cuban culture, Cuban family—first entered my life by way of my mentor and dear friend Douglas Rodriguez. Back in the late 1990s, I landed and then lost my first executive chef job in New York City. I overreached and wiped out. It was humbling, to say the least. Still, I was determined to give the restaurant business another shot, my best shot, and fill in the gaps in experience and leadership that had been my downfall. So I started over, as a twelve-buck-an-hour line cook.

Lucky for me, my new boss was none other than Douglas Rodriguez, a Cuban-American chef-restaurateur making a big name for himself as a culinary pioneer, the godfather of an emerging cuisine called *Nuevo Latino* (Latin Fusion). I was in awe of this guy and everything he'd achieved, and I gave my all in the kitchens at Pipa and Chicama, his two New York restaurants. Douglas took note, took interest, and took me under his wing.

He was a great mentor, sharing his expertise, fostering my talent, and pushing me to strive (and kicking my ass now and then). Traveling with him to various events taught me a lot about the publicity side of the culinary industry. When these travels took us to Miami, I got my first glimpses of the robust community of Little Havana, a vast and vibrant neighborhood that is a cultural capital for Cuban Americans.

And it would be Douglas who gave me my big break: bringing me aboard to help launch a high-concept restaurant—Alma de Cuba—for Stephen Starr in Philadelphia and to run the place as executive chef once it opened. This was huge: new city, new cuisine, new shot at the big time. Hell-bent on proving worthy of all the faith Douglas was investing in me, I took what little time and money I could scrape together and made a pilgrimage to Cuba.

The country was just emerging from a period of severe economic crisis and deprivation brought on by the dissolution of the Soviet Union. Still, Havana, with all its crumbling colonial buildings and hulking jalopies, had this joyous, upbeat vibe that amazed me. Great live music was everywhere. In public squares I saw Afro-Cuban women in elaborate traditional costumes, singing their hearts out between drags on big fat cigars. And there were countless bars and clubs where ensembles played *son*, salsa, conga, mambo, and on and on. While the mojitos certainly did not disappoint, restaurant food was pretty mediocre. But once I had the help and company of a local guide, I discovered *paladares* (home restaurants) in and around Havana and elsewhere on the island. So it was at the dining room tables of modest Cuban homes, usually alongside a few Canadian and German tourists, that I had my best meals—and got my introduction to various hearty, full-flavored staples of Cuban home cooking: *tostones*, *moros y cristianos*, *frijoles colorados*, *pernil asado*, *langosta a la plancha*, and more.

A week later, I was back in Philly, soulful Cuban *son* ringing in my ears, rich Cuban flavors lingering on my tongue. I was full of inspiration and had a great time working with Douglas to develop the menu for Alma. After the twists and turns in my career path over the previous few years, this foray into Cuban food was a definitive move. That much I knew. What I did not know was that another Cuban connection was just around the corner: right there at Alma de Cuba I'd meet *mi esposa cubana*, and before long we'd be raising two Cuban-Ecuadorian-American kids in a house that's as often filled with the savory scent of *arepas* sizzling on the stove as it is with the rich aroma of *ropa vieja* stewing in the pressure cooker.

Today, family—immediate and extended—is for me every bit as much Cuban as it is Ecuadorian. I hit the jackpot in the in-law department: Beatriz's parents and her vast yet close-knit family are a wonderful bunch and I have been fully adopted into the fold. They all live in Miami, so we get down there as often as possible, and her parents visit us in Philadelphia regularly. Wherever we get together, I never cease to marvel at how festive any gathering is. There is always an abundance of food, affection, high spirits, and animated conversation—they really make a celebration of life.

This direct and intimate connection to Cuban culture has deepened and broadened my experience and firsthand knowledge of Latin cuisine. And it fuels my desire to know more, especially about the full range of Caribbean cuisine, the various styles and influences throughout the islands.

Meantime, back home, Cuban food is a dinner option any night of the week. The menus in this chapter include some of our favorite dishes. I hope they inspire you to get this exuberant and supremely savory cuisine into your mealtime rotation as well.

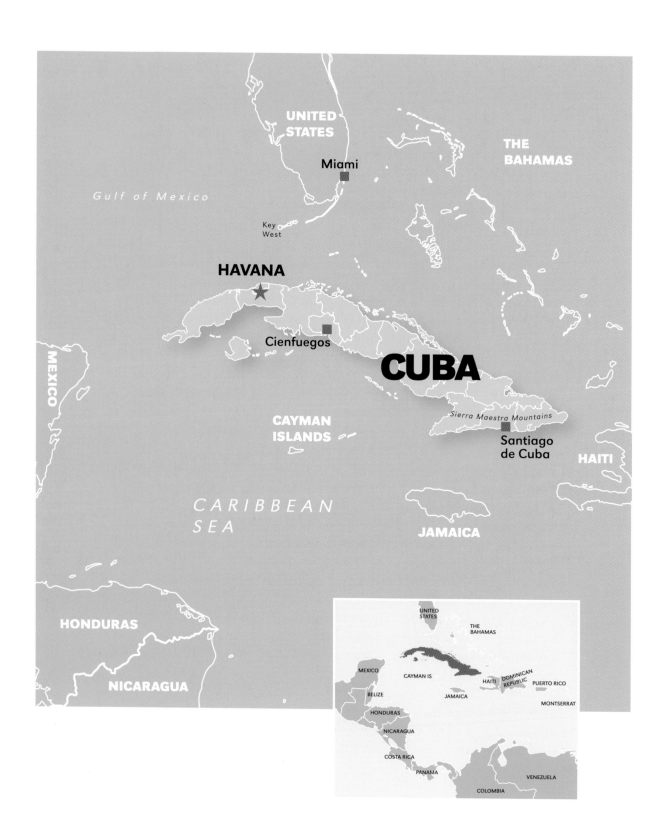

QUICK INFO

LAND

• An archipelago, with the main island surrounded by groups of smaller ones

• Largest island in the Caribbean, with just over 2,300 miles of coastline

• Tropical climate and volcanic soil; landscape mostly flat plains, with the Sierra Maestra Mountains in the southeast

• Principal cities: Havana, Santiago de Cuba

PEOPLE

• Current population is over 11 million

• Main ethnic groups are white (Spanish immigration continued long after Cuban independence), Afro-Cuban, and mixed race. Also a significant Asian population, originating with Chinese workers who came on labor contracts in the early twentieth century

FOOD

• Creole-style blend of African, Spanish, Chinese, and indigenous traditions

• Native people farmed corn, yuca, calabaza (squash) and chiles; all still staples. Local tropical fruits, such as papaya, coconut, avocado, pineapple, plantains, and guava also integral to the cuisine, along with seafood

• Spanish brought beans, rice, citrus, mangoes, coffee, and sugarcane

• Livestock such as horses, cattle, chicken, and pigs came from Europe

---

500 BCE–1492 CE
Prior to Spanish conquest, Cuba's inhabitants were the indigenous Taino.

1494 CE
Columbus claims the island for Spain; by 1514, conquistador Diego Velázquez has enslaved the Taino, who are then largely wiped out within a generation by disease and privation.

1494-1902 CE
Spain retains possession of Cuba for 400 years, importing African slaves who eventually comprise about 40 percent of the population.

1902 CE
Cuba becomes a fully independent state.

HAVANA

Vieiras con Rabo Encendido y Tamal en Cazuela | SCALLOPS WITH BRAISED OXTAIL AND PORRIDGE

Plátanos Maduros | FRIED SWEET PLANTAINS

Of all the dishes Douglas Rodriguez and I created at Alma de Cuba, this might be my favorite. A surf-and-turf number that's served up and savored all together, it evolved, as did much of the Alma menu, from a series of ideas tossed back and forth across a table in the back corner of the restaurant while the space was still under construction. That day, Douglas was all about *tamal en cazuela*. In its typical form, this staple of Cuban home cooking is a resourceful way of reconstituting leftover *tamales* into a porridge-casserole. Douglas had already reimagined the traditional *tamal*, using white cornmeal and chicken stock to refine it into a smoother and more elegant porridge, almost like a soft polenta. Certain this *tamal* belonged on the menu, he puzzled over what its role would be.

This was my first encounter with any *tamal*—I'd worked for Douglas for two years, at two restaurants, neither of them Cuban—and I loved it and agreed that we should build a dish around it. So we brainstormed away, pairing the *tamal* with another Cuban classic: *rabo encendido*. In English it's usually called braised oxtail, but the more literal translation, "tail ablaze," tells you a whole lot more about what makes this zesty rich dish a favorite of Cubans everywhere. I'd happily discovered *rabo* for myself just a week or two prior in Havana, on a trip I made to Cuba as sort of a crash course in Cuban food and culture.

Like any savory Cuban dish, *rabo* is always served with fried plantains, so the *plátanos maduros* were definitely our garnish here. But the idea of topping it all off with roasted scallops came to me pretty much out of the blue. Scallops would provide a delicate foil, a way of complementing the hearty flavors and textures of the oxtail and *tamal* and offsetting their heft just a bit. Plus, although it's not at all traditional to combine *rabo* with scallops, there is a strong tradition of *mar y montaña* ("sea and mountain," aka surf and turf) in Cuban food and in Latin cooking in general. This seemed like a perfect riff on that tradition: the beef and the corn and the plantains are very much of the earth, while the scallops bring the clean brininess of the ocean. Douglas was fully on board with the idea and the dish came together right then and there. We gave it a starring role on the menu, and it was one of our most popular dishes. It was exactly the kind of food that made the restaurant a big success, eventually.

I say eventually because at first Alma did not receive an especially warm reception. True to their reputation as staunch home-team loyalists, Philadelphians didn't come out in droves to see what the two chefs imported from Manhattan had to offer. In fact, a few months after opening, business was still on the slow side and Steve was threatening to reconcept the place as Asia de Cuba. But the Philly tide soon turned, and the customers and good reviews came our way. Meanwhile, I'd made the acquaintance of a certain Cuban gal on the wait staff at Alma—the lovely Beatriz Mirabal, who was working her way through dental school. I'm happy to say that things worked out well all around: Alma de Cuba remains a successful pillar of the Starr Restaurant Group, and Beatriz and I have been married since 2002.

VIEIRAS CON RABO ENCENDIDO Y TAMAL EN CAZUELA

SCALLOPS WITH BRAISED OXTAIL AND PORRIDGE

A pressure cooker is a must-have, both for this recipe and in general; it is the quickest and surest way to transform tough cuts of meat into meltingly tender stews. Oxtails are available from most butchers, who can separate them into discs for you if they haven't already been cut apart. After you've cooked and shredded the meat, it is important to keep it separate from the braising liquid; if it is left sitting in the warm liquid and then reheated before serving rather than just folded in at the very end, it is likely to overcook and dry out. And a word about scallops: diver scallops tend to be freshest, but any type will do so long as they are fresh. (My advice is to steer clear of frozen scallops—always.) Note that both the *rabo* and the *tamal* can be made in advance and rewarmed, while the scallops and plantains need to be made immediately before serving. SERVES 4

OXTAILS

3 lb	oxtails
	Kosher salt and freshly ground black pepper
2 Tbsp	vegetable oil
1	large Spanish onion, diced
1	small red bell pepper, diced
1	small green bell pepper, diced
2 Tbsp	minced garlic (4 to 6 cloves)
2	plum tomatoes, diced
1/2 cup	dry white wine
1/2 cup	dry red wine
6 cups	Beef Stock (page 363)
1 Tbsp	minced fresh oregano
1 tsp	cumin seeds, toasted (see page 368) and ground
1	fresh bay leaf
2 Tbsp	unsalted butter

TAMAL

2 Tbsp	unsalted butter
1	Spanish onion, finely diced
	Kernels cut from 3 ears fresh white sweet corn or 2 cups thawed frozen white corn kernels, puréed in a blender
7 1/2 cups + 1/2 cup	Chicken Stock (page 362)
1 cup	yellow instant cornmeal
	Kosher salt and freshly ground black pepper

ROASTED SCALLOPS

2 Tbsp	vegetable oil
8	large fresh sea scallops (about 3/4 lb)
	Kosher salt

TO SERVE

	Fried Sweet Plantains (recipe follows)
2	scallions (white and green parts), thinly sliced on the diagonal
	Cilantro leaves, for garnish

TO PREPARE THE OXTAILS, if the butcher has not already done this for you, trim off the excess fat and cut the oxtails into 1- to 2-inch segments at the joints.

Heat the oil in a pressure cooker over medium-high heat. Season the oxtails with salt and pepper, sear them on all sides for 1 to 2 minutes per side, and transfer them to a plate.

Add the onion, bell peppers, and garlic to the pressure cooker and sauté, stirring frequently, until translucent, about 10 minutes. Stir in the tomatoes and simmer, uncovered, to cook off all the juices, 5 to 7 minutes. Stir in the red and white wines and continue simmering until the liquid has reduced by half, about 10 minutes. Add the beef stock, bring to a boil, and simmer until the liquid has reduced by one third, 10 to 12 minutes.

Return the oxtails to the pressure cooker, stir in the oregano, cumin, and bay leaf, and season with salt and pepper. Lock down the lid of the pressure cooker and cook the stew over medium-high heat for 45 minutes.

MEANWHILE, TO MAKE THE TAMAL, melt the butter in a saucepan over medium heat and cook the onion and corn kernel purée until the onion is translucent, about 5 minutes. Add 7 1/2 cups of the chicken stock and bring to a boil over high heat. Slowly whisk in the cornmeal and continue stirring until the mixture begins to thicken.

Decrease the heat to low and cook, stirring frequently, until the tamal is very thick and creamy, 35 to 40 minutes. Add the remaining 1/2 cup chicken stock and stir to incorporate. Season to taste with salt and pepper. Keep warm until serving time, or cover and refrigerate for up to 2 days and rewarm over medium-low heat, adding more stock as needed to restore the creamy texture.

TO CONTINUE PREPARING THE OXTAILS, prepare an ice bath in the kitchen sink. Transfer the still-sealed pressure cooker from the stove to the ice bath, immersing it in the cold water and leaving it to cool for 5 minutes. Lift the pressure cooker out of the ice bath, carefully unseal it, and remove the lid.

Use a slotted spoon to lift out the oxtails. Shred and set aside the meat, discarding the bones. Strain the liquid into a clean saucepan, discarding the solids from the sieve. Skim the fat from the surface and set the braising liquid aside separately from the meat. (At this point the meat and the liquid can be kept refrigerated in separate airtight containers for up to 2 days or frozen up to 3 months.)

TO ROAST THE SCALLOPS, preheat the oven to 450°F. Heat the oil in an ovenproof skillet over high heat. Season the scallops with salt and when the oil begins to shimmer, place them in the pan and sear them for about 1 minute. Without moving the scallops, transfer the pan to the oven and roast until their centers are opaque, about 3 minutes. Remove them from the pan and set aside, tented with aluminum foil to keep warm.

MEANWHILE, TO FINISH THE OXTAILS, return the saucepan of braising liquid to the stove, warm it over medium heat, fold in the shredded oxtails and the butter, and cook just until the butter is melted and the meat is warmed through.

TO SERVE, divide the tamal among four shallow bowls, add a spoonful of stew, two scallops, and a few pieces of fried plantain to each bowl. Garnish with the scallions and cilantro leaves.

PLÁTANOS MADUROS
FRIED SWEET PLANTAINS

Thick slices of overripe plantains fried to golden perfection are a classic staple of Latin cooking. Their starchy sweetness complements any savory dish. Serve them piping hot, immediately after frying, while they are crisp on the outside and soft on the inside. SERVES 4

1/4 cup	vegetable oil, plus more as needed
2	overripe plantains, peeled and thickly sliced on the diagonal
	Kosher salt

Heat the oil to 375°F in a heavy-bottomed sauté pan over medium-high heat, using a candy or deep-fry thermometer to monitor the temperature. Line a baking sheet with parchment paper.

Fry the plantain slices in batches (do not crowd the pan) until golden and crispy, turning once, 2 to 3 minutes per side. Carefully lift the plantains out of the oil with a skimmer or slotted spoon and set them on the baking sheet to drain briefly.

Season to taste with salt and serve.

CAFÉ CUBANO

Café cubano, aka *cafecito* (it's served in a little cup) is Cuban-style espresso: dark, intensely flavorful, and very sweet. It is made in a stovetop espresso pot or an espresso machine, and the distinctive mellow sweetness comes from the Demerara sugar that is spooned into the bottom of the pot the coffee drips into. The first few drops of coffee to fall into the pot are vigorously stirred into the sugar to create the *espumita*, a sweet froth that rises to the top when the coffee is poured into the demitasse.

I am a devoted fan of the sweet punch of a good *café cubano*, and it's something I take every opportunity to enjoy whenever we visit my in-laws. Conveniently enough, they live just around the corner from La Carreta, one of the many walk-up windows around Miami that sells Cuban coffee and assorted tasty snacks. At most windows you can order a *pastel* (pastry, often filled with guava paste), *pan tostado* (griddled buttered Cuban bread), or a *croqueta* (savory filled and fried roll) to go with your coffee.

With Cuban coffee comes conversation. This is a cultural thing—for Cubans, coffee isn't just a beverage, it's a social ritual. If you visit family or friends, coffee will be served; if you bump into a friend on the street the two of you will duck into a café to catch up over coffee. And when you pop over to the walk-up window and buy yourself a coffee, you are immediately chatted up and pulled into a lively conversation with assorted patrons, *cafecitos* in hand, out there on the sidewalk.

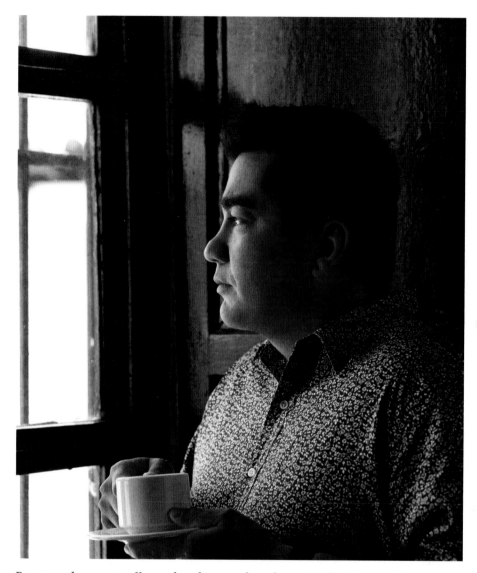

Between the great coffee and such warmth and conviviality from total strangers, I always feel for a moment like I'm back in Havana again.

Cuban coffee can really refer to any drink that uses the classic presweetened espresso as its base. First thing in the morning, there's *café con leche*, which is a *cafecito* with a small cup or glass of hot milk on the side (you pour the coffee into the milk and dunk your *pan tostado*). A *cortadito* is a *cafecito* cut with steamed milk—anywhere from a tablespoon or two of milk to equal parts milk and coffee. A *colada* is a large cup of *café cubano* sold with smaller cups for sharing. *(Recipe follows.)*

CAFÉ CUBANO

CUBAN COFFEE

You can brew the coffee in a stovetop espresso pot (if you don't have one, they are quite cheap) or an espresso machine. It's important to use coarse, raw Demerara sugar to get the right warm, caramelly flavor. SERVES 4

2 cups	whole milk
4	(1-oz) shots steaming hot espresso
2 Tbsp	Demerara sugar

If you don't have an espresso machine to steam the milk, pour the milk in a large heatproof glass jar with a tight-fitting lid. Shake the milk in the jar vigorously, until the milk is frothy and has nearly doubled in volume, about 30 seconds. Remove the lid and place the jar in the microwave. Microwave on high for 1 to 2 minutes, watching the milk closely to be sure it doesn't overflow, until the milk is steaming (140° to 150°F).

Combine the hot espresso with the sugar and stir vigorously until the sugar is dissolved and the espresso is frothy. Serve with steamed milk to taste.

CIENFUEGOS

Enchilado de Langosta | LOBSTER IN SPICY TOMATO SAUCE

Cachuchas Fritas | FRIED STUFFED CHILES

Ensalada de Garbanzos | GARBANZO BEAN SALAD WITH LEMON-DIJON DRESSING

I first had *enchilado de langosta* at the end of a long day of car travel from Havana to Cienfuegos, a city located on Cuba's southern coast and known for its impressive array of Spanish colonial architecture. I was traveling with a great local guy, Rudy, whom I'd hired in Havana to help get around. After a couple of busy sightseeing days and festive nights in and around Havana, I wanted to venture forth and see what life, the people, and the food were like in different parts of Cuba. First stop: Cienfuegos, across the island and down the coast.

Cienfuegos is only about 155 miles from Havana, but sketchy road conditions and a near total absence of signage can make for a grueling journey, even if you've got a knowledgeable guide and you're not rumbling along in a 1950s Plymouth (vintage cars were still very much the norm). The roads had a way of suddenly changing from more-or-less paved to rut-riddled dirt. And on more than one occasion, a highway-like stretch of comparatively high-speed road ended abruptly when a town appeared smack in the middle.

Suffice to say, the trip to Cienfuegos was one of our more challenging driving days, and by the time we finally arrived and sorted out a place to stay, we were tired, parched, and ravenous. Thankfully, Rudy quickly found us a great *paladar* (in-home restaurant) and before long we were feasting on big, wide steaming bowls of a tomato-y seafood stew. Shell-on hunks of lobster awash in a rich red sauce that was infused with lobster flavor soaked its way into every grain of the mound of rice at the bottom of the bowl.

Restored by the *enchilado*, Rudy and I thanked our gracious hostess and her family and headed back out into the city streets that, as night fell, were filling with people and great music—singing, guitars, horns, bongos, piano. We winded our way to a small square with an outdoor bar, and there we enjoyed another night of music and mojitos. In the midst of it all, I had a moment of clarity, realizing how right I'd been in striking out on this adventure. In a matter of days, I'd be back in Philadelphia, my new home, working with Douglas Rodriguez to bring the flavors of Havana to Philadelphia's buttoned-up Rittenhouse Square. Now I could report for work at Alma de Cuba, Stephen Starr's newest venture, with the spirit of the place fresh in my mind.

Sure enough, the Alma menu featured an *enchilado*. That *enchilado*, like the one here, was faithful to the traditional Cuban creole preparation, the only twist being the garnish—the fried *cachuchas fritas*, which add a fun and tasty pop to the savory seafood stew. The light, fresh flavors and textures of the garbanzo bean salad round out the meal.

P. 184 Cachuchas Fritas

P. 182 Enchilado de Langosta

ENCHILADO DE LANGOSTA

LOBSTER IN SPICY TOMATO SAUCE

Live lobsters are essential for this recipe. The method given here is, by the way, the most humane way to go about offing a lobster (killing them instantly being far preferable to boiling them alive) (see photo, page 181). SERVES 4

ENCHILADO SAUCE

1 Tbsp	extra virgin olive oil
1/2	Spanish onion, diced
2 Tbsp	minced garlic (4 to 6 cloves)
2 Tbsp	tomato paste
2	plum tomatoes, finely chopped
1 cup	dry white wine
2 cups	Fish Stock (page 365) or good-quality low-sodium fish stock
1 Tbsp	dried oregano
1 Tbsp	crushed red pepper
	Kosher salt and freshly ground black pepper

LOBSTER

	Kosher salt
2 Tbsp	extra virgin olive oil
2	live 1-lb lobsters
1/2	Spanish onion, diced
1	jalapeño chile, seeded and finely diced
1 Tbsp	minced garlic (2 to 3 cloves)
2 Tbsp	(4 to 6 cloves) Roasted Garlic (page 366)
1	jarred roasted red bell pepper, drained, rinsed (if packed in oil), seeded, and chopped
2 Tbsp	chopped fresh cilantro
1 Tbsp	minced fresh oregano
	Freshly ground black pepper

TO SERVE

	White Rice (page 367)
	Fried Stuffed Chiles (recipe follows)

TO MAKE THE ENCHILADO SAUCE, heat the oil in a large stainless-steel skillet over medium heat. Add the onion and garlic and cook, stirring frequently until translucent, about 10 minutes. Stir in the tomato paste and tomatoes and cook for another 2 to 3 minutes. Add the wine, bring to a low boil, and simmer to reduce by half, about 10 minutes. Add the stock and simmer to again reduce by half, about 10 minutes more. Stir in the oregano and red pepper and season to taste with salt and pepper.

TO PREPARE THE LOBSTERS, use a large and very sharp chef's knife to split them in half lengthwise: insert the tip of the knife just behind the eyes and bring the blade down through the length of the body; this kills them instantly. Remove and discard the innards and rinse the lobsters clean under cold running water.

TO COOK THE CLAWS AND KNUCKLES, prepare an ice bath and bring a saucepan of lightly salted water to a boil. Twist off the claws and knuckles of the lobsters and cook them, shell on for 5 to 7 minutes. Transfer them to the ice bath to cool. Remove and discard the shells and set aside the meat.

TO COOK THE LOBSTER BODIES, season the cut side of the lobsters with salt and pepper. Heat the oil in a large stainless-steel skillet over medium heat and sear the cut side of the lobsters until browned, about 5 minutes. Turn the lobsters, add the onion, jalapeño, raw and roasted garlic, and roasted peppers and cook, stirring frequently, for another 5 minutes. Stir in the reserved claw and knuckle meat and the enchilado sauce and cook just to warm through.

Gently stir in the cilantro and oregano, season to taste with salt and pepper, and serve with white rice and fried stuffed chiles.

CACHUCHAS FRITAS
FRIED STUFFED CHILES

A few handy tips for this recipe: First, *ajís cachuchas* look like habaneros but are more fruity than fiery; they are available in Latin grocers. Second, panko breadcrumbs make a crisp, light, tempura-like crust for the *cachuchas*; just be sure to finely grind the panko in a blender before measuring. Third, if you don't have a pastry bag, just put the filling in a zip-top bag, press out excess air and seal the top, and snip off one of the corners; this will work just as well for filling the peppers. Last but not least, I encourage you to try these poppers as a cocktail snack, especially with beer or mojitos (see photo, page 181). SERVES 4

FILLING

8 oz	cream cheese
	Kernels cut from 1 small ear fresh white sweet corn or 1/4 cup frozen white corn kernels, steamed
2 Tbsp	minced fresh chives
1 Tbsp	minced fresh cilantro
	Kosher salt and freshly ground black pepper

PEPPERS

1/4 lb	cachucha chiles (8 to 10 chiles) (see Sources)
1 1/2 qts	vegetable oil
1 cup	all-purpose flour
2	large eggs, beaten
1 cup	finely ground panko breadcrumbs
	Kosher salt

TO MAKE THE FILLING, combine the cream cheese, corn, chives, and cilantro in a mixing bowl and season to taste with salt and pepper. Transfer to a piping bag fitted with a small plain tip.

TO STUFF THE PEPPERS, use a paring knife to cut a small slit in the side of each pepper. Pipe in the filling no more than two-thirds full: filling the peppers all the way can cause them to explode when frying.

Heat the oil to 350°F in a stockpot over medium-high heat, using a candy or deep-fry thermometer to monitor the temperature. Line two baking sheets with parchment paper.

Set out three small, deep plates. Put the flour in the first, the eggs in the second, and the panko in the third. Gently roll each stuffed chile in the flour, dip in the egg to coat, and roll in the panko to cover. Set the filled chiles on one of the baking sheets.

Fry the chiles in batches until golden brown and crispy, 2 to 3 minutes, turning frequently. Drain on the other baking sheet, season to taste with salt, and serve immediately.

ENSALADA DE GARBANZOS

GARBANZO BEAN SALAD WITH LEMON-DIJON DRESSING

Any time you use fresh corn rather than frozen, don't throw out the cobs—stockpile them in a large zip-top bag in the freezer so you can make corn stock for Mexican *esquites* (page 252). SERVES 4

SALAD

3 cups	cooked garbanzo beans, drained and rinsed
1 cup	cherry tomatoes, quartered
	Kernels cut from 1 small ear fresh white sweet corn or 1/4 cup frozen white corn kernels, steamed
1	jarred roasted red bell pepper, drained, rinsed (if packed in brine or oil), seeded, and chopped

DRESSING

1 tsp	minced garlic (1 clove)
2 Tbsp	freshly squeezed lemon juice
2 Tbsp	extra virgin olive oil
1 tsp	Dijon mustard
1 tsp	cumin seeds, toasted (see page 368) and ground

TO SERVE

2 Tbsp	minced fresh flat-leaf parsley
2 Tbsp	minced fresh cilantro
	Kosher salt and freshly ground black pepper
4	scallions (white and green parts), thinly sliced on the diagonal

TO MAKE THE SALAD, combine the garbanzo beans, tomatoes, corn, and roasted pepper in a bowl and mix well.

TO MAKE THE DRESSING, combine all the ingredients in a blender and purée until the mixture is smooth and emulsified.

TO SERVE, pour the dressing over the salad, add the parsley and cilantro, and toss to combine. Season to taste with salt and pepper and garnish with the scallions.

CUBANO

For me, no visit to Miami is complete without at least one *cubano* at Latin American Cafeteria in Little Havana.

I hanker after the layered magnificence of the sandwich itself, the whole mouthwatering experience, starting with the moment I walk in the door and get that first hit of roasty pork aroma overlaid with the tang of Swiss cheese yielding to the steamy heat of the *planchas* (presses). I marvel at the stamina of the two guys who frantically work the side-by-side slicers: marinated, slow-roasted pork stacking up at the one, sugar-cured ham at the other. Onto butter- and mustard-slathered Cuban bread go the piles of rich meat, then come thinly sliced pickles and cheese, and into the *plancha* it goes for a few minutes to toast the bread and warm those tasty layers enough to melt the cheese and steam up the meat. *Que bueno. (Recipe follows.)*

CUBANO

CUBAN SANDWICH

Directly inspired by the *cubanos* served at Latin American Cafeteria, the Cuban sandwich on the menu at Garces Trading Company is my way of bringing one of the treats of Little Havana to Philadelphia. It took some doing, since the essential Cuban bread is not to be had outside of Miami, but we found a bakery that follows a legit Cuban recipe to make it for us to order. All of the other ingredients are house-made—from the roast pork and cured ham to the pickles and mustard.

To approximate the *cubano* at home, follow the recipe to make the absolute key ingredient: the marinated, moist, and deeply flavorful roast pork. (Note: plan for several hours' marinating time; you'll end up with enough pork for a second round of sandwiches or the main component of another meal.) For the next-best thing to the real deal *pan cubano*, get some good crisp-crusted bakery rolls with a light, airy texture. Pick up some best-quality domestic ham, along with Dijon mustard, Swiss cheese, and dill pickles, and you will have yourself some amazing sandwiches (see photo, page 186). MAKES 4 SANDWICHES

ROAST PORK

2 Tbsp + 1 Tbsp	kosher salt
2 Tbsp	granulated sugar
1 Tbsp	ground mustard
2 lb	boneless pork shoulder, tied in an even roll
1/2 cup	Dijon mustard
1 tsp	ground mace
2 Tbsp	freshly ground black pepper
1 Tbsp	Spanish smoked sweet paprika

SANDWICH

4	(6-inch) light crisp-crusted bakery rolls
2 Tbsp	Dijon mustard
3/4 lb	best-quality domestic ham (unglazed), thinly sliced
1/4 lb	Swiss or Gruyère cheese, thinly sliced
1	large dill pickle, thinly sliced lengthwise
2 Tbsp	unsalted butter

TO CURE THE PORK, combine 2 tablespoons of the salt with the sugar and ground mustard. Rub the mixture all over the meat, cover, and set it in the refrigerator to cure for 6 hours.

Place a rack in the middle position and preheat the oven to 325°F.

TO ROAST THE PORK, rinse it under cold running water to remove the seasoning. Pat dry with paper towels. Combine the Dijon mustard, mace, black pepper, paprika, and the remaining 1 tablespoon salt. Rub the mixture all over the meat. Set the pork in a roasting pan, cover tightly with aluminum foil, and cook until the internal temperature reaches 175°F, about 45 minutes. Allow the meat to cool completely before slicing.

TO MAKE THE SANDWICHES, heat a sandwich press or griddle to medium-high. Split the bread lengthwise and pull it open. Spread the mustard on 1 side of each roll and layer on the roast pork, ham, cheese, and pickles. Spread the butter all over the outside of the sandwiches and griddle until the cheese is melted and the meats are warmed through, 3 to 4 minutes. (Alternatively, wrap the sandwich in foil and toast in a 350°F oven for 5 to 7 minutes.) Slice each in half on the diagonal and serve.

SANTIAGO DE CUBA

Ensalada de Palmito | HEARTS OF PALM WITH COCONUT VINAIGRETTE

Ropa Vieja con Frijoles Colorados | SHREDDED BEEF STEW WITH RED BEANS

A quintessentially Cuban dish, *ropa vieja* is the epitome of meaty, rib-stickin' down-home goodness, and—no exaggeration—every Latin home cook seems to have their own version, my Ecuadorian mom included. Her *ropa vieja* was in steady weeknight rotation throughout my childhood. (I must have been well into my twenties before it dawned on me that *ropa vieja* was Cuban food.) The name *ropa vieja* means "old clothes," and refers to how the meat, peppers, and onions resemble a multicolored pile of rags; it also gets across just how homey this dish is.

My mom's version is saucier than the typical Cuban *ropa*, which tends to be on the drier side. I've always split the difference, going for a sauciness level that's somewhere in between Mom's stewy rendition and the classic Cuban style. I also like to use short ribs rather than the traditional flank steak or skirt steak, because those cuts have a tendency to dry out and toughen, whereas the marbling in short ribs means they stay reliably tender and juicy.

How I go about cooking *ropa vieja* is another story: my approach has completely changed of late, thanks to my wife, Beatriz, who is Cuban and has some bona fide kitchen chops of her own (having learned to cook at about age ten). Bea and I cook together on weekends, keeping each other company while we work independently on separate dishes. One recent evening I was midway through preparing a *ropa vieja* in much the same manner I've used for years, when Bea cast an appraising glance at the numerous pots bubbling slowly along, including the meat I'd had gently braising in tomato sauce since earlier in the afternoon. "In Cuba, we'd put all that," she gestured at the separate pots of meat and beans, "in a pressure cooker together and it was done in about an hour." You could say that Bea enlightened me, but in all honesty, I got schooled. It wasn't the first time and surely won't be the last, and I am glad of it. She was right: it's done a lot quicker her way. What's more, the flavors are richer and more balanced.

So here's my new and improved *ropa vieja*, with its streamlined method perfect for a weeknight supper. To sum it up, the beans and meat go into the pressure cooker together with some key flavoring agents and beef stock. While they cook, they also flavor each other. Meanwhile, you put together a quick sauce and a pot of white rice. After an hour, you pull the meat out of the cooker, shred it, and fold it into the sauce while the beans simmer down a little further. Soon after, everything's done, on the table, and you've got one of the best meals you could ask for. The *ensalada de palmita* is a cool, fresh thing to have on the side, balancing out the richness and bulk of the *ropa vieja*. I've named the menu for Santiago de Cuba, the second largest city in Cuba, where *paladares* (home restaurants) are the best places to eat and chances are you'd be served a hearty peasant dish like *ropa vieja*.

P. 194 Ropa Vieja con Frijoles Colorados

P. 193 Ensalada de Palmito

ENSALADA DE PALMITO
HEARTS OF PALM SALAD WITH COCONUT VINAIGRETTE

Head to an international market for the unsweetened coconut milk, coconut water, fresh coconut, and hearts of palm for this delectable, refreshing salad. Make sure the coconut water (the juice from a fresh coconut) is plain, with no pulp and no flavoring. Fresh coconut sold in shrink-wrapped chunks is ideal for grating the small amount needed for this salad; select a piece that's recently cut, not dried out. Frozen grated coconut, often carried in Asian markets, is another good option. Fresh hearts of palm—not jarred or canned—are key. They come in sealed bags and make a delicious addition to any tossed salad, bean salad, or tomato-based pasta dish, so you'll have no trouble using them up. For the best results, make the vinaigrette ahead and chill it thoroughly, keep the other components cold as well. SERVES 4

COCONUT VINAIGRETTE

1/4 cup	canned unsweetened coconut milk
1/4 cup	coconut water
2 Tbsp	freshly squeezed lime juice
1 Tbsp	Dijon mustard
2 Tbsp	honey
1/2 cup	vegetable oil
1	shallot, finely diced
	Kosher salt

SALAD

2 to 3	fresh hearts of palm, thinly sliced (2 cups)
2	heads frisée, coarsely chopped
2	bunches watercress, stemmed (1/2 lb)
1/4 cup	cooked and drained, chopped thick-cut bacon (6 to 8 slices)
8	dried dates, pitted and quartered
1	small red onion, thinly sliced
1/4 cup	grated fresh coconut or thawed frozen grated coconut
2 Tbsp	minced fresh flat-leaf parsley
	Kosher salt and freshly ground black pepper

TO MAKE THE DRESSING, purée the coconut milk, coconut water, lime juice, mustard, and honey in a blender. Slowly drizzle in the oil and purée until completely emulsified. Fold in shallots and season to taste with salt. Refrigerate 1 to 2 hours before use.

TO MAKE THE SALAD, combine the hearts of palm, frisée, watercress, bacon, dates, onion, grated coconut, and parsley in a large bowl. Dress with the coconut vinaigrette and season to taste with salt and pepper.

ROPA VIEJA CON FRIJOLES COLORADOS

BRAISED SHREDDED BEEF STEW WITH RED BEANS

Here, again, the pressure cooker is an absolute necessity: it expedites the cooking and makes the meat tender and the whole dish deeply flavorful (see photo, page 192). SERVES 4

BRAISED BEEF

2 Tbsp + 2 Tbsp	vegetable oil
2 lb	boneless beef short ribs
	Kosher salt and freshly ground black pepper
1/4 lb	thick-cut bacon, diced small
1	large Spanish onion, diced small
1	red bell pepper, diced small
1	green bell pepper, diced small
2 Tbsp	minced garlic (4 to 6 cloves)
2 Tbsp	(4 to 6 cloves) Roasted Garlic (page 366)
1/4 cup	tomato paste
2 Tbsp	whole cumin seeds, toasted (see page 368) and ground
2 Tbsp	cider vinegar
2 qts	Beef Stock (page 363)
1/2 lb	dried red kidney beans, soaked overnight, drained, and rinsed (2 cups)

SAUCE

2 Tbsp	vegetable oil
1	large Spanish onion, thinly sliced
1	large green bell pepper, thinly sliced
1	large red bell pepper, thinly sliced
2 Tbsp	minced garlic (4 to 6 cloves)
1/4 cup	tomato paste
2 Tbsp	chopped fresh parsley
2 Tbsp	chopped fresh cilantro
5	plum tomatoes, seeded and diced small
	Kosher salt and freshly ground black pepper

TO SERVE

	White Rice (page 367)
	Fried Sweet Plantains (page 175)
2	scallions (white and green parts), thinly sliced on the diagonal

TO PREPARE THE BRAISED BEEF, heat 2 tablespoons of the oil in a large cast-iron skillet over medium-high heat. Generously season the meat with salt and pepper. Sear it until well browned, 3 to 4 minutes per side. Set aside.

Heat the remaining 2 tablespoons oil in a pressure cooker over medium-high heat until it shimmers. Add the bacon, onion, bell peppers, and raw and roasted garlic. Cook until the onion is translucent, about 10 minutes, stirring frequently. Stir in the tomato paste, cumin, and vinegar and cook until the mixture is lightly caramelized, about 5 minutes. Add the stock, seared short ribs, and kidney beans. Close and seal the pressure cooker and cook over medium-high heat for 1 hour.

Prepare an ice bath in the kitchen sink. Transfer the still-sealed pressure cooker to the ice bath and leave it to cool for 5 minutes. Lift the pressure cooker out of the ice bath, carefully unseal it, and remove the lid.

Lift the short ribs out of the cooker; the meat should be soft to the touch and fork-tender. While the meat is still hot, shred it with a fork and set aside. Measure out 1 quart (4 cups) of the braising liquid and set aside (return any beans to the pot).

To finish the beans, transfer the contents of pressure cooker to a saucepan and cook over medium heat, stirring occasionally, until the liquid thickens, 18 to 20 minutes.

MEANWHILE, TO MAKE THE SAUCE, heat the oil in a large sauté pan over medium-high heat. Add the onion, bell peppers, and garlic and cook until translucent, about 10 minutes, stirring frequently. Stir in the tomato paste and cook until the mixture is caramelized, about 5 minutes. Add the reserved braising liquid and cook until reduced by about half, about 15 minutes. Add the meat and stir to incorporate. Fold in the parsley, cilantro, and tomatoes and season to taste with salt and pepper.

SERVE THE ROPA VIEJA and beans with rice and plantains, garnished with scallions.

MIAMI

La Tormenta | DARK AND STORMY MOJITO

Frituras de Malanga | MALANGA FRITTERS

Frituras de Bacalao | SALT COD FRITTERS

Sopa de Calabaza con Cangrejo | ROASTED SQUASH SOUP WITH CRAB AND ZUCCHINI

Lechón Asado | ACHIOTE- AND CITRUS-MARINATED ROAST SUCKLING PIG

Moros y Cristianos | BLACK BEANS AND RICE

Yuca con Mojo Criollo | YUCA WITH SOUR ORANGE MOJO

Tostones | CRISPY FRIED GREEN PLANTAINS

Pasteles de Guayaba | GUAVA AND CREAM CHEESE TURNOVERS

Roasting a pig in the backyard is the Cuban way to celebrate most any special occasion, and it's a cherished tradition among Cuban Americans for Christmas Eve dinner. The pig is marinated overnight in a tangy *mojo*, then it's slowly roasted, sometimes over hot coals in a pit dug in the ground, but more often in an ingenious device called a Chinese roasting box, which situates the pig beneath the heat rather than above it, and cooks the animal to crackling, succulent perfection in less than half the time.

Douglas Rodriguez introduced me to the caramelized splendor of a whole

pig cooked in a Caja China–brand roasting box when I was working with him at Alma de Cuba. Cuban American, raised in Miami, a renowned chef, and pioneer of *Nuevo Latino* cuisine, Douglas has a whole lot of whole-hog enthusiasm and know-how to share, and he has spread the gospel of the Caja China far and wide. At Alma we sometimes offered a roast pig–centered menu on summer weekends and holidays. We'd fire up a massive Caja China in the alleyway out back, right there on Moravian Street.

When it's done properly, roasting a pig in a Caja China yields unparalleled results. To this day, the top-down roasting technique is essential to the way I cook whole pig and various cuts of pork, as well as other meats.

In the years since my Alma days I've enjoyed many Cuban Christmas Eves, complete with whole roast pig. It's one of the many perks of being married to Beatriz, whose entire family is Cuban and faithfully upholds the pig roast tradition with a huge annual Christmas Eve celebration in Miami.

For many years, Bea's Tía Carmita always hosted the feast. Soon after Bea and I got married, we and her parents thought it was time to give Tía Carmita a break, with the Mirabals (Bea's parents) hosting while I handled the pig. Douglas has restaurants in Miami, and Roberto Guerra manufactures Caja Chinas right there in the area, so I'd be able to arrange everything I needed before flying down from Philly.

What I hadn't factored into the plan was Douglas's fondness for practical jokes. The 140-pound hog he got for me was twice the size I needed! It took three of us (big guys) to hoist, brine, and marinate that beast; then we had to wrestle it into the Caja China.

The Caja China does cook a pig way faster than other ways of pit-roasting, but this pig was so huge that I got up at five o'clock in the morning to put it in, tended to it throughout the day, and it still wasn't done twelve hours later. By about seven in the evening, I could see that serious hunger had taken hold and the relatives were getting a bit agitated. Luckily, the pig had crisped up nicely at that point, so we hauled it out of the Caja China. I was ready for some relief at this point, but nobody seemed interested in stepping up to the task of carving—it's a messy job and they were dressed up, I guess. Not that their fancy clothes kept them from going vulture, reaching over me to pluck up bits of meat and skin while I hacked away at the carcass with a lousy blade, wishing I'd brought my knife kit. I ended up drenched in sweat and pig juice, with blisters all over my hands. I was totally done in and passed out right after dinner.

But the pig was incredibly delicious—and there was plenty to go around!

Here's a scaled-down version for suckling pig (including an oven-roasting method) plus recipes for all the fixin's for a true Cuban feast: fritters, beans and rice, yuca, *tostones*—the works!

LA TORMENTA

DARK AND STORMY MOJITO

If you want to serve a festive Cuban-style feast, it is a simple fact that you have got to be able to make a good mojito, as the traditional Cuban highball is known. This particular mojito deviates from the classic bright and summery feel while maintaining an essential mojito-ness. Keith Raimondi, an extremely talented mixologist I've been glad to have aboard since 2007, helped me put this together as a more year-round drink. In addition to the requisite mint, it's flavored with toasted cardamom and aromatic bitters (Keith recommends Fee Brothers Whiskey Barrel–Aged Bitters), which add rich, lively fragrance and just a hint of spice, as does the Demerara rum, an especially dark, deeply aromatic, and potent rum from Guyana on the north Atlantic coast of South America. Note that you will have enough syrup left to make another round. SERVES 8

CARDAMOM-MINT SYRUP

6	cardamom pods
1 cup	water
1 cup	granulated sugar
4	sprigs mint

MOJITO

8	springs mint, plus more for garnish
1 1/2 cups	Demerara rum
1 cup	freshly squeezed lime juice (about 10 limes)
	Ice
1 cup	club soda
	Aromatic bitters

TO MAKE THE CARDAMOM-MINT SYRUP, toast the cardamom pods in a dry saucepan over low heat until fragrant, 3 to 5 minutes, shaking the pan frequently to prevent scorching. Add the water, sugar, and mint and cook over low heat until the sugar has dissolved, about 5 minutes. Remove the pan from the heat and allow the syrup to cool completely. Remove and discard the cardamom pods and mint sprigs. Measure out three-quarters cup of the syrup and store the remainder in an airtight jar in the refrigerator for later use.

TO MAKE THE MOJITOS, muddle the mint in a large pitcher: stir it firmly with a wooden spoon or muddler with enough force to bruise the leaves, bringing out the herb's essence and oils. Add the rum, lime juice, and syrup. Add ice to fill and mix vigorously.

TO SERVE, put fresh ice in eight 12-ounce glasses and pour in the mojito. Top off each glass with club soda, add a dash of bitters, and garnish with a mint sprig.

FRITURAS DE MALANGA

MALANGA FRITTERS

Malanga, a staple root vegetable throughout much of the Caribbean, is one of many foods that Cubans are fond of frying up in fritters. The roots are brown and a bit hairy on the outside and creamy white, yellow, or pink on the inside, depending on the variety. They all make light, tasty fritters (see photo, page 202).

SERVES 8

BÉCHAMEL

2 Tbsp	unsalted butter
2 Tbsp	all-purpose flour
1 cup	whole milk

FRITTERS

2 qts	vegetable oil, for frying
2 lb	malanga, peeled and finely grated (see Sources)
1/4 cup	minced garlic (12 to 16 cloves)
2	jalapeño chiles, seeds and ribs removed, minced
	Grated zest of 2 navel oranges
1/2 cup	all-purpose flour
2 tsp	baking powder
1/4 cup	chopped fresh cilantro
1 Tbsp	kosher salt
1/4 tsp	freshly ground black pepper

TO MAKE THE BÉCHAMEL, melt the butter over low heat in a small nonreactive saucepan and whisk in the flour. Cook, stirring constantly, until it no longer tastes of raw flour, 2 to 3 minutes. Slowly whisk in the milk and cook over low heat, stirring frequently, until it thickens enough to coat the back of a spoon, about 5 minutes. Remove from the heat and allow to cool. If not using right away, store in an airtight container in the refrigerator until needed, up to 3 days.

Heat the oil to 350°F in a stockpot over medium-high heat, using a candy or deep-fry thermometer to monitor the temperature. Line a baking sheet with parchment paper.

TO MAKE THE FRITTERS, combine the grated malanga, garlic, béchamel, jalapeños, orange zest, flour, and baking powder and mix well. Fold in the cilantro and season with the salt and pepper.

Use two spoons to form the batter into small fritters and carefully drop them into the hot oil. Fry in batches until golden brown and crispy, about 3 minutes. Drain the fritters on the baking sheet and season to taste with salt. Serve immediately.

FRITURAS DE BACALAO

SALT COD FRITTERS

The salt cod needs to be soaked overnight, so plan accordingly. Also be sure to mind the seasoning: It's important to salt the batter to taste before you fry it and to taste before sprinkling any additional salt on the finished fritters (see photo, page 202). SERVES 8

2 lb	boneless, skinless salt cod fillet, soaked (see page 132), drained, and shredded (4 cups)
4 Tbsp	unsalted butter
1/2	Spanish onion, finely diced
2	jalapeño chiles, seeds and ribs removed, finely diced
2 Tbsp	minced garlic (4 to 6 cloves)
2 qts	vegetable oil, for frying
2 cups	all-purpose flour
3/4 tsp	baking powder
1 cup	whole milk
2	large eggs
	Kosher salt

Bring a saucepan of unsalted water to a boil and poach the salt cod over medium-high heat for 15 minutes. Drain the fish, return it to the pot with fresh water, bring to a boil then lower the heat to a simmer. Continue cooking it until the fish is very soft and the salt flavor has diminished, about 15 minutes more. Drain the fish, rinse it, and drain again thoroughly.

Melt the butter in a stainless-steel sauté pan over medium heat. Add the onion, jalapeños, and garlic and cook, stirring occasionally, until translucent, about 10 minutes. Add the cod and cook for 5 minutes more. Set aside to cool while you make the batter.

Heat the oil to 350°F in a stockpot over medium-high heat, using a candy or deep-fry thermometer to monitor the temperature. Line a baking sheet with parchment paper.

Sift together the flour and baking powder into a large bowl. In a separate bowl, whisk together the milk and eggs. Fold them gently into the dry ingredients to form a batter. Fold the cod mixture into the batter and season to taste with salt.

Use two spoons to form the batter into small fritters and carefully them drop into the hot oil. Fry in batches until golden brown and crispy, about 3 minutes. Drain them on the baking sheet and serve immediately.

P. 200 Frituras de Malanga

P. 201 Frituras de Bacalao

SOPA DE CALABAZA CON CANGREJO

ROASTED SQUASH SOUP WITH CRAB AND ZUCCHINI

Calabaza, a tropical squash commonly known as Cuban pumpkin, is popular in creamy stews. Butternut squash, similarly dense, mellow, and slightly sweet, makes a good North American substitute. Here, the sweet, delicate lump crabmeat garnish is like icing on the cake. Lump crabmeat comes refrigerated in little tubs, pasteurized and precooked. You can also use canned (see photo, page 203). SERVES 8

ROASTED SQUASH SOUP

2	butternut squash, peeled, halved, seeded, and diced (8 cups)
1/4 cup	vegetable oil
2 Tbsp	kosher salt, plus more as needed
8 Tbsp	unsalted butter
2	large Spanish onions, diced
2	Granny Smith apples, peeled, cored, and diced
1/4 cup	minced garlic (12 to 16 cloves)
1/4 cup	(12 to 16 cloves) Roasted Garlic (page 366)
2 tsp	cayenne pepper
3 qts	Vegetable Stock (page 364)
2 cups	heavy cream
1/2 cup	honey

TO SERVE

1 lb	cooked jumbo lump crabmeat
1/4 cup	minced fresh chives
1/4 cup	Arbequina olive oil (see Sources)
2	small zucchini, diced small (1 cup)
1/2 cup	toasted salted pepitas (pumpkin seeds)
1/4 cup	pumpkin seed oil or extra virgin olive oil

Place a rack in the middle position and preheat the oven to 350°F.

TO ROAST THE SQUASH, combine the squash, vegetable oil, and 2 tablespoons salt in a bowl and toss to combine. Spread the squash in a single layer on a large rimmed baking sheet. Bake until tender and lightly caramelized, 10 to 15 minutes.

TO MAKE THE SOUP, melt the butter in a stockpot over medium heat. Add the onions, apples, and the raw and roasted garlic and cook until translucent, about 10 minutes. Stir in the cayenne and cook until the spice gives off a toasty aroma, 2 to 3 minutes. Add the stock and roasted squash and simmer until reduced by one-quarter. Stir in the heavy cream and cook for 10 minutes more.

Working in batches, transfer the soup to a blender and purée until very smooth. Alternatively, use a handheld immersion blender to purée the soup in the pot. Strain the soup through a fine-mesh sieve lined with cheesecloth into a clean pot. Stir in the honey and season to taste with salt.

TO SERVE THE SOUP, toss the crabmeat with the chives and Arbequina olive oil to lightly dress. Divide the soup among eight warmed bowls, garnish each with the crab mixture, zucchini, pepitas, and pumpkin seed oil, and serve.

LECHÓN ASADO

ACHIOTE- AND CITRUS-MARINATED ROAST SUCKLING PIG

If you are new to roasting a pig, here are a few tips to guarantee your first venture is a hit. First and foremost, fully submerge that pig in the brine! Brining from snout to tail, ears to hoofs in a combination of salted water and sugar is triply essential: It seasons the meat through and through, bringing out flavor; it tenderizes the meat by beginning to break down the proteins; and it ensures moisture retention so after hours over the fire the pork is not only tasty and tender, but also juicy (rather than dried out). Brining requires 24 to 48 hours, and an additional overnight soak is needed for the marinating step.

Also essential is the *mojo*, because it brings all the delicious flavors of the citrus, garlic, cumin, and herbs (especially oregano), but most importantly because its pronounced acidity is a perfect counterbalance to the fattiness of the meat.

Have your butcher clean and dress the pig, and be sure to ask that it be butterflied, so you don't have to do the work of splitting the animal's backbone yourself.

The Caja China is on my list of great culinary implements of all time, but you don't have to have one to make yourself a great roast pig; instructions are provided for an oven method as well (see photo, page 210). SERVES 8

BRINE

4 gallons	water
4 cups	kosher salt
2 cups	granulated sugar

1	whole suckling pig (about 20 lb), cleaned, dressed, and butterflied

MARINADE

1/4 cup	achiote paste (see Sources)
1 cup	minced garlic (2 heads)
1 cup	dried oregano
1 qt	vegetable oil
2 cups	freshly squeezed orange juice
1/2 cup	kosher salt

SEASONING

2 cups	extra virgin olive oil
	Kosher salt

TO SERVE

1/4 cup	Arbequina olive oil (see Sources)
	Sea salt
2 cups	Mojo Criollo (recipe follows)
	Black Beans and Rice (page 213)

TO BRINE THE PIG, combine the water, salt, and sugar in a nonreactive container (such as a clean plastic 30-gallon trashcan) large and deep enough for the pig to be submerged. Mix until salt and sugar are completely dissolved. Slide the pig into the brine, cover, and refrigerate, fully submerged, for 24 to 48 hours.

Line a large baking sheet with parchment paper.

TO MAKE THE MARINADE, combine the achiote paste, garlic, oregano, vegetable oil, orange juice, and salt and mix well. Lift the pig out of the brine, discard the brine, and pat the pig completely dry. Place the pig on the baking sheet or in a large nonreactive container and pour the marinade over it, using your hands to rub the marinade all over, inside and out, to completely coat. Cover and refrigerate overnight.

Remove the pig from the marinade, discarding any marinade left in the container.

TO ROAST THE PIG IN A CAJA CHINA or other roasting box, set up the box and preheat according to the manufacturer's instructions. Season the pig inside and out with the extra virgin olive oil and kosher salt. Arrange the pig skin-side down in the cooking cage, place it in the Caja China, and cover. Roast the pig until cooked through (the meat will be falling off the bone), 2 1/2 to 3 hours.

Turn the cage over and continue to cook the pig until the skin is crispy, about 30 minutes more. Carefully remove the pig from the roasting box, take it out of the cage, and set it on a carving board. Allow the pig to rest for 10 minutes before carving.

TO ROAST THE PIG IN A CONVENTIONAL OVEN, preheat the oven to 375°F. Line a large roasting pan with aluminum foil and set a heavy-duty rack in the pan. Place the pig skin-side up on the rack and brush the skin with the extra virgin olive oil and salt. Cover the roasting pan tightly with aluminum foil and roast the pig for 1 hour.

Lower the heat to 325°F and continue roasting for 1 hour more.

Remove the foil and roast until the skin is crispy and the meat is falling off the bone, about 1 hour more. Remove the pig from the oven and allow it to rest for 10 minutes before carving.

Once the roasted pig is properly rested, carefully remove the skin in its entirety, one side at a time, using a pair of tongs and a kitchen knife; cut or tear the skin into individual-size portions. From there, simply pull the meat away from the bone.

SEASON THE CARVED PORK with Arbequina olive oil and sea salt. Serve with beans and rice and mojo, and garnish with crispy skin.

MOJO CRIOLLO
SOUR ORANGE MOJO

The potent flavors and acidity of a Cuban *mojo* sauce make it the perfect marinade and barbecue sauce for both pork and chicken; if you have some left over from the pig roast, serve it with crispy grilled chicken or with scrambled eggs and tortillas. There are as many variations of *mojo* as there are of American barbecue sauce, and it's also a traditional dressing for yuca (page 214), potatoes, and other starchy vegetables. MAKES ABOUT 1 QUART

8	navel oranges
1 cup	freshly squeezed Seville orange juice (about 4 Seville oranges) (see Sources)
1 cup	extra virgin olive oil
2 Tbsp	whole cumin seeds, toasted (see page 368) and ground
1/2 cup	minced garlic (about 2 whole heads)
8	shallots, thinly sliced
2 Tbsp	minced fresh oregano
2 Tbsp	minced fresh flat-leaf parsley
2 Tbsp	minced fresh cilantro
4	scallions (white and green parts), thinly sliced on the diagonal

TO SEGMENT THE NAVEL ORANGES, use a large sharp chef's knife to cut off the tops and bottoms so that the fruits will stand upright on a cutting board. Stand an orange on the board and slice away the peel from top to bottom, following the curve of the fruit and removing the pith along with the rind. Trim away any remaining white pith. Holding the orange in your hand, cut each fruit segment out from between the dividing membranes with a paring knife into a bowl. Repeat with the remaining oranges. Squeeze the juice remaining in the segments into a bowl and set the segments aside.

Combine the Seville orange juice, oil, cumin, garlic, and shallots in a small bowl and mix well.

Heat a stainless-steel sauté pan over high heat. Pour the juice mixture into the hot pan and cook for 1 minute, stirring constantly. Remove from the heat and stir in the orange segments, oregano, parsley, cilantro, and scallions.

P. 206   Lechón Asado

MOROS Y CRISTIANOS

BLACK BEANS AND RICE

Yes, *Moros y Cristianos*, the common Cuban name for this ubiquitous side dish, translates as "Moors and Christians." And yes, the black beans are taken for the dark-skinned Moors while the white rice grains are the lighter-complected Christians. And that's all I have to say about that. The dish itself, though, I could talk about all day; it is easy, absolutely delicious, and part-and-parcel of any proper Cuban barbecue. The base is a classic Cuban sofrito of onions, tomatoes, peppers, garlic, chiles, herbs, and spices. The resting step at the end helps make the rice moist yet fluffy. SERVES 8

2 Tbsp	extra virgin olive oil
1	large Spanish onion, diced
2	green bell peppers, diced
2 Tbsp	minced garlic (4 to 6 cloves)
2	serrano chiles, seeds and ribs removed, finely diced
10	plum tomatoes, diced
4 tsp	whole cumin seeds, toasted (see page 368) and ground
6	sprigs thyme
2	fresh bay leaves
2 cups	long-grain white rice
2	(15-oz) cans black beans (preferably organic), drained and rinsed
1 qt	Chicken Stock (page 362)
1/4 cup	cider vinegar
1 Tbsp	kosher salt
1/4 tsp	freshly ground black pepper

Heat the oil in a large, heavy-bottomed saucepan over medium heat. Add the onion, bell peppers, garlic, and chiles and cook until translucent, about 10 minutes.

Stir in the tomatoes, cumin, thyme, and bay leaves and cook until fragrant, about 3 minutes.

Add the rice, beans, stock, vinegar, and salt and pepper. Bring to a boil over high heat, then lower the heat to a simmer and cook, covered, until the rice is tender, about 20 minutes.

Allow the beans and rice to rest uncovered for 2 to 3 minutes before serving.

YUCA CON MOJO CRIOLLO

YUCA WITH SOUR ORANGE MOJO

Yuca is known both as manioc and cassava. It becomes soft and fragile when it cooks; take care not to squish it—or give yourself a steam burn—when lifting it out of the steamer basket. SERVES 8

4 lb	yuca, peeled and cut into 1-inch pieces
2 cups	Sour Orange Mojo (page 209)
	Kosher salt and freshly ground black pepper

Place the yuca in a steamer basket in a stockpot and add water up to the bottom of the basket. Bring to a boil and steam the yuca, covered, until fork-tender, 25 to 30 minutes, adding water if necessary.

Meanwhile, gently heat the mojo in a small nonreactive saucepan.

Carefully transfer the yuca to a serving dish, toss with the hot mojo, adding the sauce 1/2 cup at a time until the yuca is dressed to your taste. Season to taste with salt and pepper and serve immediately.

TOSTONES

CRISPY FRIED GREEN PLANTAINS

Sliced green plantains oxidize and turn brown very quickly so it's important to get them right into the oil. The first fry at a lower temp tenderizes the plantains, much like blanching a French fry. Refrying at a higher temperature makes them crispy on the outside. SERVES 8

2 qts	vegetable oil
4	green plantains, peeled (see page 67)
	Kosher salt

Heat the oil to 300°F in a stockpot over medium heat, using a candy or deep-fry thermometer to monitor the temperature. Line a baking sheet with parchment paper.

Cut the plantains into 2-inch pieces and fry them in batches until soft, 5 to 7 minutes.

Use a slotted spoon to transfer the hot plantains directly to a work surface and press them with the bottom of a saucepan to form patties about 1/2-inch thick.

Increase the heat under the pot to medium-high to raise the temperature of the oil to 375°F.

Refry the plantains in batches until golden brown and crispy, about 3 minutes. Drain the tostones on the baking sheet and season to taste with salt. Serve immediately.

PASTELES DE GUAYABA

GUAVA AND CREAM CHEESE TURNOVERS

Pasteles may not be the traditional dessert for Cuban Christmas Eve, but I've included them here because they are such a big favorite in our household—my kids go completely bananas for the ones my in-laws bring from Miami. Filled with sticky-sweet guava paste, quite a confection on its own (and available in any Latin grocery), these flaky and delicious little pies are pretty easy to make but plenty impressive for company, so they're a good way to go for a prep-heavy occasion like a pig roast with all the trimmings. MAKES 8 PASTELES

1	large egg
1 Tbsp	cold water
2	(12 by 12-inch) sheets frozen puff pastry
1/4 lb	guava paste (about 1/2 cup)
4 oz	cream cheese
2 Tbsp	turbinado sugar

Line two baking sheets with parchment paper. Beat together the egg and water to make a wash.

Unfold the puff pastry on a large cutting board or other work surface and use a sharp knife or pizza cutter to cut each sheet into four 6 by 6-inch squares. Brush each square lightly with some of the egg wash. Spoon equal parts (about 1 Tbsp each) of guava paste and cream cheese onto the pastry squares, just off center. Fold each square over corner to corner, forming a triangle, and seal by pressing the edges together. (If at any point the puff pastry gets too soft, put back into the freezer for 10 minutes.) Crimp the edges of the pastries with a fork; brush the tops with the remaining egg wash and sprinkle with the sugar. Arrange the pasteles on the baking sheets and chill them in the freezer for 30 minutes.

While the pasteles are chilling, preheat the oven to 400°F.

Bake the pasteles, rotating the sheets once, until golden and puffed, about 15 minutes. Serve warm or at room temperature.

MEXICO

MENU 1
VERACRUZ

Sopa de Tortilla | TORTILLA SOUP

Pescado a la Veracruzana | RED SNAPPER IN TOMATO SAUCE

Ejotes | WARM GREEN BEAN SALAD

MENU 2
TAMPICO

Ceviche de Pulpo | OCTOPUS CEVICHE WITH AVOCADO

Carne Asada a la Tampiqueña | GRILLED MARINATED SKIRT STEAK

Arroz Rojo | RED RICE

Refritos | REFRIED BEANS

MENU 3
TENOCHTITLAN

Ensalada de Nopales | CACTUS PADDLE SALAD

Camarones al Ajillo | PAN-ROASTED SHRIMP WITH TEQUILA

Papas con Chorizo | ROASTED POTATOES WITH CHORIZO

MENU 4
DISTRITO FEDERAL

Margarita de Chile Verde | SPICY MARGARITA

Margarita de Mango | MANGO MARGARITA

Nachos de Pollo | CHIPOTLE CHICKEN NACHOS

Guacamole y Tortillas | GUACAMOLE AND TORTILLAS CHIPS

TACO BAR
Carnitas | BEER- AND CITRUS-BRAISED FRIED PORK

Alambres de Camarones | SHRIMP SKEWERS

Rajas con Hongos | ROASTED POBLANO CHILES WITH MUSHROOMS

Frijoles Borrachos | BEER-BRAISED BEANS

Tortillas de Maíz | CORN TORTILLAS

Salsas | CLASSIC SALSA | ROASTED TOMATO SALSA WITH TOMATILLOS | TOMATILLO SALSA

Acompañamientos | ACCOMPANIMENTS

Pastel de Tres Leches | TRES LECHES CAKE

ESSENTIALS | Pozole PG 237 | Antojitos PG 248 | El Mercado de la Merced PG 260

As a kid, I encountered Mexican food early and often, thanks mainly to my dad and the fact that my family lived in a series of multiethnic melting-pot Chicago neighborhoods. On weekends, Pops and I teamed up on the grocery shopping, heading first to the big Jewel supermarket for basic household supplies, then to Carnicería Jimenez, the Mexican grocery at Central Park and Fullerton, where we'd work our way through my mom's list of Latin provisions for the week—from plantains and yuca to *queso fresco* and hominy, *achiote* and avocados, to *arracheras* (skirt steak) and roast pork shoulder.

It was in this friendly, bustling establishment, amid the columns of corn tortillas and swags of dried chiles that I first fell in love with food markets. Sealing the deal was the taco stand—right there inside the store. The offerings were simple and delicious: steak, chicken, or pork filling with a sprinkling of chopped white onions and cilantro and a squirt of lime. Pops and I would knock back a few tacos and be on our way, lugging all the grocery bags home.

Once in a while my father would take the family out for Mexican food at one or another of the low-key neighborhood restaurants around town he was fond of, places that featured rustic, home-style Mexican meals. Wherever we went, we always had traditional guacamole and *salsa mexicana* with our meal, and Pops or my older brother ordered the *carne asada a la Tampiqueña* (page 244). Other family favorites included *camarones al ajillo* (page 258), chicken tacos, and *pescado a la veracruzana* (page 233).

Then there was the late-night taco ritual. We were part of a group of Ecuadorian families that took turns hosting parties that went on until all hours, and on the way home my father had a habit of swinging by a taco place for a midnight snack. I'd wake up in the wee hours, sandwiched between my brothers in the back seat, one of my parents saying "Here, Josecito, take this . . ." as a taco came toward me over the blue vinyl headrest of our Chevy Malibu. Depending on what part of town we were coming from and how late it was, we could be parked outside a *taquería* or, just as easily, pulling through the drive-thru at Jack-in-the-Box. As much as Pops enjoyed real-deal Mexican food, when it came to the essential post-party taco, he was no stranger to the fried shell with crumbled hamburger, shredded iceberg, and American cheese.

From my late teens and into my early twenties, my own late-night food ritual veered into Tex-Mex by way of Chicago's network of great burrito joints. Burritos are mighty fine post-party grub. Those were decadent years; my favorites were pretty heavy duty, usually a *burrito suizo* (cheese-covered, baked, and eaten with a knife and fork) or that ever-popular staple of late-night dining, the steak burrito (basically a tortilla-clad analogy to the Philly cheesesteak). Now and then I'd branch out and go for something like *queso fundido* (Mexican chorizo, soft corn tortillas, lots of Chihuahua cheese). Such is youth!

I first encountered Mexican food from the cooking side in the mid-1990s, when I spent the better part of a year as an intern for the chef Stephan Pyles at Star Canyon, his Southwest restaurant in Dallas. I was just beginning to learn how to be a professional line cook and I'd never witnessed a Mexican prep team at work. (As any honest person in the industry will tell you, few of America's great restaurants would shine as they do were it not for the legions of Mexican cooks in their kitchens.) Their knife skills were phenomenal, and I was just amazed at the way they cranked out production with breakneck speed and seamless precision. This kitchen was doing 300 to 400 covers a night. I ended up staying at Star Canyon more than twice as long as I'd originally planned, soaking up everything this crew had to teach me. When I headed back to school to finish up my degree, I had acquired some serious skills—I could kill it on the line.

Back in Chicago, just as I was finishing up my culinary degree, Rick Bayless was becoming a big star. He'd been a major presence in my hometown since the late 1980s, when he opened Frontera Grill and Topolobampo, serving deeply traditional Mexican cuisine the likes of which most Americans had never known. Rick's fame grew as he published a series of authoritative cookbooks. I read each and every one of them avidly, and that's how I discovered that indigenous techniques are intrinsic to Mexican cuisine, having been passed down from ancient times, preserved throughout Spanish conquest and colonization, and carried onward to the present day. This revelation, and the complexity and sophistication of the food itself, deepened my appreciation for the tacos and other Mexican restaurant standards that were such a big part of my childhood— and sparked my interest in exploring this cuisine more fully as a chef.

Fast-forward six years to Philadelphia in 2003: With my first restaurant launch officially a success—Douglas Rodriguez and I had opened Alma de Cuba for restaurateur Stephen Starr and the place was humming along—I was raring to get going on a new venture. But this time around I wanted to hatch my own idea. So I scouted out a space on an up-and-coming stretch of Thirteenth Street and came up with a couple of concepts: Spanish tapas versus modern Mexican, neither of which was part of the restaurant landscape in Center City (downtown Philly) at the time. Steve took a liking to the Mexican notion, though it was a challenge to pry him away from Tex-Mex and convince him, through a series of tastings and arguments, that Philly was ready to find out how much more there is to Mexican cuisine than fast-food burritos and enchiladas.

Developing the menu for the new restaurant, I studied Mexican culinary traditions intensively, cooking (and eating) my way through recipes by Diana Kennedy, Zarela Martinez and, of course, Rick Bayless, to get myself informed and inspired, and fully versed in this venerable and highly complex cuisine. For good measure, I headed back to Chicago for a few days to do trails (spend full shifts observing and working in the kitchen) at Frontera Grill and Topolobampo, making sure I had a lock on all of the fundamentals.

When El Vez opened eight months later, Philadelphians proved me right: they have quite the appetite for Mexican fare that melds rich traditions with modern possibilities. The place is going strong to this day, and while I certainly savor that success, it's always bittersweet. Striking out on my own when the time came meant leaving El Vez, my first creation, behind.

It took me a few years to open a modern Mexican restaurant of my very own. When the right opportunity came along, I revisited the modern Mexican concept from a new angle. This time, I traveled to Mexico for my research and teamed up with fellow chef Tim Spinner and restaurant designer Jun Aizaki. This proved to be a great way to develop the menu I'd originated with El Vez in a new direction, with its own personality and true sense of place. We created a restaurant inspired by Distrito Federal: Mexico City—a vibrant, rollicking cosmopolis where all the regional cuisines of Mexico are represented. Distrito opened in 2008 and has been a joy since day one.

I'm still very much a student of traditional Mexican cooking and I look forward with great anticipation to investigating the multitude of individual regional cuisines in depth over the coming years. In the meantime, the Mexican dishes I've come to know thus far are among the foods I most enjoy preparing and eating with friends and family. This chapter is a selection of those recipes, a handpicked and fine-tuned sampling of mostly traditional home-cooked meals.

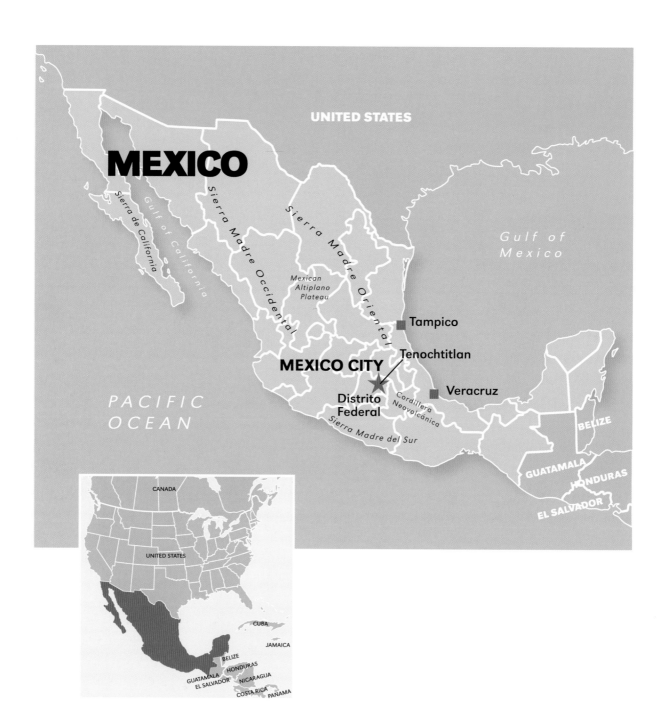

QUICK INFO

LAND

• Major mountain ranges include the Sierra Madre Occidental and the Sierra Madre Oriental along the west and east, with the vast Mexican Altiplano (plateau) between them; the Cordillera Neovolcánica across central Mexico; the Sierra Madre del Sur in the south; and the Sierra de California on the Baja Peninsula

• Divided into temperate and tropical zones by the Tropic of Cancer, with climatic diversity throughout by virtue of elevation and rainfall—from coastal plain to mountain peak, subtropical highland to desert valley, tropical rain forest to arid plateau

PEOPLE

• Current population is over 113 million people with over 20 million in Mexico City alone. The world's most populous Spanish-speaking country; more than sixty indigenous languages are also recognized

• Large majority of Mexicans are of mixed indigenous and European heritage: following the revolution of 1920, a national identity was established officially embracing *mestizaje*—Mexico's ethnic and cultural mixture of indigenous and European

FOOD

• Cuisine strongly based in ancient traditions, blended over the past 500 years with foods introduced during the colonial period

• Present-day staples include indigenous foods that date back millennia, such as corn, beans, squash, tomatoes, avocados, chiles, and chocolate, as well as peanuts, various cacti, and assorted tropical fruits

• Spanish introductions include wheat, grapes, olives, rice, onions and garlic, sugar cane, and livestock, such as pigs, cattle, and chickens

1500 BCE–1519 CE
Over some 3,000 years, an overlapping succession of ancient civilizations—including Olmec, Teotihuacán, Toltec, Maya, and Aztec—reign over various parts of present-day Mexico and adjacent lands.

1519 CE
Spanish explorers arrive and in two years conquer the Mexica, who ruled the Aztec Empire from the Valley of Mexico, and proceed to colonize the entire region.

1821 CE
New Spain wins its independence, taking its name from the capital—Mexico City, which three hundred years prior had been the site of the great Aztec capital crushed by the conquest.

VERACRUZ

Sopa de Tortilla | TORTILLA SOUP

Pescado a la Veracruzana | RED SNAPPER IN TOMATO SAUCE

Ejotes | WARM GREEN BEAN SALAD

Back in 2003, restaurateur Stephen Starr green-lit a modern Mexican concept I'd dreamed up and it was down to me to create a kick-ass menu that would make El Vez (named for the famous Mexican Elvis impersonator) a big new arrival on the Philadelphia scene rather than a passing curiosity. The way I saw it, El Vez would fill the city's void in authentic Mexican fare with food that was decidedly contemporary but deeply rooted in tradition.

I was especially intent upon featuring a truly superb rendition of the classic tortilla soup, a dish I'd enjoyed in restaurants all my life but never once attempted to cook. I set about unlocking the magic of this comforting concoction, the epitome of soul food *a la mexicana*, to create a version that manifested everything I'd always relished about *sopa de tortilla*—all the deep, nuanced flavors and intermingled textures. Making a study of this homespun, complex dish was a great way to kick my self-schooling in Mexican cooking into overdrive. When I emerged from the process, I not only had a terrific take on tortilla soup but also a heightened understanding of what it is I find so compelling about Mexican cuisine—and what sets it apart so distinctly from other Latin cooking traditions.

At the crux of the best tortilla soups, and a great many other classic Mexican dishes, are key ingredients that have been prepared in particular ways before being combined. There are, say, onions, garlic, tomatoes, and chiles, all of which have been charred, roasted, or toasted before being incorporated. Applying direct flame or dry heat to these produce staples is an ingenious and age-old technique for concentrating and subtly transforming their flavors and aromas. A distinctive practice—one not found in other Latin culinary traditions—it is one of the ancient Indian ways at the very heart of Mexican cooking.

And with chiles, the treatment goes further. The variety of fresh and dried chiles is more extensive than in any other Latin cooking style—from fiery-hot (like habanero) to straight-ahead spicy (like serrano) to fruity-mellow (like guajillo) and all gradations in between. Most chiles (except for a few of the hottest types) are not just toasted or roasted, but also stemmed and seeded; soaked or steeped; pressed or pulped; strained, blended with spices, and transformed into a paste. Converting chiles to this condensed form preserves them (the pastes keep for ages) and produces a compact agent of intense, multidimensional flavor. Chile pastes are indispensable staples in the Mexican kitchen, used to build salsas and moles, flavor soups and stews, season meat and chicken, and so on.

As these elementary principles of Mexican cooking became part of my daily life, certain aspects of the prep I'd experienced in other kitchens made a whole new world of sense to me. No wonder the walk-in at Star Canyon (the Southwest restaurant where I'd interned way back in cooking school) had always been so packed with tubs of chile paste—guajillo, pasilla, ancho, chipotle, árbol, and more. And no wonder there were always so many sheet trays full of vegetables and chiles picking up char under the broiling units at Topolobampo and Frontera Grill (renowned Bayless restaurants where I'd recently done trails).

As my recipe research progressed, I discovered another element crucial to the very best tortilla soups: tortillas. Not the typical and delicious use of crispy tortilla chips on top of the finished soup, but rather the neat trick of incorporating crumbled, stale corn tortillas chips into the broth. This move probably originated as a resourceful way to make use of leftovers. (This makes a lot of sense when you consider that, until fairly recently, tortillas were made from scratch daily, in a labor-intensive process that involved soaking whole corn kernels in a lime solution to hull them, then grinding the grains into *masa* for the dough. By the end of the day, any tortillas that hadn't been eaten were irretrievably stale, but throwing them out was not only a waste of time and effort, it was an extravagance that most families simply could not afford.) Pieces of tortilla (fried or unfried) stirred into the stock dissolve in a matter of minutes, beautifully enhancing the body of the soup and infusing it with toasty corn flavor.

Then came the garnishes, a specific assortment of which I established as mandatory for the soup. They delivered a perfectly balanced bite in every spoonful: freshly fried tortilla strips, silky avocado, tender shredded chicken, salty *queso fresco*, tangy *crema*, herbaceous cilantro, and zingy lime.

As my tortilla soup recipe and my expertise in Mexican cuisine evolved, so did my career ambitions. By the time El Vez opened and the *sopa de tortilla* achieved the popularity I'd hoped it would, my desire to eventually launch restaurants of my own had morphed into a much more immediate objective. Inside of two years, I established my own restaurant group, which within a few more years grew to include my very own modern Mexican concept, Distrito. Since the doors opened in 2008, we've served countless bowls of tortilla soup, closely based on that original formative recipe. Here's a version that I've reworked just a bit for simpler home prep, plus a classic Veracruz-style preparation for whole fish in a gorgeous, flavorful sauce, as well as *ejotes*, which are a really nice bright fresh complement to both the soup and the fish.

P. 230 Sopa de Tortilla

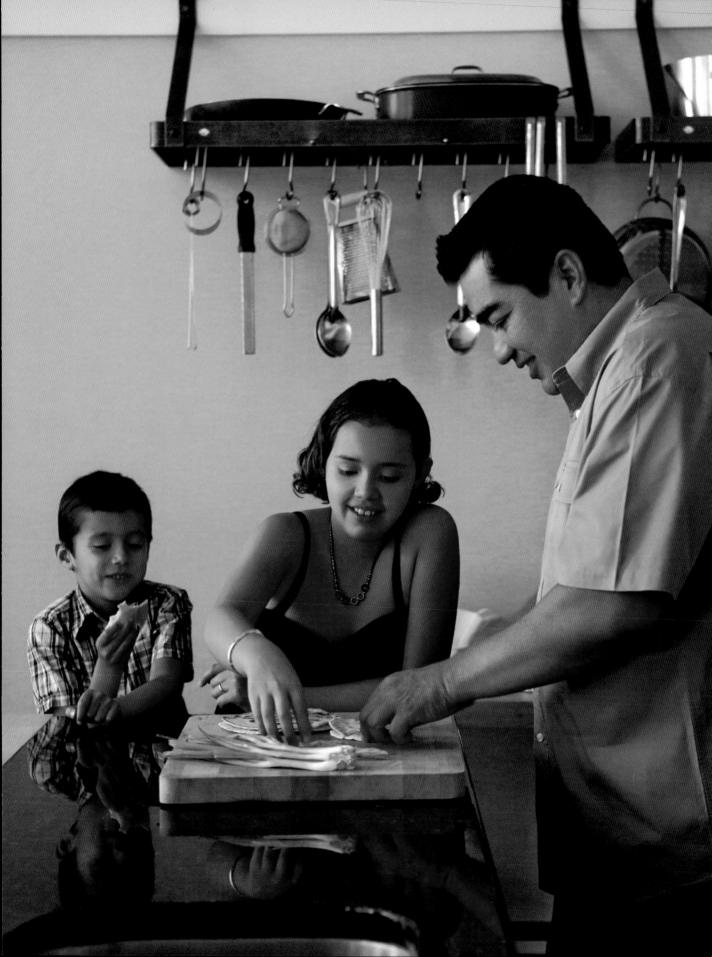

SOPA DE TORTILLA

TORTILLA SOUP

Keeping chile pastes and roasted garlic on hand makes Mexican dishes an easier proposition in general. For this soup, you can poach the chicken and make the chips in advance to help speed the prep along— or you can make the entire soup up to three days ahead of time, leaving just the garnish (including the crispy tortilla strips) to be prepped right before serving. Packaged chips can really mar the soup's flavor and texture; if you must use something from a bag, use a high-quality, minimally processed, unsalted chip. Mexican *crema* and *queso fresco* are both sold at Latin groceries (see photo, page 228). SERVES 4

POACHED CHICKEN

1	Spanish onion, coarsely chopped
1	fresh bay leaf
	Kosher salt
1 1/2 lb	boneless, skinless chicken thighs

SOUP

2 Tbsp	vegetable oil
2 Tbsp	(4 to 6 cloves) Roasted Garlic (page 366)
1	Spanish onion, halved, charred (see page 368), and chopped
3	beefsteak tomatoes (about 1 1/2 lb), charred (see page 368) and chopped
1/4 cup	tomato paste
1/4 cup	pasilla Chile Paste (page 369)
1	canned chipotle chile in adobo, with sauce (see Sources)
2 qts	Chicken Stock (page 362)
8 to 10	tortillas home-fried into chips (page 274), preferably stale
	Kosher salt

CRISPY TORTILLA STRIPS

1 1/2 qts	vegetable oil, for frying
4 to 6	small (about 6-inch) corn tortillas
	Kosher salt

TO SERVE

1/4 cup	Mexican crema
1/4 lb	grated queso fresco (1/2 cup)
2	avocados, diced
2 Tbsp	chopped fresh cilantro
	Lime wedges

TO POACH THE CHICKEN, bring a large saucepan of water to a boil. Add the onion, bay leaf, and 3 to 4 tablespoons salt. Add the chicken and simmer for 10 to 12 minutes, until just cooked through. Lift the chicken out of the water, drain it, and allow it to cool. Shred it by hand into bite-size pieces. (Discard the cooking water.)

TO MAKE THE SOUP, heat the oil in a stockpot over medium-high heat. Add the garlic, onion, and tomatoes and cook until softened, about 10 minutes, stirring occasionally. Stir in the tomato paste, chile paste, and chipotle chile with sauce and cook for 10 minutes more. Add the stock and bring to a boil. Lower the heat and simmer, uncovered, for 30 minutes.

TO MAKE THE TORTILLA STRIPS, heat the oil to 375°F in a stockpot, using a candy or deep-fry thermometer to monitor the temperature. Line a baking sheet with paper towels. Use a sharp knife or a pizza cutter to slice the tortillas into strips about 1/4-inch wide. Fry the strips briefly, 30 to 60 seconds, just to crisp them. Use a slotted spoon to carefully transfer the strips from the oil to the baking sheet to drain.

Stir the tortilla chips into the soup and cook for another 5 minutes. Take the pot off the heat and use a handheld immersion blender to purée the soup until it is very smooth. Strain through a fine-mesh sieve and season to taste with salt. (At this point, the soup can be cooled and stored in the refrigerator in an airtight container for up to 3 days.)

TO SERVE, rewarm the soup over medium heat, stirring often. Garnish each serving with crema, cheese, avocado, shredded chicken, cilantro, lime wedges, and tortilla strips, or pass the garnishes at the table.

PESCADO A LA VERACRUZANA
RED SNAPPER IN TOMATO SAUCE

Cooking the fish whole makes for a dramatic presentation and also imparts flavor and richness from oils that come forth from within the skin and bones of the fish as it roasts. Use any fish with firm white flesh—branzino or black sea bass, whatever looks fresh (avoid darker oily fish like mackerel and trout; their full flavor will overshadow the sauce). The chunky tomato-based sauce with capers, olives, and jalapeños, is very light and aromatic. Both the sauce base and the marinade can be made in advance. The accompanying plantains and green beans round things out nicely with their sweetness. SERVES 4

GARLIC-PARSLEY MARINADE

2	cloves garlic, crushed
1/2 cup	chopped fresh flat-leaf parsley
1/2 cup	minced fresh cilantro leaves
2 Tbsp	minced fresh oregano
3/4 cup	vegetable oil

FISH

2	whole fresh fish (about 1 1/2 lb each), cleaned and scaled
2 Tbsp	vegetable oil
	Kosher salt and freshly ground black pepper

VERACRUZANA SAUCE

1/4 cup	extra virgin olive oil
1	Spanish onion, diced
2 Tbsp	minced garlic (4 to 6 cloves)
2 Tbsp	tomato paste
1/2 cup	dry white wine
8	plum tomatoes, diced
2	(14.5-oz) cans stewed tomatoes, chopped, with juice
2 cups	bottled clam juice (2 [8-oz] bottles)
2 Tbsp	dried Mexican oregano

SACHET

6	sprigs thyme
1	2-inch piece canela (Mexican cinnamon stick), toasted and ground (see page 368)
1 tsp	whole allspice berries, toasted (see page 368)
2 tsp	whole black peppercorns, toasted (see page 368)
4	whole cloves, toasted (see page 368)
4	bay leaves (preferably fresh)

TO SERVE

1/4 cup	halved grape tomatoes (about 4 tomatoes, depending on size)
1/4 cup	pitted and quartered Manzanilla or other green olives, (8 to 10 olives, depending on size)
2 Tbsp	Pickled Jalapeños (page 367)
	About 12 caperberries (see Sources)
	White Rice (page 367)
	Fried Sweet Plantains (page 175)

TO MAKE THE MARINADE, combine the garlic, parsley, cilantro, oregano, and vegetable oil in a blender and purée until very smooth. If not using immediately, set aside, refrigerated, in a covered container, up to 48 hours.

Set the fish in a shallow glass dish or other nonreactive container, cover with the marinade, turn to coat, and refrigerate for 1 hour.

TO MAKE THE SAUCE, combine the olive oil, onion, and garlic in a saucepan over medium heat and cook, stirring often, until translucent, about 10 minutes. Add the tomato paste and white wine and continue cooking to reduce by half, about 5 minutes. Stir in the plum tomatoes, stewed tomatoes, clam juice, and oregano.

TO MAKE THE SACHET, wrap the thyme, canela, allspice, peppercorns, cloves, and bay leaves in a piece of cheesecloth, tie securely into a sachet, and add to the sauce. Continue simmering until reduced by one-third, 12 to 15 minutes. Remove from the heat, discard the sachet, and season to taste with salt. (At this point the sauce can be cooled and stored in an airtight container in the refrigerator for up to 3 days.)

TO COOK THE FISH, preheat the oven to 425°F, heat a stovetop grill pan over medium-high heat, and lightly oil a baking sheet.

Lift the fish out of the marinade and season generously with salt and pepper. (Discard the marinade.) Grill the fish in the pan, turning once, until the skin is well browned, 4 to 5 minutes per side. Transfer the fish to the baking sheet and roast them in the oven 10 to 12 minutes, until they are very firm to the touch and opaque to the center.

Meanwhile, combine the sauce with the grape tomatoes, olives, jalapeños, and caperberries in a saucepan and cook over medium heat just to warm through.

TO SERVE, ladle the sauce onto a large platter and top with the fish. Pass the rice and fried plantains at the table. To portion out the fish, use a dinner fork and spoon to carefully remove the flesh—in chunks or as a whole fillet—from the top side of each fish. The skeletons will easily lift away from the bottom halves of the fish, leaving whole fillets that lift away from the skin.

EJOTES
WARM GREEN BEAN SALAD

Serve this dish slightly warm, with the egg freshly cooked sunny-side up so that the yolks are nice and oozy. SERVES 4

GARLIC-LIME VINAIGRETTE

2 Tbsp	(4 to 6 cloves) Roasted Garlic (page 366)
2 Tbsp	freshly squeezed lime juice
2 Tbsp	extra virgin olive oil
2 Tbsp	honey
	Kosher salt and freshly ground black pepper

BEANS

1 lb	haricots verts or very thin green beans, stem ends trimmed
2	jarred roasted red bell peppers, drained, rinsed (if packed in brine or oil), seeded, and chopped
1/4 lb	queso fresco (1/2 cup)
1	large shallot, thinly sliced
	Kosher salt

TO SERVE

4	large eggs
4 tsp	butter
2 Tbsp	grated Cotija cheese
	Kosher salt
	Pequín chile powder (see Sources)

TO MAKE THE VINAIGRETTE, combine the roasted garlic, lime juice, oil, and honey in a blender and purée until the mixture is smooth and completely emulsified. Season to taste with salt and pepper.

TO COOK THE BEANS, prepare an ice bath and bring a large saucepan of generously salted water to a boil. Boil the beans for 1 minute, then drain and immediately transfer them to the ice bath for several minutes to cool. Drain the beans again and let them sit, allowing them to come to room temperature.

Combine the beans, roasted peppers, cheese, and shallots and toss with the vinaigrette. Season to taste with salt.

Just before serving the beans, fry the eggs sunny-side up in the butter (the yolks should be oozy).

TO SERVE, divide the beans among four plates and garnish each with a warm egg, some Cotija, and a little chile powder. Serve immediately.

POZOLE

Pozole is a hearty hominy soup, a fiesta food so popular all over Mexico that entire restaurants, called *pozolerías*, specialize in it, as do many street stands and market stalls. Meaty and chile-infused, this is rich, robust stuff with origins dating back to long before Spanish colonization; the name comes from the ancient Nahuatl word *potzolli* for "foam" or "bubble."

There are three basic types of *pozole*, with many regional specialties and variations among them—most are made with lots of pork (some traditional recipes specifically call for *cabeza*, the pig's head), though chicken is also common. Generally speaking, a *pozole rojo* features red chiles, while a *pozole blanco* has a clear broth, and a *pozole verde* is tinged green from a mixture of tomatillos, green chiles, and pepitas (hulled pumpkin seeds). Garnishes, which are crucial and often piled on in quantity, may include shredded lettuce or cabbage, radishes, onions, oregano, chiles, cilantro, avocado, *tostadas* (deep-fried corn tortillas), and *chicharrones* (fried pork rinds).

A great bowl of *pozole*, with its earthy savor, is quintessential comfort food. I'd put the best tortilla soups in this category as well. The comforting feel of these dishes reminds me of the soothing *locros* (rustic Ecuadorian potato soups) I grew up on, though those stews were bulkier and much more rustic than a deftly wrought *pozole* or *sopa de tortilla*.

I've tinkered quite a bit with various types of *pozoles*. So far, my favorite interpretation is a vibrant *verde* with which I've taken some liberties. While retaining the traditional tomatillos and green chiles along with copious amounts of cilantro, I've replaced the traditional pork broth with crab stock. And as much as I enjoy the rich nutty flavor and thickening power of pepitas, I've set them aside in this rendition, instead incorporating crabmeat and clams, which lend a sweet yet delicate richness of their own. The fresh garnishes—radish, cabbage, oregano, onion, cilantro, and avocado—bring flavors and textures that really complete the dish. *(Recipe follows.)*

POZOLE VERDE CON CANGREJO
GREEN HOMINY SOUP WITH CRAB

Note that the hominy needs to soak for 2 days, then simmer for 3 hours, before being used in the soup; you can do this in advance and store the cooked hominy and cooking liquid separately in airtight containers in the refrigerator for up to 3 days. The finished *pozole* also keeps well for up to 3 days in an airtight container in the refrigerator. It's a renowned hangover remedy (see photo, page 236). SERVES 8

HOMINY

4 cups	dried hominy (see Sources)

CLAM BROTH

10	fresh quahog clams, scrubbed and rinsed under cold water
1	large Spanish onion, diced small
2	celery stalks, diced small
1 cup	crushed garlic cloves (2 heads)
1 cup	dry white wine
1 Tbsp	whole white peppercorns
2 1/2 qts	cold water

SOUP

2	Spanish onions, diced
1/4 cup	minced garlic (12 to 16 cloves)
2 lb	tomatillos, husked and washed (see page 288)
1	poblano chile, seeded and roughly chopped
4	serrano chiles, seeded
2 tsp	dried Mexican oregano
2 cups	fresh cilantro leaves
1/4 cup	extra virgin olive oil
	Kosher salt
32	fresh littleneck clams, scrubbed to remove all dirt and sediment
2 lb	jumbo lump crabmeat
1/4	small head green cabbage, finely shredded

TO SERVE

2	avocados, sliced
1/2 cup	sliced radishes (about 4 radishes)
1/4 cup	fresh oregano leaves
1	Spanish onion, finely diced
1/2 cup	minced fresh cilantro

TO SOAK THE HOMINY, rinse and drain it. Place it in a deep container and cover with enough cold water to completely submerge the hominy. Soak the hominy, covered, in the refrigerator for 2 days.

TO COOK THE HOMINY, rinse and drain the soaked hominy and combine it in a stockpot with cold water to cover by 8 to 10 inches. Bring to a boil, then decrease the heat to low and simmer, partly covered, until the hominy is tender and opens up into blossoms, about 3 hours. Ladle out 1 quart (4 cups) of the cooking liquid, strain it through a fine-mesh sieve, and set aside. Drain the hominy of all remaining liquid. (The strained cooking liquid and hominy can be stored in separate airtight containers in the refrigerator for up to 3 days.)

TO MAKE THE CLAM BROTH, combine the quahogs, onion, celery, garlic, white wine, and white peppercorns in a stockpot and bring to a boil. Cook until the clams just begin to open and the wine is reduced by half.

Add the cold water and bring to a simmer. Cook over low heat until all the clams are open, about 20 minutes. Discard any that don't open. Lift the clams out of the broth and set them aside. Strain the broth through a fine-mesh sieve lined with a double layer of cheesecloth. Remove the clams from their shells and discard the shells. Chop the clams into bite-size pieces and set aside.

TO MAKE THE SOUP, combine the clam broth, reserved hominy cooking liquid, and cooked hominy in a stockpot and bring to a boil over medium heat. Lower the heat and simmer for 30 minutes.

Meanwhile, combine the onions, garlic, tomatillos, poblano and serrano chiles, and dried oregano in a blender and purée the mixture until it is very smooth. Add the cilantro and continue puréeing until the cilantro is completely incorporated and the mixture is vibrant green. Slowly add the oil in a thin stream until the purée is emulsified. Season to taste with salt.

Add the purée to the hominy and cook 5 minutes. Add the chopped quahog clams and littlenecks to the soup and cook just until the littlenecks open, 2 to 3 minutes. Discard any that don't open. Stir in the crabmeat and the cabbage and heat the soup just to warm through. Season to taste with salt.

TO SERVE, divide the soup among eight warmed soup bowls and garnish with the avocados, radishes, oregano, onion, and cilantro.

TAMPICO

Ceviche de Pulpo | OCTOPUS CEVICHE WITH AVOCADO
Carne Asada a la Tampiqueña | GRILLED MARINATED SKIRT STEAK
Arroz Rojo | RED RICE
Refritos | REFRIED BEANS

Bistec a la Tampiqueña was originally created by José Luis Loredo, a Mexico City restaurateur who named the dish for his birthplace, Tampico, a port city in northeastern Mexico. The dish has become classic Mexican restaurant fare, and it is especially prized in *my* hometown, Chicago, where the meat component is typically skirt steak—well marinated for big flavor and quickly grilled for juicy tenderness. Then there's all the other goodies on the plate, which might include an enchilada with mole as well as some manner of rice, beans, avocados or guacamole, a pile of salad or grilled onions, and so on. When served in Mexico, the presentation tends to conform to the original and includes grilled *panela* cheese with the *bisteca*, which is often a tenderloin cut. In any case, it's by definition quite a sizable combo platter.

For me, *Tampiqueña* harkens back to the frequent Mexican restaurant outings of my childhood and the comically predictable ordering habits of the Garces males: one or more plates of *Tampiqueña* were a sure bet every time.

Revisiting this delicious, nostalgic old standby and devising my own rendition was one of the many great pleasures of opening my own Mexican restaurant. Firmly established in the "Tradicionales" section of the Distrito menu, my take on *carne a la Tampiqueña* centers on a finely tuned marinade that infuses the steak with robust, complex yet balanced flavors.

It's pretty simple, really. Grind up a paste that combines the distinctive near-fruitiness of guajillo chiles with the rich sweetness of roasted garlic, the fragrance of rosemary and thyme, a strong punch from black pepper, and the mellowing effects of honey and olive oil. Slather paste on steak. Marinate overnight. Grill briefly. Rest and slice. And the accoutrements are easy: rice tinged with tomato and chile de árbol powder, canned beans fried up with a little lard for richness and body, a few choice garnishes—crumbled Cotija cheese, cilantro leaves, radish slivers, avocado slices—and warm tortillas. What more could you ask for?

I suspect that part of the appeal of the dish to me and my brothers when we were kids was the zany musicality of the name, which I admit I still enjoy announcing in an exaggerated way whenever I make this dish at home: "*Carrrrne a la Tam-pi-queña!!!*" The vocal flourish is optional, of course, but highly recommended. Regardless, I do encourage you to go with the full menu here, starting with the octopus ceviche, which can mostly be prepared in advance and makes for a fun and fantastic meal.

P. 242 Ceviche de Pulpo

CEVICHE DE PULPO

OCTOPUS CEVICHE WITH AVOCADO

For this Mexican-style *ceviche de pulpo*, you may need to order fresh (or high-quality frozen) Spanish or Mediterranean octopus from your fishmonger a week or more in advance. Then use my cooking technique, which I've perfected over the course of several years, to make the octopus super tender. Dressed with the perfect balance of green chiles and citrus, the finished ceviche is light and refreshing, and the crispy garlic chips and creamy avocado espuma bring additional flavor and texture dimensions to the plate. Consider making the garlic chips ahead, as they take about an hour to marinate (see photo, page 241). SERVES 4

GARLIC CHIPS

3	cloves garlic, sliced paper thin
2 Tbsp	canned unsweetened coconut milk
2 cups	vegetable oil, for frying
	Kosher salt

AVOCADO ESPUMA

1/2 cup	whole milk
1/2	bunch cilantro, stemmed (about 1 cup leaves)
1/2	jalapeño chile, split lengthwise, seeds and ribs left in
2 Tbsp	freshly squeezed lemon juice
1	avocado, diced
	Kosher salt

LIME VINAIGRETTE

1/4 cup	extra virgin olive oil
1/4 cup	freshly squeezed lime juice (2 to 3 limes)
1 tsp	granulated sugar
	Kosher salt and freshly ground black pepper

OCTOPUS

	Octopus Boil (page 125), prepared through chilling, sliced lengthwise into thin strips about 2 inches long and 1/4-inch thick
1 to 2	scallions (white and green parts), thinly sliced on the diagonal
1	large jalapeño chile, sliced crosswise into rings
2 Tbsp	chopped fresh cilantro
1/4	small red onion, finely diced

TO MAKE THE GARLIC CHIPS, marinate the garlic slices in the coconut milk for 1 hour.

Heat the vegetable oil to 275°F in a saucepan over medium heat, using a candy or deep-fry thermometer to monitor the temperature. Line a plate with a double layer of paper towels. Drain the garlic thoroughly in a fine-mesh sieve, discarding the coconut milk. Carefully fry the garlic (the slices are delicate, and their moisture will cause the oil to spit when you drop them in), stirring frequently with a slotted spoon, until the chips begin to turn golden brown, 1 to 2 minutes. Remove the chips from the oil and drain thoroughly on paper towels. Season to taste with salt. May be stored in a paper towel–lined airtight container at room temperature (don't refrigerate) until needed, up to 1 week.

TO MAKE THE AVOCADO ESPUMA, combine the milk, cilantro, jalapeño, and lemon juice in a blender and purée on high until the mixture is very smooth. Add the avocado and continue puréeing until the espuma is creamy. Season to taste with salt. Refrigerate in an airtight container until needed.

TO MAKE THE LIME VINAIGRETTE, whisk together the olive oil, lime juice, and sugar and season to taste with salt and pepper.

COMBINE THE OCTOPUS in a mixing bowl with the scallions, jalapeño, cilantro, red onion, and lime vinaigrette and mix well.

To serve, divide the ceviche among four chilled salad plates and garnish with a spoonful of avocado espuma and a few garlic chips. Serve immediately.

CARNE ASADA A LA TAMPIQUEÑA

GRILLED MARINATED SKIRT STEAK

This is my version of the iconic house specialty from Mexico City's legendary Tampico Club: a nice piece of grilled skirt steak with a red chile marinade that adds a lot of flavor. Note that the marinade will keep in an airtight container in the refrigerator for up to 2 weeks. If you make the marinade ahead of time, you can marinate the steak one night and on the next evening turn this meal out, sides and all, in about 30 minutes. For the tortillas, homemade is best but not always doable; the corn or flour ones available from Latin groceries are your best alternative, rather than the mass-produced and often preservative-laden ones sold in chain supermarkets (see photo, page 246). SERVES 4

GUAJILLO CHILE MARINADE

4	guajillo chiles, seeded
5 cloves	Roasted Garlic (page 366)
1 Tbsp	minced fresh rosemary
1 Tbsp	minced fresh thyme
1 Tbsp	freshly ground black pepper
1 Tbsp	honey
2 Tbsp	extra virgin olive oil
	Kosher salt

STEAK

1	beef skirt steak (about 2 lb)
	Kosher salt and freshly ground black pepper

TO SERVE

	Fresh Corn Tortillas (page 286)
	Red Rice (recipe follows)
	Refried Beans (page 247)
2 oz	Cotija cheese, grated (1/2 cup)
2	avocados, sliced
3 to 4	radishes, cut into thin strips
1/4 cup	minced fresh cilantro

TO MAKE THE MARINADE, put the chiles in a small heatproof bowl. Heat a kettle of water to scalding but not boiling. Pour the hot water over the chiles to cover by about 1 inch and let soak until the chiles are very soft and pliable, 5 to 10 minutes. Drain the chiles over a bowl to catch the soaking liquid. Transfer the chiles to a blender and purée, adding enough of the soaking liquid to form a smooth paste. Strain the chile paste through a fine-mesh sieve, pressing on the solids with the back of a wooden spoon.

Wipe the blender clean. Transfer the chile paste back to the blender and add the garlic, rosemary, thyme, and pepper. Purée until well combined. Slowly add first the honey, then the oil, each in a thin stream, and blend until the marinade is emulsified. Season to taste with salt. (The marinade will keep for up to 2 weeks in an airtight container in the refrigerator.)

Combine the steak and the marinade in a large zip-top bag. Seal the bag, put it in the refrigerator, and leave it to marinate overnight.

TO COOK THE STEAK, allow the steak to come to room temperature. Heat a stovetop grill pan over medium-high heat. Season the meat generously with salt and pepper and cook to desired doneness, 3 to 4 minutes per side for medium rare. Allow the steak to rest for 2 minutes before slicing.

Warm the tortillas over low heat in a nonstick sauté pan moistened with a little cooking spray.

SERVE THE STEAK with the warm tortillas, red rice, refried beans, Cotija cheese, avocado, radish, and cilantro.

ARROZ ROJO
RED RICE

A classic Mexican rice dish. Make sure you use a smooth tomato paste with no added flavorings. SERVES 4

2 Tbsp	vegetable oil
1 cup	long-grain white rice
1/4	Spanish onion, diced small
1 Tbsp	minced garlic (3 to 4 cloves)
2	plum tomatoes, diced
1 tsp	plain tomato paste
1 1/2 cups	Beef Stock (page 363)
1/2 tsp	chile de árbol powder or other spicy chile powder
	Kosher salt

Heat the oil in a wide saucepan over medium heat. Add the onion and garlic and cook, stirring frequently, until the vegetables are translucent, about 10 minutes. Add the rice and toast, stirring frequently, until the grains are golden brown, about 5 minutes. Stir in the tomatoes, tomato paste, stock, and chile powder and season to taste with salt. Bring to a boil, decrease the heat to low, cover, and cook until the rice is tender, 18 to 20 minutes. Keep warm until ready to serve.

REFRITOS
REFRIED BEANS

In this super quick dish, lard is essential for both flavor and richness. It is typically kept near the dairy section at the supermarket. Most major supermarkets also stock canned chipotles in adobo. You can make the *refritos* up to 3 days ahead and store in an airtight container in the refrigerator. Warm them through before serving, adding a little chicken stock to loosen them up a bit. SERVES 4

2 Tbsp	lard
1/2	Spanish onion, diced small
1	canned chipotle chile in adobo, with sauce (see Sources)
2	(15-oz) cans pinto beans (preferably organic), with liquid
	Kosher salt

Melt the lard in a medium saucepan over high heat. Add the onion and cook, stirring constantly, until lightly caramelized, about 5 minutes. Add the chipotle chile and sauce and continue cooking and stirring for another minute. Add the beans and their liquid and season to taste with salt. Cook until the beans are warmed through and remove from heat. Use a handheld immersion blender to purée the beans until smooth. Adjust the seasoning with salt if necessary and serve warm.

ANTOJITOS

If any one type of dish epitomizes Mexican gastronomy, it's got to be the *antojito*. For starters, the term itself is a Mexican invention, derived from the Spanish word *antojo*, meaning "craving," and its very existence says a lot about the food culture of Mexico.

Much as the term "tapas" is unique to Spain and tells you that the bar food there is something extraordinary, a place where there's a special term for "snacks-to-go" is a place where between-meal hankerings are serious business. Sure enough, when it comes to ubiquity, variety, and sheer deliciousness of food-on-the-go, Mexico has no rival—not in the Western Hemisphere, anyway.

In Mexico City, food vendors are everywhere: stalls and stands, pushcarts and trucks, shacks and huts that line the streets and plazas, marketplaces and parks of the cities and towns, and even the roadsides out in the country. We're basically talking street food here, though you can serve *antojitos* at home or toss back a few at a cantina. The range of *antojitos* sold is as diverse as the Mexican cuisine itself—from something as simple as a roasted ear of corn (*elote*) or a chunk of mango sprinkled with chile salt, to a more involved taco or *torta* (sandwich), a mini *huarache* corn cake covered with *crema* and stringy Oaxaca cheese, even a mole-filled tamale or a rich *pozole*. The defining feature is portability. So a ceviche or stew, so long as it's dispensed in and consumed from a plastic cup or paper cone, is as much an *antojito* as more obvious finger food like a *flauta* (an elongated tortilla filled, rolled, and deep-fried into a crisp flute-shaped cylinder) or a *tostada* (a tortilla that's fried flat, then piled with toppings and garnish).

Two prime examples of *antojitos* that I've especially enjoyed in Mexico City are *quesadillas* and *esquites*. In the D.F. (Distrito Federal, as the capital is known) a *quesadilla* is a savory pastry, like a turnover or empanada, fried and crispy, made of fresh *masa* dough enveloping a tasty pocket of just about anything— from beans and cheese to squash blossoms or cactus, from pickled pork fat (*cueritos*) or diced shark meat to *huitlacoche* (an inky black fungus that grows on corn). One of the Mexico City–style *quesadillas* I was inspired to create for the Distrito menu uses a combination of Oaxaca cheese and a peppery Mexican green called *huazontle*. I've included an adaptation of the recipe here. It makes a terrific cocktail snack.

Something resembling *esquites* can be found in any American city with a significant Mexican immigrant population, but nothing I'd experienced stateside compared to the *esquites* I had in Mexico City within hours of landing there for the first time. My friend and fellow chef Tim Spinner and I had found our way to the hotel where we'd be staying throughout our ten-day research trip. Curious to have a look around and hungry for a snack that didn't smell and taste of jet fuel, we dumped our bags in our rooms and headed out to have a look around the neighborhood. Honing in on the nutty, sweet scent of roasted corn within a block or two of the hotel, we followed our noses to a little square packed with street vendors. Wedged among them was a giant pushcart where a guy peered over a wide steaming vat filled with a buttery-looking mixture of fresh sweet corn, *epazote* (a pungent Mexican herb), and oregano. "*¡Dos!*" we agreed, and the vendor layered the brothy corn mixture into waxed paper cones along with *queso fresco* and a little mayo. He handed over these gorgeous, aromatic parfaits and gestured toward the condiments: a shaker of chile pequín powder and a bowl of lime wedges. So we dusted and spritzed, and down the hatch those *esquites* went. Stellar street food. Back in Philadelphia, *esquites* most definitely went on the menu at the new restaurant, Distrito. Even better, now that we've rolled out Guapos Tacos, a taco truck, we've got *esquites* out on the street, where they truly belong. (*Recipes follow.*)

QUESADILLAS DE HUAZONTLE

QUESADILLAS WITH PEPPERY GREENS AND BLACK BEANS

Huazontle is a peppery-tasting braising green native to Mexico that has long stems topped by sprigs of little seed-like flowers. Broccoli rabe can be substituted if your Latin grocery does not carry *huazontle* or it isn't in season. Prepare and form the tortilla dough according to the instructions on page 286, but leave the plastic wrap on each uncooked round so that you can stack them without having them stick together. SERVES 8 AS AN APPETIZER

FILLING

2 Tbsp	vegetable oil
2 cups	coarsely chopped huazontle (about 1 lb)
3 Tbsp + 1 Tbsp	Roasted Garlic (page 366)
	Kosher salt
1 lb	Oaxaca cheese, grated (2 cups)
2 cups	cooked black beans, rinsed and drained
1/2 cup	Mexican crema
1/2 cup	Caramelized Onion (page 366)
1/4 cup	chopped fresh cilantro
2 qts	vegetable oil, for frying
	Fresh Corn Tortilla dough (page 286), formed into 16 4-inch rounds but not cooked
	Minced parsley, for garnish

TO MAKE THE FILLING, heat the oil in a large sauté pan over high heat and cook the greens with 1 tablespoon of the roasted garlic, until the leaves are just wilted, 3 to 5 minutes. Season to taste with salt as the huazontle cooks. Drain the cooked huazontle thoroughly. Combine the drained huazontle with the cheese, beans, crema, onions, the remaining garlic, and the cilantro and mix well. Season to taste with salt.

Heat the oil to 375°F in a stockpot over medium-high heat, using a candy or deep-fry thermometer to monitor the temperature. Line a baking sheet with paper towels.

TO FORM THE QUESADILLAS, scoop 2 tablespoons of the filling into the center of each tortilla round. Gently fold the dough over and seal the edges with a fork to form a half-moon.

Fry the quesadillas in batches, turning once, until they are golden brown and crispy, about 3 minutes. Drain the quesadillas on the baking sheet, season with salt to taste, and garnish with parsley before serving.

ESQUITES

SWEET CORN WITH CHIPOTLE MAYONNAISE AND SMOKED TROUT

Incorporating smoked fish into *esquites* is an idea we came up with in an Iron Chef America battle. Here I've used smoked trout; it has a smoky sweetness that pairs beautifully with the corn. Leftover corn stock keeps well in the freezer and makes a great base for risottos and soups. There will also be a bit of chipotle mayo left over, which makes a delicious sandwich spread or dip for vegetables—you can also slather it on corn on the cob, sprinkle with Cotija cheese, and finish with a squirt of lime. SERVES 8 AS AN APPETIZER

CORN STOCK

2 qts	water
4	ears fresh white sweet corn, kernels removed and reserved, cobs chopped into 3- to 4-inch chunks
1	Spanish onion, chopped
2	cloves garlic
1 tsp	saffron threads
	Kosher salt

CHIPOTLE MAYONNAISE

1/2	canned chipotle chile in adobo, with sauce (see Sources)
1 tsp	freshly squeezed lime juice
1/4 cup	prepared mayonnaise
	Kosher salt

ESQUITES

2 Tbsp	unsalted butter
1/2	Spanish onion, finely diced
1/2 lb	smoked trout fillet, skin and bones removed, flaked
1/4 lb	queso fresco, grated (1/2 cup)
1/2 tsp	pequín chile powder (see Sources)
	Grated zest of 2 limes

TO MAKE THE STOCK, combine the water, corncobs, onion, garlic, and saffron in a stockpot and bring to a low boil. Lower the heat and simmer, uncovered, for 1 hour.

Strain the stock through a fine-mesh sieve. Season to taste with salt. Measure out 1 cup of stock and store the rest for another use. (Store frozen in an airtight container for up to 3 months.)

TO MAKE THE CHIPOTLE MAYONNAISE, combine the chile and lime juice in a blender or food processor and purée until very smooth. Transfer the purée to a mixing bowl, add the mayonnaise, and whisk to combine. Season to taste with salt. Measure out 1/4 cup of the chipotle mayonnaise and keep the remainder for another use. (Store in an airtight container in the refrigerator for up to 1 week).

TO MAKE THE ESQUITES, melt the butter in a medium saucepan over low heat. Add the onion and cook, stirring often, until translucent, about 10 minutes. Add the reserved corn kernels and cook, stirring often, 5 minutes. Add 1 cup corn stock and bring to a simmer. Cook until tender, 12 to 15 minutes. Season to taste with salt.

TO SERVE THE ESQUITES, layer mayo, corn, smoked trout, and cheese, parfait-style, in eight small glasses. Top each serving with a pinch of the chile powder and a sprinkle of the lime zest. Serve immediately.

TENOCHTITLAN

Ensalada de Nopales | CACTUS PADDLE SALAD

Camarones al Ajillo | PAN-ROASTED SHRIMP WITH TEQUILA

Papas con Chorizo | ROASTED POTATOES WITH CHORIZO

The starter for this menu showcases *nopales* (aka prickly pear cactus), a very popular ingredient in Mexican cuisine that remains largely unknown here in the United States. A common wild plant throughout the arid and semiarid parts of Mexico (and familiar to anyone who's spent time in Southern California), this sprawling succulent is an important crop, cultivated for both its fruit (known in Spanish as *tuna*) and the spiny, fleshy, oval pads or paddles (*nopales*). The prominent role of *nopales* in Mexican cuisine dates back centuries, as does its cultural significance: the plant has the singular distinction of appearing in the country's national seal. Check it out next time you see the Mexican flag or a Mexican coin; you'll see an eagle that's perched on a cactus and holding a snake. This exact scene, legend has it, was the divine signal that compelled the Aztec to establish the capital city of Tenochtitlan on the site now occupied by Mexico City.

While the plant's seedy little pear-shaped fruits are incorporated into sweet street treats such as *aguas frescas* (soft drinks) and *paletas* (popsicles), the paddles show up in all sorts of dishes. Stripped of their spines, they are charred on the grill alongside meat, simmered in soups and stews, battered and deep-fried, stirred into scrambled eggs, folded into tacos, stuffed to form a sort of cactus sandwich, and (my favorite) served cold in salads.

Aside from the spines, which are easy to remove (see page 256) there is another potential impediment to enjoying *nopales*: the inherent moisture that makes them so nice and tender and juicy also makes them kind of slimy. This brings on inevitable comparisons to okra, and we all know how most people feel about okra. Before I lose you completely, believe me when I say that: 1) whereas okra is a vegetable I am not fond of (for me, it just doesn't offer much to like in the texture or flavor departments), I love the tender texture and delicate flavor of *nopales*; and 2) *nopalitos* (cut-up *nopales*) are much more reminiscent of green beans than okra. Further strengthening the case for *nopales*, there are various ways of minimizing the slime factor, including boiling them with a tiny pinch of baking soda prior to use. And grilling them pretty much scorches off the slimy moisture while also bringing out a really nice flavor. But I like *nopales* best in a cool, refreshing salad. My approach is to cure the paddles in a salt-and-sugar solution before cutting them up, then be sure they are thoroughly chilled when they get incorporated with a select combination of complementary salad ingredients (tomato, avocado, radish). These steps, plus a dressing that combines a little zip from jalapeños with some acidity from lime juice and a touch of sweetness from agave, brings everything into delicious balance.

So don't let a little slime get in the way of enjoying a delightful salad! And, while you're at it, for the second dish on this menu, if you can override any squeamishness that would keep you from cooking the shrimp head-on and twisting off the heads and slurping out the tasty meat, please do. The flavor is simply amazing. And for the third dish, indulge in a simple yet heavenly combo of potatoes and chorizo that rounds out the whole meal.

ENSALADA DE NOPALES

CACTUS PADDLE SALAD

Nopales are sold at most any Mexican grocery. For tender flesh and delicate flavor, be sure to select small cactus paddles—no bigger than your hand—that are bright green and firm; avoid those that are big and thick or at all faded, soft, or wrinkly. The *nopalitos* need at least 18 hours to cure, after which, keep them well chilled, and don't let the salad sit for long, or the acidity from the lime juice will begin to break down the tomatoes. SERVES 4

NOPALES

4	fresh cactus paddles
2 cups	granulated sugar
2 cups	kosher salt

SALAD

1/2 cup	quartered cherry tomatoes (about 8 tomatoes)
1 oz	queso fresco, finely diced (1/4 cup)
1/4	small red onion, thinly sliced
2 Tbsp	Pickled Jalapeños (page 367)
1	radish, cut into thin matchsticks
2 Tbsp	freshly squeezed lime juice
2 Tbsp	extra virgin olive oil
2 Tbsp	agave nectar (see page 72)
	Kosher salt

If the spines have not already been removed from the cactus paddles, wear a thick glove or oven mitt on the hand you'll be holding the paddles with. Use a sharp knife to trim around the edge of each cactus paddle. Hold a large knife nearly flat against the paddle to scrape off all the spines.

TO CURE THE NOPALES, combine the sugar with the salt and mix well; spread a thin layer of this mixture across the bottom of a shallow nonreactive (preferably glass) dish. Add the cactus paddles in a single layer, and cover with the remaining sugar-salt mixture completely. Set the dish in the refrigerator covered with plastic wrap and leave the paddles to cure for at least 18 hours but no more than 24 hours.

Lift the cactus paddles out of the dish, rinse thoroughly under cold running water, and pat dry with paper towels. (At this point the cured paddles can be stored in an airtight container in the refrigerator for up to 1 week.)

TO MAKE THE SALAD, cut the cactus paddles into strips 1/4-inch thick (they should look like short linguine). You want to end up with 2 cups of strips. Stir together the tomatoes, nopalitos, cheese, onion, jalapeños, radish, lime juice, oil, and agave nectar in a bowl. Season to taste with salt. Serve immediately.

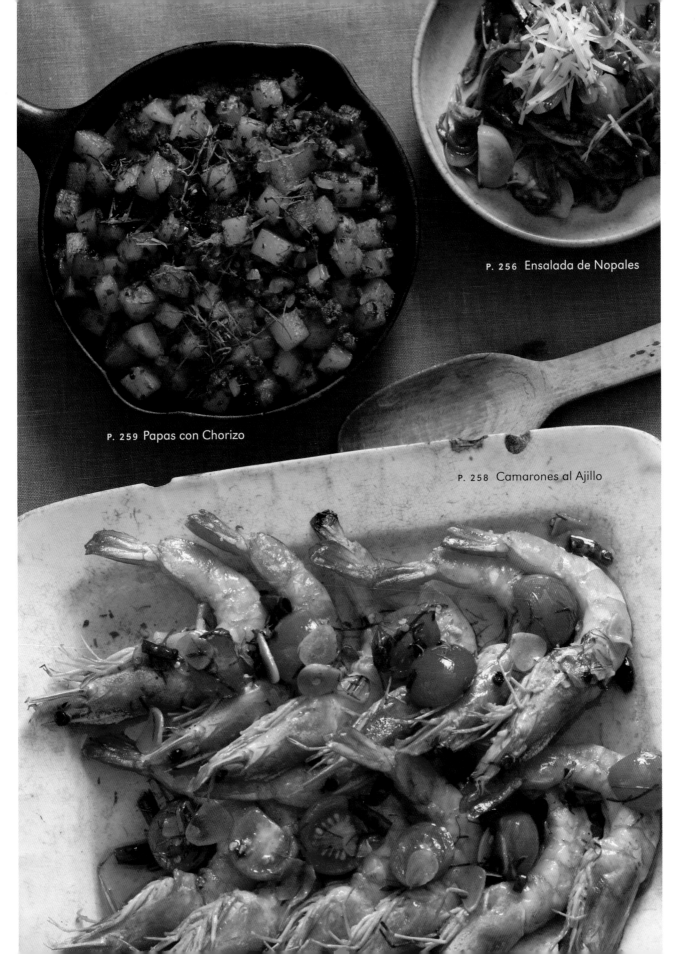

P. 256 Ensalada de Nopales

P. 259 Papas con Chorizo

P. 258 Camarones al Ajillo

CAMARONES AL AJILLO

PAN-ROASTED SHRIMP WITH TEQUILA

Ask your fishmonger specifically for U-10 size shrimp (this is a standard seafood measure that means there are fewer than ten shrimp per pound). A *cazuela*, or terra cotta casserole dish, is the ideal pan for this preparation because the brick-like earthenware provides a uniquely steady, even heat across its surface. *Cazuelas* are quite inexpensive and can be found in larger Latin groceries as well as online. You can use a *cazuela* for any oven-baked dish and as a serving vessel for anything that needs to stay warm on the table (see photo, page 257). SERVES 4

SHRIMP

1 1/2 cups	extra virgin olive oil
2 Tbsp	sliced garlic (4 to 6 cloves)
6	chiles de árbol, crushed
1 1/2 lb	fresh U-10 shrimp, peeled and deveined, heads and tails left on
	Kosher salt
2 Tbsp	tequila blanco (see page 270)
8	cherry tomatoes, halved (about 1/2 cup)
2 Tbsp	chopped fresh cilantro

TO SERVE

	Fresh lime wedges
	Fresh Corn Tortillas (page 286) or store-bought (see page 244)

TO PREPARE THE SHRIMP, combine the oil, garlic, and chiles in a large cazuela and set it over medium-high heat. Season the shrimp with salt. When the garlic starts to sizzle, add the shrimp and cook, turning once, until just done through (firm to the touch and opaque in the center), about 1 minute per side. Remove the cazuela from the heat. Add the tequila (use caution; do not add the alcohol while the pan is in contact with the heat, and be especially careful if you're using a gas stove, the gas can flame up). Return the cazuela to the stovetop and cook about 1 minute to burn off most of the alcohol. Add the cherry tomatoes and cilantro and gently stir to incorporate.

SERVE IMMEDIATELY, with the lime and tortillas.

PAPAS CON CHORIZO
ROASTED POTATOES WITH CHORIZO

Mexican chorizo, unlike Spanish chorizo, is ground pork that's highly seasoned but not cooked or fully cured. It is also typically sold loose rather than packed in casing. Here, the fat and the flavor from the chorizo coat the potatoes, which in turn balance out the saltiness of the sausage with their mellow starchiness and soft texture. One bite is all it takes to understand why this traditional dish has been passed down for generations (see photo, page 257). SERVES 4

4	large Yukon gold potatoes (about 1 1/2 lb), peeled and diced
2 Tbsp	unsalted butter
1 Tbsp	extra virgin olive oil
1 cup	crumbled Mexican chorizo (about 1/4 lb)
1/2	Spanish onion, diced (1/2 cup)
2 Tbsp	minced garlic (4 to 6 cloves)
1	large jalapeño chile, finely diced
1 to 2	scallions (white and green parts), thinly sliced on the diagonal
2 Tbsp	chopped fresh cilantro
	Kosher salt and freshly ground black pepper
1 oz	queso fresco, grated (1/4 cup)

Bring a large saucepan of lightly salted water to a boil. Line a baking sheet with parchment paper.

Boil the potatoes until just tender, 8 to 10 minutes. Lift the potatoes out of the pot with a slotted spoon and transfer them to the baking sheet to cool.

Heat the butter and oil in a large cast-iron skillet over medium heat. Add the chorizo and cook, stirring frequently, until lightly rendered and browned, about 5 minutes. Add the onion, garlic, and jalapeño and cook until lightly caramelized, stirring frequently, 10 to 12 minutes. Add the potatoes and cook, stirring frequently, until they are golden brown and crispy, about 6 minutes. Add the scallions and cilantro and stir to combine. Season to taste with salt and pepper and garnish with cheese.

EL MERCADO DE LA MERCED

My first visit to Mexico City was a research trip with chef Tim Spinner and restaurant designer Jun Aizaki. These two guys are top-notch pros I'm glad to count as friends, and I brought them along so that we could immerse ourselves in the city for a week, working together as a creative team to gather ideas for the restaurant concept that would become Distrito.

The sprawling, teeming megalopolis did not disappoint—from ritzy restaurants to shabby street carts, elegant enclaves to bustling barrios, and awe-inspiring cultural and historical sites like the Museo Nacional de Antropología to zany popular entertainments like the *lucha libre* (wrestling) theatrics at the Arena Mexico—the city served up nonstop inspiration that was often surreal, sometimes scary, and always intriguing. We had a total blast.

The huge central market, El Mercado de la Merced, was one of the sights we really wanted to see. When we mentioned this plan to the hotel concierge, he got a worried look on his face and unleashed an animated report on recent incidences of the criminal element preying on *los turistas* in the chaotic area around the market. So Jun and Tim and I opted to play it safe and have our driver, Luis, come along with us rather than just dropping us off. Sure enough, between the car and the market entrance was a churning mass of humanity, including plenty of shady-looking characters. We didn't realize just how sensible it was to have a streetwise local along for lookout until Luis explained why we needed to give an especially wide berth to the groups of guys wandering around with cages holding colorful birds. Apparently, the birds are a distraction, making it easy for bands of thugs to single out a vulnerable mark, slip a rope around the gringo's neck, and semistrangle the poor guy into submission so they can quickly empty his pockets or even haul him off for ransom.

Unscathed, but buzzing a bit from the adrenaline jolt, we made our way inside and found ourselves in a market complex on the grandest scale I've ever seen. Made up of interconnected warehouses, this place was like a colossal hive, packed with vendors and foodstuffs and shoppers and seething with activity. Everything—really, everything—you might think to cook or eat in Mexico was available here in massive quantity and variety. (I'm told that within La Merced you can also do your banking, hit the video arcade, get a perm, have your tarot cards read, buy a KISS t-shirt or a statue of the Virgin of Guadalupe or a live goat, and catch the subway.)

We spent a while wandering through the various parts of the market, marveling at the abundance all around us and dodging the *diableros* (handcart "devils") speeding by, piled high with teetering stacks of crated produce. The selection of dried chiles alone was astounding—dozens upon dozens of varieties arranged in baskets, bins, and cascading curtain formations. Nearby were stands selling other key ingredients for *mole*: peanuts, pepitas, almonds, sesame seeds, chocolate, and canela and other dried spices.

Many stands (there must have been at least ten or fifteen of them) offered untraditional but obviously very popular prepared *moles*. Some of them were in powder form, mounded like spicy dunes in all shades of green, gold, orange, red, and brown. Others were further processed into pastes and shaped into loaf-like bricks in an endless spectrum of deep dark sepia tones, with a slight sheen to them, some with regional labels like "Pueblo" and "Oaxaca," others identified simply as "Especial" or "Súperespecial."

Among the various *antojitos* sold at the market were a lot of *quesadillas* and *tostadas*. We headed to a place called Taco Metro, reportedly the source for some of the best *huaraches* in town. A *huarache* is a large, sandal (*huarache*)-shaped cake made of *masa* and typically filled with a thin layer of black or refried beans, then griddled and covered with assorted toppings. We sampled several, and my favorite was a sort of meat lover's delight, with chorizo, ham, *carnitas* (braised and fried pork), *queso* Oaxaca, and Mexican *crema*—decadent, delicious, and just the right kind of brash and brawny food to steady the nerves before braving the trip back past those sinister bird men. (*Recipes follow.*)

CHILANGO HUARACHE

HUARACHE WITH CHORIZO, CARNITAS, AND SERRANO HAM

Note that the masa cakes can be partially cooked, then wrapped in plastic and refrigerated for up to 2 days. SERVES 4

MASA CAKES

1/2 cup	Maseca brand white corn instant masa harina (see Sources)
1/4 tsp	chile de árbol powder
1/2 tsp	kosher salt
1/3 cup	warm water

TOPPINGS

1	large potato (about 1/2 lb), boiled in salted water, peeled, and mashed until smooth
1/2 cup	crumbled Mexican chorizo (about 1/4 lb), cooked until lightly browned and drained
1 cup	Carnitas (page 279)
4 oz	Oaxaca cheese, shredded (about 1 cup)
16	slices Serrano ham (about 1/3 lb)
2 Tbsp	Pickled Jalapeños (page 367), drained
	Microgreens, for garnish
	Bottled Mexican hot sauce

TO MAKE THE MASA CAKES, combine the masa harina, chile powder, and salt in a large mixing bowl. Slowly add the warm water, using your hands to mix the dough until smooth and form it into a ball. Cover the dough with a damp cloth and allow it to rest for 20 minutes.

Heat a lightly oiled griddle or skillet over medium heat.

Divide the dough into four equal portions. Use a rolling pin or tortilla press to flatten each portion, between two sheets of plastic wrap, into a long oval 1/16- to 1/8-inch thick. Precook each masa cake on the griddle for 2 minutes per side. If not using right away, wrap the masa cakes in plastic wrap and refrigerate until needed, up to 3 days.

Place a baking stone in the oven and preheat the oven and stone to 450°F for 1 hour.

TO TOP THE MASA CAKES, spread each with a thin layer of potato, then top evenly with the chorizo, carnitas, and Oaxaca cheese. Bake the huaraches directly on the baking stone until the bottoms of the cakes are crispy and the cheese is melted, 6 to 8 minutes. Top each huarache with 4 slices ham and sprinkle on a few slices of pickled jalapeño and microgreens. Pass hot sauce at the table.

TAMALES CON MOLE POBLANO
TAMALES WITH POBLANO MOLE

Whatever form it takes or name it's known by—*pastel* in Puerto Rico, *humita* in Ecuador—the *tamal* is essentially a starchy dough wrapped in a leaf and cooked, and I love it. Even the Chicago fast-food version made with machine-extruded *masa* and filled with heartburn-inducing mystery meat was a comforting treat in the chilly depths of winter when I was a kid.

Developing a recipe that produced a firm but perfectly tender and flavorful *tamal* was a lengthy process, but I eventually nailed it down. No way around it, making great *tamales* is a bit of a project, but they are one of those extraordinary foods that are well worth some time and labor.

As fascinated as I was by the prepared *moles* I saw at La Merced, I still make my own. Here it's a *mole poblano*, the perfect accompaniment to *tamales*. You will have plenty of this versatile sauce left over. Store it in an airtight container in the refrigerator for up to 2 weeks or in the freezer for up to 3 months. You might need to add a little stock to restore the *mole's* smooth, saucy consistency before serving it—with another round of *tamales*, or with simple roast chicken or turkey and white rice.

SERVES 8 AS AN APPETIZER, 4 AS A MAIN COURSE

(continued)

GUAJILLO CHILE SAUCE

1	guajillo chile, toasted (see page 369)
1	plum tomato, quartered
2 Tbsp	coarsely chopped Spanish onion
2	cloves garlic
1/2 tsp	whole cumin seeds, toasted (see page 368)
1 cup	water
1 Tbsp	vegetable oil
	Kosher salt

MOLE POBLANO

1/4 cup + 1/4 cup	lard
1/2	Spanish onion, chopped
2 Tbsp	(4 to 6 cloves) Roasted Garlic (page 366)
1/3 cup	each of shelled, toasted pumpkin seeds (pepitas), toasted sesame seeds, toasted peanuts, and blanched, toasted almonds, (see page 368)
1	2-inch-long stick of cinnamon, toasted and ground (2 Tbsp) (see page 368)
5	whole cloves, toasted and ground (see page 368)
5	whole allspice berries, toasted and ground (see page 368)
2	star anise, toasted and ground (see page 368)
2	mulato chiles, toasted (see page 369)
1	ancho chile, toasted (see page 369)

1	pasilla chile, toasted (see page 369)
1	guajillo chile, toasted (see page 369)
1/3 cup	raisins
1	ripe plantain, peeled
1	Granny Smith apple, peel left on, cored and chopped
1	plum tomato, chopped
2 qts	Chicken Stock (page 362)
1	(3.3-oz) tablet Ibarra sweet Mexican chocolate (see Sources), chopped
	Kosher salt

TAMALES

1 cup	Maseca brand white corn instant masa harina (see Sources)
1 1/4 cups	hot Chicken Stock (page 362)
1/2 cup	lard
1 tsp	baking powder
1 Tbsp	kosher salt
8	dried corn husks, soaked in cold water about 15 minutes or until pliable

TO SERVE

1 oz	queso fresco, grated (1/4 cup)
2 to 3	radishes, cut into thin matchsticks
	Toasted sesame seeds (see page 368)

TO MAKE THE CHILE SAUCE, combine the chile, tomato, onion, garlic, cumin, and water in a small saucepan and bring to a boil. Lower the heat and simmer for 15 minutes.

Transfer the mixture to a blender and purée to make a very smooth sauce. Heat the oil in a clean saucepan, add the sauce, and fry over high heat for 10 minutes. Take it off of the heat and add the salt, adjusting to taste. Allow the sauce to cool thoroughly and refrigerate in an airtight container until needed, up to 3 days.

TO MAKE THE MOLE, melt 1/4 cup of the lard in a large Dutch oven over medium-high heat. Cook the onion and roasted garlic, stirring often, until translucent, about 10 minutes. Stir in the pumpkin seeds, sesame seeds, peanuts, and almonds and cook, stirring occasionally, for 3 to 4 minutes. Add the cinnamon, clove, allspice, and star anise and cook, stirring now and then, for another 3 to 4 minutes. Add the toasted mulato, ancho, pasilla, and guajillo chiles, the raisins, plantain, apple, and tomato and stir to incorporate. Pour in the stock and bring to a boil. Lower the heat and simmer for 30 minutes.

Transfer the mole in batches to a blender and purée until very smooth. Strain each batch through a fine-mesh sieve, pressing on the mole with the back of a spoon.

Melt the remaining 1/4 cup lard in a clean Dutch oven over high heat until just smoking. Add the mole and chocolate. Bring to a boil, then decrease the heat to low and simmer, stirring often to prevent the chocolate from scorching, for 1 hour. Season to taste with salt.

TO MAKE THE TAMAL DOUGH, combine the masa, hot stock, and lard in a large bowl with 1/2 cup of the guajillo chile sauce (store the remainder for another use, such as marinated grilled or roasted meat or chicken), add the baking powder and salt, and mix well.

TO ASSEMBLE THE TAMALES, lay out a cornhusk with the pointed tip facing away from you. Mound 2 tablespoons of the tamal dough in the center of the husk. Fold the two sides of the husk to the center, over the dough, to overlap. Fold the top down and the bottom up, overlapping, to form a tight package.

Lay the tamales flat, in a single layer, in a bamboo steamer or other steamer basket. Bring a few inches of water to a rapid boil in a stockpot and place the steamer basket over the water. Cover and steam the tamales gently until they are firm to the touch, about 20 minutes. Transfer the steamer basket to a plate and leave the tamales to firm up, covered, for about 10 minutes.

SERVE THE TAMALES with the mole poblano and garnish with cheese, radishes, and sesame seeds.

DISTRITO FEDERAL

Margarita de Chile Verde | SPICY MARGARITA

Margarita de Mango | MANGO MARGARITA

Nachos de Pollo | CHICKEN NACHOS

Guacamole y Tortillas | GUACAMOLE AND TORTILLAS CHIPS

TACO BAR
- Carnitas | BEER- AND CITRUS-BRAISED FRIED PORK
- Alambres de Camarones | SHRIMP SKEWERS
- Rajas con Hongos | ROASTED POBLANO CHILES WITH MUSHROOMS
- Frijoles Borrachos | BEER-BRAISED BEANS
- Tortillas de Maíz | CORN TORTILLAS
- Salsas | CLASSIC SALSA | ROASTED TOMATO SALSA WITH TOMATILLOS | TOMATILLO SALSA
- Acompañamientos | ACCOMPANIMENTS

Pastel de Tres Leches | TRES LECHES CAKE

Savory filling tucked into a warm tortilla and topped *al gusto* with tasty garnishes—what could be a finer food on the go? Chalk it up to exposure early in childhood followed by thirty-five years of steady reinforcement, but I have a thing for tacos. I just love them. So rolling out Guapos Tacos, my very own taco truck, has been a thrill. My pride and joy on wheels, the truck has found taco-hungry Philadelphians all over town, from corporate types in the Center City workaday fray, to families enjoying weekend time in West Philly's public parks, to bar-crawlers roaming Northern Liberties through the wee hours of the night.

I am also a big believer in the domestic taco experience. Sure, you lose out on that gritty D.F. (the local nickname for Mexico City, aka *el Distrito Federal*) *puesto* vibe (take the taco out of the street and you pretty much do take the street out of the taco). But you gain a lot of creature comforts (like seating) in the trade-off, and a taco bar is the ideal format for an awesomely satisfying meal at home. For our family's regular taco nights, Beatriz and I keep things fairly simple: out on the countertop go fresh tortillas, some roast chicken and black beans, a couple salsas and a few key toppings—avocado and *queso fresco* and *crema*, cilantro and shredded lettuce, maybe a little onion. Everybody pulls up a stool, builds their own, eats their fill, and we are a happy crew.

Assemble a more extensive array of fillings and condiments and garnishes and you've got a taco bar fit for company—a vibrant and enticing spread. This is one of my favorite ways to entertain a group of friends because it's relaxed and unstructured but festive and fun. Everyone serves themselves, sits wherever they like, comes back for more whenever they want. I've put together this taco bar menu with just that kind of a casual and convivial evening in mind.

First come the margaritas—I've included a spicy one and a fruity one (have a pitcher of each ready, or more, depending on your crowd)—perfect for everyone to sip at while saying hello and munching on some chips and guacamole. It's great to have some good, cold Mexican beer on hand as well.

Meanwhile, you've prepped all the accompaniments and salsas earlier in the day to set out on the table just before people arrive. Days ahead of time you can get the *chicken ropa vieja* completely ready, use it either as a taco filling or on chicken nachos. The beans can also be made ahead. So those two components just need to be rewarmed and put out on the table. The *carnitas* you can braise in advance so all that's left to do before serving is the final quick frying step. The *rajas* can be made hours ahead of time (though not the day before—their texture does not improve over time once they're cooked). As for the *camarones*, so long as you make the marinade and soak the skewers earlier in the day, the shrimp can be marinated and threaded onto the skewers half an hour before cooking, and will need just a minute or two of grilling to be ready to serve.

That leaves just the corn tortillas to attend to. Now, you can certainly get by quite nicely with some fresh tortillas picked up that day from a Latin grocery and warmed in batches for serving. But making them yourself is a really nice touch. It's not too time consuming or difficult and makes for the peak taco experience, so I urge you to go for it. If you are new to making tortillas, just follow the steps carefully on page 286 and you will quickly get the hang of it—and you will wow your guests and do yourself proud, no doubt. Form and cook the tortillas earlier in the day (or make them the day before, wrap tightly in plastic wrap and refrigerate), then rewarm them in batches during the party.

Once you've set out the fillings and the tortillas, everyone can graze to their heart's content. You'll just need to keep tabs on the warm tortilla supply and replenish any garnishes that run low (like avocado, which you don't want to put out too early or in too large a quantity as it will eventually turn brown).

Toward the end of the evening, bust out that *tres leches* cake, cutting out the custardy little rounds just before serving them up with coffee or espresso.

MARGARITA DE CHILE VERDE

SPICY MARGARITA

This take on a traditional margarita with jalapeño is not only delicious but simply stunning to behold. Tequila *blanco* (aka silver) is a style of tequila bottled immediately after it's distilled from the agave plant. Keith Raimondi, mixologist extraordinaire, added another fun Mexican element to this cocktail by sweetening the drink with syrup also derived from the agave plant. Keith recommends making your own chile-infused tequila: put one slice jalapeño chile in a bottle of tequila blanco and let it sit for several hours, periodically checking the level of spiciness. Let the tequila get a touch more fiery than you'd typically prefer, as the liqueur and agave nectar will blunt the heat just a bit (see photo, page 272). SERVES 8

1 1/2 cups	chile-infused tequila blanco
2/3 cup	(5 oz) agave nectar (see page 72)
1 cup	freshly squeezed lime juice (about 10 limes)
3/4 cup	Cointreau or other orange liqueur
	Ice

TO SERVE

	Kosher salt, for rims of glasses
	Lime wedges
1	jalapeño chile, sliced crosswise into rings

Pour the tequila, agave nectar, lime juice, and orange liqueur over ice in a large pitcher and stir vigorously.

To salt the rims of the margarita glasses, pour about a quarter-inch of the salt into a saucer. Cut a little notch in the flesh of one of the lime wedges and draw it along the rim of the glass until the edge is uniformly moistened, making a nice clean line on the outside of the glass only. Hold the glass by the bottom and gently tip the outer edge into the salt, rolling to coat evenly. Tap or shake gently to remove any loose grains. Repeat with the remaining glasses.

Fill each salted glass with fresh ice, pour in the margarita mixture, garnish with a jalapeño slice and a lime wedge, and serve.

MARGARITA DE MANGO

MANGO MARGARITA

Reposado ("rested") tequila is aged for anywhere from 60 days to a full year in oak barrels that impart a golden color along with a smooth flavor that's well suited to fruit margaritas like this. To pass along the sage advice of master mixologist Keith Raimondi: always look for what's in season when you're preparing fresh fruit margaritas. If your market has gorgeous strawberries, pineapple, melon, even grapefruit—anything that you love that's fresh—feel free to swap it in for the mango. Keith also recommends tasting and adjusting each batch to make sure the balance of flavors, acidity, and sweetness is right (see photo, page 273). SERVES 8

1	mango
1 1/2 cups	tequila reposado
3/4 cup	Cointreau or other orange liqueur
1/2 cup	freshly squeezed lime juice (about 5 limes)
2/3 cup	(5 oz) Simple Syrup (page 367)
	Ice

TO SERVE

	Kosher salt, for rims of glasses
	Lime wedges

Cut the peel away from the mango. Slice the peel into 1/2-inch-wide strips and set aside for garnish. Slice the flesh of the mango away from the pit and cut the fruit into small dice. Put the mango in a large pitcher and muddle the fruit vigorously with a wooden spoon (you want the fruit to release a lot of its flavorful juices). Add the tequila, orange liqueur, lime juice, simple syrup, and ice and stir vigorously.

To salt the rims of the margarita glasses, pour about a quarter inch of the salt into a saucer. Cut a little notch in the flesh of one of the lime wedges and draw it along the rim of the glass until the edge is uniformly moistened, making a nice clean line on the outside of the glass only. Hold the glass by the bottom and gently tip the outer edge into the salt, rolling to coat evenly. Tap or shake gently to remove any loose grains. Repeat with the remaining glasses.

Fill each salted glass with fresh ice, pour in the margarita mixture, garnish with a lime wedge and a twist of mango skin, and serve.

P. 270 Margarita de Chile Verde

P. 271 Margarita de Mango

NACHOS DE POLLO
CHIPOTLE CHICKEN NACHOS

Frying up your own chips may seem a bit daunting, and those big bags available at the grocery may seem irresistibly convenient, but I urge you to give home-frying a go—it's worth it. For best results, use fresh corn tortillas from your local Latin grocery (or even your own homemade ones, page 286). Supermarket tortillas tend to be too thick and won't fry evenly. Serve the chips the same day you make them. The chicken *ropa vieja* also makes a great taco filling. SERVES 8

FRESH TORTILLA CHIPS

6 qts	vegetable oil, for frying
12 to 15	fresh (about 6-inch) corn tortillas
	Kosher salt

CHIPOTLE CHILE SAUCE

4	canned chipotle chiles in adobo, with sauce (see Sources)
1 cup	ketchup
2 Tbsp	(4 to 6 cloves) Roasted Garlic (page 366)
1 cup	Chicken Stock (page 362)
2 Tbsp	Spanish smoked sweet paprika
	Kosher salt

POACHED CHICKEN

2 lb	boneless, skinless chicken thighs
1	Spanish onion, coarsely chopped
1	fresh bay leaf
3 to 4 Tbsp	kosher salt

ROPA VIEJA

1/4 cup	vegetable oil
2	Spanish onions, chopped
2 to 3	red bell peppers, chopped
1/4 cup	minced garlic (12 to 16 cloves)
	Kosher salt

NACHOS

2 cups	Chihuahua cheese, grated
1/4 cup	fresh cilantro, finely shredded
1/2 cup	Mexican crema
2	avocados, sliced
1/2 cup	radish matchsticks (about 4 radishes)

TO MAKE THE CHIPS, heat the oil to 375°F in a stockpot, using a candy or deep-fry thermometer to monitor the temperature. Line a large baking sheet with paper towels.

While the oil is heating, working in batches, stack the tortillas so that the edges are aligned. Use a sharp knife to cut them into six relatively equal triangles.

Separate the tortilla triangles to prevent them from sticking together and fry them in small batches until slightly golden and crispy, 3 to 4 minutes. Use a slotted spoon to stir the chips often (this ensures even cooking) then carefully lift the chips out of the oil with the spoon and set them evenly on the baking sheet to drain. Season immediately with salt to taste.

TO MAKE THE CHIPOTLE SAUCE, combine the chiles, ketchup, roasted garlic, stock, and paprika in a blender and purée the mixture until very smooth. Season to taste with salt.

TO POACH THE CHICKEN, bring a large saucepan of water to a boil and add the onion, bay leaf, and salt. Add the chicken and simmer for 10 to 12 minutes, until just cooked through. Lift the chicken out of the water with a slotted spoon, drain it, and set aside to cool. (Discard the cooking liquid.) Shred it by hand into bite-size pieces.

TO MAKE THE ROPA VIEJA, heat the oil in a large sauté pan over medium heat. Cook the onions, bell peppers, and garlic, stirring often, until translucent, about 10 minutes. Add the chipotle sauce and cook at a gentle simmer until the whole mixture has reduced by one-quarter, 15 to 20 minutes. Fold in the chicken and season to taste with salt.

TO MAKE THE NACHOS, in a large shallow casserole, spread the tortilla chips in an even layer and top with the chicken ropa vieja and Chihuahua cheese. Bake until the cheese is melted and tortilla chips are lightly toasted, 8 to 10 minutes. Garnish with cilantro, Mexican crema, avocado slices, and radish.

GUACAMOLE Y TORTILLAS

GUACAMOLE AND TORTILLA CHIPS

SERVES 8

GUACAMOLE

2	jalapeño chiles, roasted and peeled (see page 369), seeded, and finely chopped
4 to 6	ripe avocados, diced
1	Spanish onion, finely diced
1/4 cup	chopped fresh cilantro
1/2 cup	freshly squeezed lime juice (about 5 limes), plus more to taste
	Kosher salt

TO SERVE

2 oz	Cotija cheese, finely grated (about 1/2 cup) for serving
	Fresh Tortillas Chips (page 274)

TO MAKE THE GUACAMOLE, combine the jalapeños with the avocados, onion, cilantro, and lime juice and mix until just combined. (Do not overmix; it should be nice and chunky.) Season to taste with salt and additional lime juice.

Transfer the guacamole to a clean serving bowl. If not using right away, cover tightly with plastic wrap so that the plastic wrap is pressed firmly against the finished dip and there are no air pockets. Refrigerate until needed, ideally no more than 1 hour.

TO SERVE, garnish with the Cotija cheese and serve with tortilla chips.

CARNITAS

CLASSIC BEER- AND CITRUS-BRAISED FRIED PORK

The meat is twice cooked: slowly braised in the oven in a super-rich broth, then quickly fried on the stovetop—so you end up with superbly tender caramelized chunks of pork finished with lime and cilantro. You can do the braising step up to 2 days in advance; store the meat in the refrigerator along with the braising liquid, then fry shortly before serving. SERVES 8

BRAISED PORK

6 lb	boneless pork shoulder
2 qts	vegetable oil
1/2 cup	lard
10	cloves garlic, crushed
2	Spanish onions, chopped
2	(14-oz) cans sweetened condensed milk
2	(12-oz) bottles Mexican lager
1 cup	freshly squeezed orange juice (about 3 navel oranges)
2	navel oranges, peel left on, quartered
2	bay leaves (preferably fresh)
2 tsp	whole black peppercorns
10	sprigs thyme
20	whole allspice berries
10	whole cloves
1/2 cup	kosher salt

CARNITAS

1/4 cup	vegetable oil
2	red onions, thinly sliced
1/4 cup	minced garlic (12 to 16 cloves)
1/2 cup	chopped fresh cilantro
2 Tbsp	freshly squeezed lime juice (about 1/2 lime)
	Kosher salt and freshly ground black pepper

Preheat the oven to 300°F.

TO BRAISE THE PORK, combine all the ingredients for the braised pork in a large roasting pan. Cover the pan snugly with aluminum foil and roast for 3 hours.

Take the pan out of the oven and allow the meat to rest in the braising liquid for 15 minutes. (At this point, the meat can be refrigerated in the braising liquid for up to 2 days.) Transfer the meat to a large platter or rimmed baking sheet and discard the braising liquid and solids. When the meat is cool enough to handle, gently pull it apart into large pieces with your fingers.

TO FINISH THE CARNITAS, heat the oil in a large cast-iron skillet over medium-high heat until it shimmers. Add the shredded pork, onions, and garlic and cook the meat to crisp it on one side, 1 to 2 minutes (it will happen quickly). Carefully turn the pork (beware of spattering oil) and add the cilantro and lime juice. Season to taste with salt and pepper (see photo, page 284).

ALAMBRES DE CAMARONES

SHRIMP SKEWERS

To transfer the cooked shrimp into a warm tortilla, hold the tortilla in one hand and a skewer of shrimp in the other and use the tortilla hand to pull the shrimp off the skewer (see photo, page 284). SERVES 8

MARINADE

4	cloves garlic, crushed
1 cup	tightly packed fresh flat-leaf parsley leaves
1 1/2 cups	vegetable oil

SHRIMP

2 lb	fresh large shrimp, peeled and deveined (about 60 shrimp)
	Kosher salt and freshly ground black pepper

TO MAKE THE MARINADE, combine the garlic, parsley, and oil in a blender and purée the mixture until it is very smooth. Keep the marinade in an airtight container in the refrigerator until needed, up to 2 days.

Soak about 30 (3- to 4-inch) bamboo skewers in water for 20 minutes.

TOSS THE SHRIMP with 1 cup of the marinade, storing the remainder in the refrigerator for another use. Thread two shrimp onto each skewer and season with salt and pepper. Proceed with cooking the shrimp, or refrigerate for up to 30 minutes.

Heat a stovetop grill pan or cast-iron skillet over medium-high heat.

Grill the shrimp until cooked through, turning once, about 1 minute per side.

RAJAS CON HONGOS

ROASTED POBLANO CHILES WITH MUSHROOMS

Rajas con hongos is a great vegetarian option for the taco bar; fresh mushrooms add meaty substance to the mix of roasted poblano strips (*rajas* means "slices"), onions, roasted garlic, and fragrant cilantro. *Salsa Verde* (page 288) makes a good accompaniment, bringing brightness and acidity that contrasts nicely with the earthiness of the mushrooms and poblanos (see photo, page 285). SERVES 8

1/4 cup	extra virgin olive oil
2	Spanish onions, thinly sliced
6 cups	cremini mushrooms, quartered (about 1 lb)
4	poblano chiles, roasted and peeled (see page 369), seeded, and cut into 1/4-inch-wide strips
1/4 cup	(12 to 16 cloves) Roasted Garlic (page 366)
1/4 cup	chopped fresh cilantro
	Kosher salt and freshly ground black pepper

Heat the oil in a large stainless-steel sauté pan over medium-high heat. Add the onion and mushrooms and cook, stirring occasionally, until the vegetables are lightly caramelized, 10 to 12 minutes. Add the poblano strips and garlic and stir to incorporate. Add the cilantro and season to taste with salt and pepper.

FRIJOLES BORRACHOS

BEER-BRAISED BEANS

When I put together a taco, I always layer in a small amount of beans first. Then I add the protein, a little salsa, and select toppings. For optimal taco pleasure, some restraint is important: pile in just a little bit of each component so that you can still get the tortilla around it and then savor each and every perfect bite— not contend with an overstuffed mess that falls apart when you try to eat it. The beans can be made a few days before serving, and they keep well in the refrigerator—just hold off on adding the tomatoes and herbs until you've gently rewarmed the beans, shortly before serving (see photo, page 284). SERVES 8

4 cups	dried pinto beans
1 lb	smoked bacon, chopped
2	Spanish onions, chopped
1/4 cup	minced garlic (12 to 16 cloves)
2	jalapeño chiles, minced
2	(14.5-oz) cans stewed tomatoes, chopped, with juice
2	(12-oz) bottles Mexican lager (preferably a more flavorful one, like Negra Modelo)
2 qts	Chicken Stock (page 362)
1 lb	plum tomatoes, chopped
1/4 cup	chopped fresh flat-leaf parsley
1/4 cup	chopped fresh cilantro
	Kosher salt and freshly ground black pepper

Soak the beans for at least 8 hours or overnight in cool water to cover by 2 inches.

Drain and rinse the soaked beans. Combine them in a large saucepan with enough water to cover by at least a couple of inches and bring to a boil. Lower the heat to a simmer and cook about 90 minutes. The beans should be not quite tender, still a bit dry on the inside.

In a stockpot over medium heat, cook the bacon just until crispy at the edges. Stir in the onions, garlic, and jalapeños and cook, stirring occasionally, until the vegetables are translucent, about 10 minutes. Add the tomatoes and beer and stir to combine. Continue to cook until the liquid has reduced by half, 15 to 20 minutes. Stir in the beans and their liquid and the stock and simmer until the beans are tender, 30 to 40 minutes more. (The beans can be prepared up to this point, cooled, and refrigerated in an airtight container for up to 3 days; rewarm over low heat, stirring frequently, before finishing.)

Just before serving, fold in the plum tomatoes, parsley, and cilantro and season the beans to taste with salt and pepper.

P. 286 Tortillas de Maíz

P. 279 Carnitas

P. 283 Frijoles Borrachos

P. 289 Salsa Roja

P. 280 Alambres de Camarones

P. 281 Rajas con Hongos

P. 288 Salsa Mexicana

P. 288 Salsa Verde

TORTILLAS DE MAÍZ
CORN TORTILLAS

A fresh homemade tortilla still warm from the griddle is quite a wonderful thing. First, get yourself a simple, inexpensive tortilla press so that you don't have to face trying to roll out the dough into paper-thin rounds. A press will run you about twenty bucks and makes the work infinitely easier— and the end product a lot more attractive. You can buy them from larger Latin groceries and just about any store or online retailer that sells kitchen equipment. Once you get the hang of it, you'll be churning out your own tortillas by the dozen. For the instant masa, we use Maseca brand at my restaurants, which I recommend highly (though I advise sticking with this recipe rather than the one on the masa bag) (see photo, page 284). MAKES ABOUT 2 DOZEN TORTILLAS

2 cups	white corn instant masa harina (see Sources)
1 cup + 2 Tbsp	water
1/2 tsp	chile de árbol powder
1 tsp	kosher salt

Combine all the ingredients in a large bowl and mix by hand into a soft moist dough. Turn the dough out onto a dry work surface and gently knead it just to get the ingredients fully incorporated and the consistency even. (If the dough appears cracked, add a little more water, 1 tablespoon at a time, until the dough is moist enough to be smooth, but not wet or sticky.) Form the dough into a smooth ball, cover with a damp kitchen towel, and allow it to rest for 20 minutes.

Heat a nonstick griddle or skillet over medium-high heat. Arrange a clean, dry kitchen towel (large enough to wrap around the hot tortillas) nearby.

Divide the dough in half and continue dividing each piece into halves until you have 24 dough balls, all of which should be about the size of a walnut (roughly 1 inch in diameter).

Cut two squares of plastic wrap large enough to overlap the plates of your tortilla press by about 2 inches. Set one sheet of plastic on the bottom plate of the press and center a dough ball on the sheet. Cover with the other sheet of plastic, close the press, and gently flatten the dough into a 4-inch round about as thick as a sheet of heavyweight paper (about 1/16 inch).

Carefully lift the tortilla, still between the sheets of plastic, off the press. Hold the tortilla in one hand and use your other hand to peel off the top sheet of plastic. Invert the tortilla, peel off the second sheet, and turn the tortilla onto the hot griddle. Repeat the process with the remaining dough balls, cooking in batches just until they begin to puff, about 1 minute per side. Transfer the cooked tortillas directly to the towel and wrap snugly to keep warm until ready to serve. (The tortillas can be kept this way up to about 1 hour. To store, cool the tortillas, wrap tightly in plastic wrap, and refrigerate for up to 3 days. To rewarm them, moisten the griddle with a little cooking spray to help resoften the tortillas and heat over medium heat for only 10 to 15 seconds per side.)

SALSA MEXICANA

CLASSIC SALSA WITH TEQUILA AND LIME

The traditional use of tequila in this salsa gives it a nice sharp bite. The salsa needs to be used the same day it's made because the tequila and lime juice break down the vegetables, fading and softening them over time (see photo, page 285).
MAKES 3 CUPS

2	jalapeño chiles, roasted and peeled (see page 369), seeded, and finely chopped
1 lb	plum tomatoes, finely chopped
1/2	red onion, finely diced
1/4 cup	chopped fresh cilantro
2 Tbsp	freshly squeezed lime juice
3 Tbsp	extra virgin olive oil
2 tsp	tequila blanco (see page 270)
	Kosher salt

Combine all the ingredients in a nonreactive bowl and mix well. Season to taste with salt. Refrigerate until well chilled, at least 30 minutes, before serving.

SALSA VERDE

TOMATILLO SALSA

Tomatillos, which look like little green tomatoes housed in papery coverings, are stocked at Latin groceries and some supermarkets, and can be found at farmers' markets when in season. Select small firm fruits with snugly fitting husks and keep them in the refrigerator (remove the husks before refrigerating; they trap moisture and promote rapid spoilage). Tomatillos taste quite different than tomatoes—tangy and lemony-herbal when green and unripe, which is how they are used here. A versatile condiment that has a bright and fresh flavor-heightening power, *salsa verde* must be served the same day it's made (see photo, page 285). SERVES 8

16	small green tomatillos, husked and washed
1/2	Spanish onion, coarsely chopped
2	cloves garlic
2	jalapeño chiles, halved lengthwise
1	bunch cilantro, stemmed (about 2 tightly packed cups leaves)
1/4 cup	extra virgin olive oil
	Kosher salt

Combine the tomatillos, onion, garlic, and jalapeños in a blender and purée until smooth. Add the cilantro and with the machine running, pour in the oil in a thin stream and purée until the salsa is emulsified. Season to taste with salt. Refrigerate for at least 30 minutes before serving.

SALSA ROJA
ROASTED TOMATO SALSA
WITH TOMATILLOS

This robust, spicy salsa is best made the day before serving to allow the rich flavors to come into balance. It keeps well in the refrigerator in an airtight container for up to 2 days (see photo, page 284). MAKES 3 CUPS

4	beefsteak tomatoes, charred (see page 368) and cooled
1	small Spanish onion, halved, charred (see page 368), and cooled
4	tomatillos (see page 288), husked, charred (see page 368), and cooled
2	jalapeño chiles, charred (see page 368) and cooled
2	chiles de árbol, toasted (see page 369)
2	canned chipotle chiles in adobo, with sauce (see Sources)
2	cloves garlic, crushed
1/4 cup	chopped fresh cilantro
	Kosher salt

Combine the tomatoes, onion, tomatillos, jalapeños, chiles de árbol, chipotles, and garlic in a blender and purée until smooth. Add the cilantro and purée to thoroughly incorporate it into the salsa. Season to taste with salt and chill for at least 30 minutes before serving.

ACOMPAÑAMIENTOS
ACCOMPANIMENTS

In the quest for the perfect bite, a few choice toppings judiciously sprinkled on before you close up that taco are critical. I nominate the following as essential options at any taco bar. SERVES 8

1 cup	Mexican crema
4 oz	queso fresco, crumbled (1 cup)
	Leaves of 2 bunches cilantro
4	avocados, sliced or diced
10 to 12	radishes, cut into thin matchsticks
1	head crisp lettuce, such as romaine, shredded
1	Spanish onion, diced
6 to 8	scallions (white and green parts), thinly sliced on the diagonal (about 1 bunch)
4	limes, cut into small wedges

PASTEL DE TRES LECHES

TRES LECHES CAKE

This traditional Mexican treat is as convenient a make-ahead option as it is an impressive ending for a festive evening. It's soaked in a rich combination of heavy cream, evaporated milk, and sweetened condensed milk, which is why it's known as "three-milk" cake. As noted below, you can complete the cake a few days in advance—as long as it's been properly soaked and tightly covered, it will keep perfectly. Hold off on cutting until you're ready to serve. SERVES 8

CAKE

3	large eggs, separated
1 2/3 cups	granulated sugar
1 1/3 cups	all-purpose flour
1 3/4 tsp	baking powder
1/4 cup + 1 Tbsp	whole milk
1 tsp	pure vanilla extract

TRES LECHES SOAKING LIQUID

1 cup	heavy cream
1	(12-oz) can evaporated milk
3/4 cup	sweetened condensed milk (half a 12-oz can)
1 cup	firmly packed dark brown sugar
1 Tbsp	ground cinnamon or canela
1/2 tsp	freshly grated nutmeg
1/4 tsp	kosher salt
1/4 cup	dark rum or mezcal (optional)

Place a rack in the middle position and preheat the oven to 325°F.

TO MAKE THE CAKE, whip the egg whites on high speed in a clean, dry bowl while slowly adding the granulated sugar. Continue whipping the mixture until it is fluffy, shiny, and firm but not dry. With the mixer still running, slowly add the yolks.

Sift the flour with the baking powder and fold into the egg mixture. Whisk in the milk and vanilla.

Lightly coat a 9 by 9-inch square cake pan or casserole with cooking spray and pour in the batter. Bake until the center of the cake springs back to the touch and a wooden skewer inserted into the middle comes out clean, 40 to 45 minutes, rotating the pan 180 degrees about halfway through the baking time.

Cool the cake in the pan on wire rack for 10 minutes.

TO MAKE THE SOAKING LIQUID, while the cake is still warm, whisk together all the ingredients for the soaking liquid until the sugar dissolves. Poke the top of the cake 8 to 10 times with a fork to make evenly spaced holes, then pour the soaking liquid over the warm cake to completely saturate it. Leave the cake to soak at room temperature until the liquid is fully absorbed and the cake has cooled to room temperature. Cover the pan tightly with plastic wrap and refrigerate for at least 2 hours and up to 3 days.

Fifteen to 20 minutes before serving, take the cake out of the refrigerator and leave it to sit and soften at room temperature. Cut the cake into individual rounds (see photo) or squares and serve.

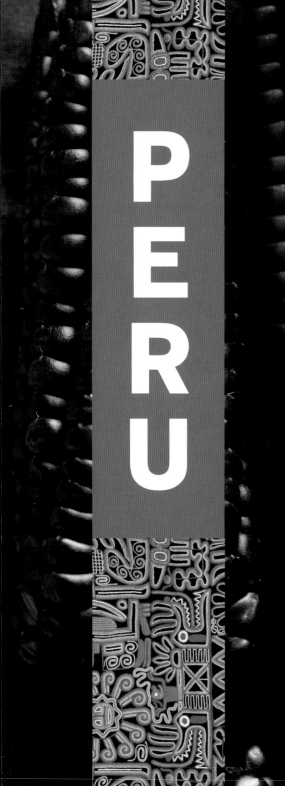

PERU

MENU 1
CHICAMA

Ceviche de Corvina | CORVINA CEVICHE

Cebollas Rojas Encurtidas | PICKLED RED PEARL ONIONS

Aguadito de Pato | STEWED DUCK WITH POTATOES, PEAS, AND CHILES

Mantequilla de Rocoto | RED CHILE BUTTER

MENU 2
LIMA

Tiradito de Lubina | BLACK BASS CEVICHE WITH YUZU

Lomo Saltado con Arroz | SOY STIR-FRIED BEEF WITH RICE

MENU 3
CUZCO

Solterito | EDAMAME SALAD WITH GARLIC VINAIGRETTE

Parihuela | SEAFOOD CHOWDER

Pan Tostado de Ajo | GARLIC TOAST

MENU 4
HUANCAYO

Chicha Morada | PURPLE CORN PUNCH

Yuquitas | FRIED YUCA

Ceviche de Pargo con Salsa de Maracuyá | PINK SNAPPER CEVICHE WITH PASSION FRUIT

Pachamanca | ROASTED MEATS IN BANANA LEAVES

Salsa Chimichurri | ROSEMARY-MINT CHIMICHURRI

Salsa de Huancaina | SPICY CHEESE SAUCE

Picarones con Miel | PERUVIAN DOUGHNUTS

Peru and Ecuador share a border and a lot of ancient history, but their cuisines don't really have much in common aside from a few staple ingredients. This was a startling discovery for me back when I was eight years old and first sat down to dinner at the Carreras family table.

My parents had met Armida and Roberto Carreras, who were both from Lima, through a group of Chicago-area South American immigrants who socialized together. The two couples became great friends, and there was a stretch when we regularly spent weekends with them in Hanover Park, a little ways outside Chicago.

Between the suburban setting and the rowdy Carreras offspring, these visits were big fun. To city kids like me and my brothers, the townhouse complex they lived in was a wonderland—all winding sidewalks, shrubby greenery, and traffic-free places to run around. In my memory, the moms were always in the kitchen and the dads, beers in hand, were either out back shooting the breeze or in the den watching a game. My big brother Jorge and the middle Carreras kid, Roberto Jr., played soccer nonstop. Roberto's little sister Jessica and I were the same age and great pals, tearing around outside like wild things or sprawled on the shag carpet playing endless rounds of SORRY! and Uno.

When dinnertime rolled around, the meals looked somewhat like the Ecuadorian food my family ate at home—often a ceviche followed by a soupy rice dish—but tasted totally different and not, in my juvenile opinion, in a good way. Whereas Mom's cooking was rich and comforting, with *ají* (chile) available on the side if you cared to add a little heat, everything Señora Carreras served seemed overwhelmingly robust and fiery hot. Even the ceviche was a minefield of spicy chiles.

Family weekends at the Carreras place tapered off by the time I was in middle school, and over the next decade and a half my early experiences of Peruvian food receded into memory. Come the late 1990s, I was a young chef trying to make a go of it in New York City. I'd racked up experience in various Mediterranean and American regional cuisines when I got an incredible opportunity: taking over for Larry Kolar at Bolivar, a hybrid combo of Peruvian ceviche bar and Argentinean grill. It was my first crack at executive chef—and my first time working with South American food.

Day one on the job, Larry and his crew got right down to schooling me in the fundamentals, starting with the rundown on Peru's distinctive chiles (*rocoto, amarillo, panca, mirasol*), then moving on to making some idiosyncratic ceviches and other classic preparations that epitomize Peruvian cuisine's complex *criollo* blend—its extraordinary intermingling of Indian and Spanish traditions with African and European influences as well as prominent Asian elements. As we prepped and sampled the first few dishes, the bold flavors, colors, and aroma—all distantly familiar from back in the day—really grabbed me. These dishes were way more vibrant and compelling than anything I'd done as a chef in quite some time. Maybe ever. Larry and the guys proceeded onward with some Argentinean basics. They marched me through composing my first *salsa chimichurri* and I marveled at how brilliantly this herbaceous, acidic, pungent sauce complemented a simple grilled steak.

The Bolivar job ended up fizzling out in about six months, but the experience was key: it transformed my perspective on food, ignited my passion for Latin cuisine, and reset my compass to new coordinates. My next move was a big step backwards in rank (line cook!), but a great leap forward career-wise. Not only did I get hired by Douglas Rodriguez, a major force in creating and popularizing *Nuevo Latino* cuisine, but I climbed aboard just as he launched a daring new venture: Chicama, a Peruvian-inspired restaurant with a spectacular, temple-like ceviche bar.

Douglas soon had me working shoulder to shoulder with the ace chefs he'd assembled: Raymond Mohan, Máximo Tejada, Jorge Adriazola, Adrian Leon, Jose Messina, and Romiro Jimenez. These guys were the best Latin chefs in New York City, and the formidable force of their talent and creativity was directed at South American-inspired fare—especially ceviche. Added to this was the ultimate seafood connection: Douglas's fish purveyor was a Chilean guy named Patricio Osis, whose dad was a fisherman back home in Chile and would haul in a day's catch and air-ship it to Manhattan. This meant that all the fish and shellfish at Chicama was not just supremely fresh, it was exotic, amazing South American stuff; there was nothing like it anywhere else in the city—*merluza* (hake), *conchas negras* (black clams), *picorocos* (giant acorn barnacles), and on and on. What's more, there was the Chicama menu, featuring signature dishes like Viagra Ceviche—oysters, various fresh clams, and calamari, all awash in a beautiful squid ink sauce. Fantastic. This wild inventiveness may have been the element that put the whole Chicama scenario over the top, to the point where it became a seriously happening hotspot and unleashed a ceviche craze.

By the time I headed to Philadelphia to open another restaurant with Douglas,

I'd amassed boatloads of inspiration—and some entrepreneurial acumen—that has carried through in everything I've done since. I had also acquired a desire to explore Peruvian cuisine further, from my own vantage point.

Jump forward a dozen years or so to 2008. I'd been out on my own for a while, my first three restaurants—Amada, Tinto, and Distrito—were humming along, and I was mulling over possible ideas for a venture number four. Ever since Chicama, I'd been itching to revisit Peruvian cuisine, and judging from what I was seeing in the press, the time had come. Peruvian gastronomy was gaining major international recognition. Next stop: Lima.

I suppose I could have kept the culinary research step simple, with chef Chad Williams and myself taking on Lima in much the same way we'd hit the Basque Country a couple years prior, when we were getting ready to open Tinto. But I opted to make a group expedition of it: Chad, Beatriz and myself, and my old buddy Joe Erlemann and his wife, Roopa.

We had less than a week for our culinary mission in the capital and we sure as hell made the most of it, aided and abetted throughout by our inexhaustible guide, Pollo. From the night we first landed and toasted our arrival at a touristy *taberna* with a few rounds of pisco sours (the national cocktail), Pollo had us eating and drinking our way through Lima like there was no tomorrow: ultramodern new restaurants and iconic bastions, quaint *huariques* and upscale bistros, trendy hotspots and obscure *puertas cerradas* (unmarked restaurants), smoky street carts and thatch-roofed *cevicherías*, kitschy *chifas* on the Calle Capón (Lima's Chinatown) and sleek Peruvian-Japanese restaurants in swank Miraflores. And we still managed to shoehorn in a three-day, soul-rocking side trip to the wondrous heights of Machu Picchu and the Sacred Valley of the Incas.

In 2009, I did open that fourth restaurant: Chifa, which takes its name from the term that Limeños and other Peruvians use for both Peruvian-Cantonese cooking and the establishments that serve it. Developing the concept was a golden opportunity for me to dig into the Latin-Asian crossover aspect of Peruvian gastronomy. Since the restaurant launched, the menu has evolved in various directions, and this has fed rather than quelled my curiosity about the permutations and possibilities of this cuisine. Peru beckons further investigation, as does Ecuador (always), not to mention Colombia, Brazil, Argentina, Chile…

My experience of Peruvian cooking may have begun long ago, but I think my real exploration of this cuisine is just getting started. This chapter sums up some of my favorite Peruvian-inspired dishes so far, some of them first encountered when I was just a kid, others picked up in the course of my early years as a chef, plus more I discovered in Peru itself, from the Pacific shores of Lima up into the heights of the Andes.

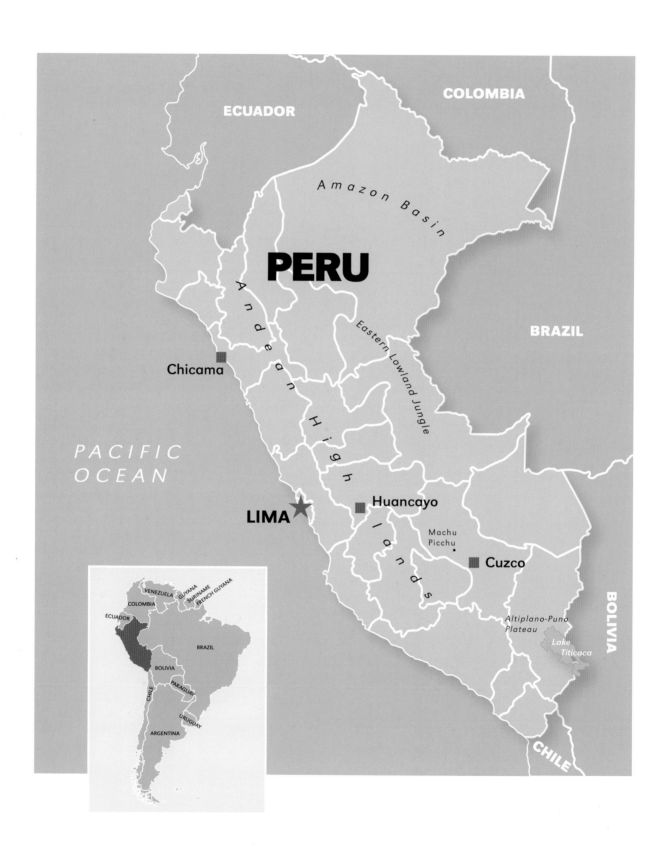

PERU

Amazon Basin

Eastern Lowland Jungle

Andean Highlands

Chicama

PACIFIC
OCEAN

LIMA ★

Huancayo

Machu
Picchu •

Cuzco

Altiplano-Puna
Plateau

Lake
Titicaca

ECUADOR

COLOMBIA

BRAZIL

BOLIVIA

CHILE

VENEZUELA
GUYANA
SURINAME
FRENCH GUYANA
COLOMBIA
ECUADOR
BRAZIL
BOLIVIA
CHILE
PARAGUAY
URUGUAY
ARGENTINA

QUICK INFO

LAND

• Terrain divided by the Andes into three primary zones: western coastal plain (*costa*), with 1,500 miles of South Pacific coastline; central Andean highlands (*sierra*), including the Altiplano-Puna Plateau (location of Lake Titicaca, the world's highest navigable lake); and eastern lowland jungle (*selva*), the tropical Amazon basin, which constitutes more than half the country's area

• Microclimatic along the coast and through the Andes by virtue of equatorial latitude, ocean currents and El Niño, topographical features, and other factors

PEOPLE

• Current population is approaching 30 million; nearly 10 million in Lima alone

• Multiethnic nation—majority is *indígena* (Amerindian), many of whom speak Quechua and other ancient languages of the highlands and the Amazon; next are *mestizo* (mixed native and European); other groups include Afro-Peruvian, Asian, and white

FOOD

• Extraordinary quality and diversity of cuisine due to peculiar geography and ecology that creates abundance and variety of foods; and interaction of multiple culinary influences over several centuries

• Current food staples cultivated in ancient times include native crops such as potatoes, quinoa, corn, chiles, peanuts, yuca, and squash; primary animal protein sources are fish, cuy (guinea pig), and llama

• Spanish introductions include olives, grapes, beef and dairy, pork, chicken, rice, wheat, and citrus

• Additional culinary influences: African (via slaves brought by Spanish colonists); Moorish and Sephardic (also with Spaniards); Chinese, Japanese, Italian, Basque, and French (via immigration)

1430 CE
Incas, one of many advanced cultures in the region over several millennia, begin their military expansion and rapidly overtake much of western South America, becoming the largest empire in the pre-Colombian Americas.

1526 CE
Within 100 years, Spanish arrival and subsequent conquest ends the Inca empire; exploitive feudal system make the land—and native inhabitants—property of Spanish colonists.

1542–1824 CE
Native resistance persists but proves futile during the viceroyalty of Peru; exploitation and successive waves of disease decimate population; colonists import African slaves to work plantations and mines.

1826 CE
Latin American colonies eventually win independence from Spanish rule; Peru, with Lima the capital of the viceroyalty, is the last to be surrendered.

CHICAMA

Ceviche de Corvina | CORVINA CEVICHE

Cebollas Rojas Encurtidas | PICKLED RED PEARL ONIONS

Aguadito de Pato | STEWED DUCK WITH POTATOES, PEAS, AND CHILES

Mantequilla de Rocoto | RED CHILE BUTTER

This menu is an homage to Armida Carreras, a wonderful Peruvian-born home cook whom I've known just about my entire life. I stayed at the Carreras' house in the Chicago suburbs with my family on many a weekend when I was growing up, and it was at that dinner table, packed in with my two brothers and the three Carreras kids, that I first tasted Peruvian food. Showcased here are a couple of Señora Carreras's specialties, two Peruvian classics that, although I did not take a shine to them when I was little, have since become big favorites of mine.

As I understand all too well now that I have young children of my own, unfamiliar foods can pose a real challenge. I think what made it especially unsettling for me was that the meals at the Carreras's looked like Ecuadorian stuff my mom made, but smelled and tasted a lot different. Take the *ceviche*: Peruvians go for a lot more acidity and chile heat than Ecuadorians do, so Señora Carreras's ceviche to me seemed crazy sour and hot as hell. I had no objections to the starchy garnish: chunky *choclo* kernels and tender cubes of sweet potato might not have been the salty *tostado* I was looking for, but made for acceptable and palatable bland substitutes. But what was up with that glass of cloudy, chile-specked fish juice on the side? At home, our ceviche was soupy, but you spooned up the juices from the bowl, along with the fish. No way was I up for a fishy beverage.

Years later, of course, I fell madly in love with the vibrancy of Peruvian ceviche and recognized *leche de tigre*—that shot of limey-fishy-spicy juice collected from the ceviche and knocked back as a chaser—for the stroke of gastronomic genius that it is.

Then there was the *arroz verde con pato*. "This," I vividly remember thinking, "is the worst thing I have ever tasted." Nowadays, I adore everything that made it awful to me back then: a funky, stewy mélange of rice and potatoes with gamey-rich duck leg, yeasty lager, chiles, and pungent cilantro—what's not to love?

Armida remains one of my mom's dearest friends. So, with love and thanks (and apologies for my shenanigans as an eight-year-old), here is a meal in her honor. The *aguadito de pato* main dish is based on Armida's stewed duck. While the corvina ceviche bears some resemblance to ceviches I had at the Carreras table, it probably owes more to the ceviches I encountered when I first started working for Douglas Rodriguez. The menu is named Chicama as a nod both to the beautiful coastal town of Chicama in northwestern Peru and to Douglas' Peruvian-inspired restaurant of the same name.

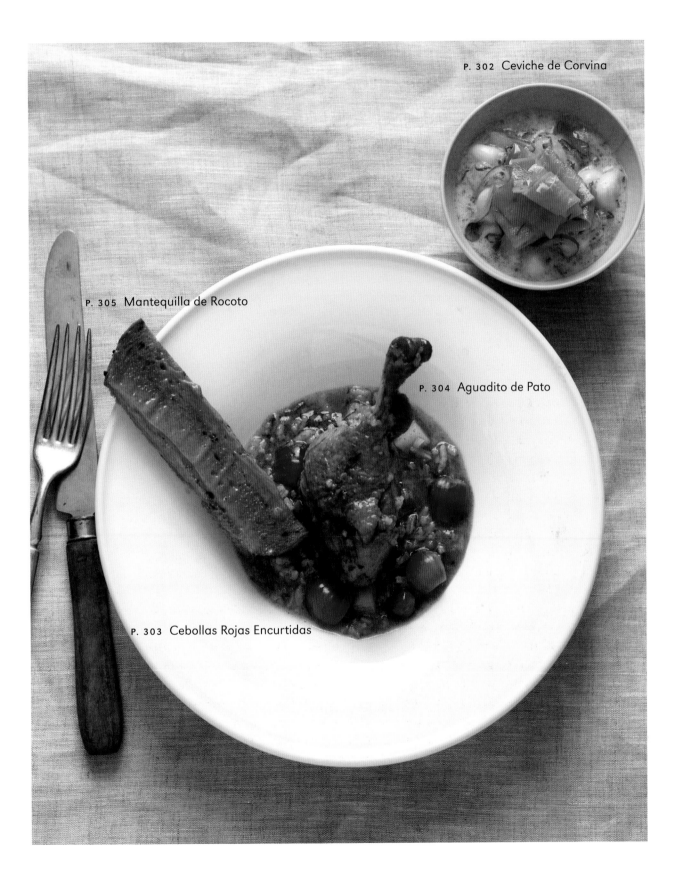

CEVICHE DE CORVINA

CORVINA CEVICHE

Aside from pristinely fresh fish, the key component to this style of ceviche is the *leche de tigre* (literally translated: "tiger's milk")—the juices collected from the marinating step. In Peru, *leche de tigre* is served in a small glass alongside the ceviche. I like to build up the *leche de tigre* by making a purée of additional fish (you can use trimmings from the ceviche) along with supplemental amounts of the other ceviche ingredients, plus some water and ice. Be sure to use bottled water to avoid any hint of mineral flavor, which is often present in tap water and would mar the delicate taste. *Choclo* (oversized, chewy South American corn kernels) is usually sold frozen in Latin groceries; thaw it overnight in the refrigerator, or at room temperature on the countertop if you're pinched for time. SERVES 4

CHOCLO

	Kosher salt
1/4 cup	choclo, thawed if frozen (see Sources)

SWEET POTATO RIBBONS

	Kosher salt
1	sweet potato (about 1/2 lb), peeled and sliced into thin ribbons on a Japanese mandoline

LECHE DE TIGRE

6 to 8 oz	fresh boneless, skinless white fish, coarsely chopped (2/3 cup)
2/3 cup	freshly squeezed lime juice (6 to 8 limes)
1	large Spanish onion, finely diced
1 1/2 Tbsp	minced peeled fresh ginger
1	jalapeño chile, seeded and coarsely chopped
2 1/2 cups	bottled spring water
1 Tbsp	granulated sugar
	Kosher salt

CEVICHE

1/2 lb	fresh skinless corvina or sea bass fillet, pin bones removed, sliced very thinly on the diagonal
2 Tbsp	grapeseed oil

TO SERVE

1/4	small red onion, finely diced
1	jalapeño chile, seeds and ribs removed, finely diced
1 to 2	radishes, thinly sliced
2 Tbsp	chopped fresh cilantro
	Coarse sea salt
2 Tbsp	Pickled Red Pearl Onions, quartered (recipe follows)
	Toasted Corn Nuts and Fava Beans (page 50)

TO PREPARE THE CHOCLO, bring a small saucepan of salted water to a boil and prepare an ice bath. Cook the kernels until tender, about 30 minutes. Use a slotted spoon to transfer the choclo to the ice bath to cool. Drain the choclo. (At this point the choclo can be stored in an airtight container in the refrigerator, up to 2 days.)

TO MAKE THE SWEET POTATO RIBBONS, bring a large saucepan of lightly salted water to a boil and prepare an ice bath. Cook the ribbons until just tender, 15 to 20 seconds. Use a slotted spoon to transfer the ribbons to the ice bath to cool for 15 to 20 seconds. Drain the ribbons. (At this point the ribbons can be stored in an airtight container in the refrigerator until needed, up to 1 day.)

TO MAKE THE LECHE DE TIGRE, prepare an ice bath in a deep, wide bowl. Combine the chopped fish, lime juice, onion, ginger, jalapeño, water, and granulated sugar in a blender and purée until very smooth. Transfer the purée to a small stainless-steel bowl, set the bowl in the ice bath, and allow the mixture to chill for 30 minutes. Strain the chilled leche de tigre through a fine-mesh sieve (discard the solids) and season to taste with salt.

TO MAKE THE CEVICHE, combine the sliced fish, leche de tigre, and oil in a bowl and allow the mixture to marinate for 10 minutes. Add the choclo, sweet potato ribbons, onion, jalapeño, radish, and cilantro and mix well.

TO SERVE, divide the ceviche into four small bowls, garnish with pickled red onions and corn nuts and fava beans, and serve immediately.

CEBOLLAS ROJAS ENCURTIDAS
PICKLED RED PEARL ONIONS

Small, lightly pickled onions are a common garnish at ceviche stalls in Peru. Pickling the onions quickly is a great way to blunt their sharp raw flavor but retain some nice crunch. The pickled onions add a nice touch of acidity along with their pretty purple color. MAKES ABOUT 1/4 CUP ONIONS

1/2 cup	water
1/4 cup	red wine vinegar
1/4 cup	granulated sugar
2 tsp	kosher salt
1/4 cup	red pearl onions, peeled

Bring the water, vinegar, sugar, and salt to a boil in a small saucepan. Pour the pickling liquid over the onions and allow to cool, about 1 hour. Chill thoroughly before use.

AGUADITO DE PATO

STEWED DUCK WITH POTATOES, PEAS, AND CHILES

This dish was inspired by Armida Carreras's *arroz verde con pato*. My version is an *aguadito*—a soupier rice dish. Note that you can divide the prep over a couple of days: cook the *aguadito* until the duck legs are tender, cool to room temperature and park the covered pot in the refrigerator for a couple of days; proceed with making and adding the purée and finishing the dish just before serving. SERVES 4

DUCK

4	whole duck legs
	Kosher salt and freshly ground black pepper
2 Tbsp	vegetable oil
1	large Spanish onion, finely diced
4 to 6	cloves garlic, minced
1	jalapeño chile, finely diced
1 Tbsp	whole cumin seeds, toasted (see page 368) and ground
1 Tbsp	ají amarillo chile paste (see Sources)
2	(12-oz) cans or bottles lager-style beer
2 qts + 1 qt	Chicken Stock (page 362)

CILANTRO PURÉE

2 cups	tightly packed chopped fresh cilantro
2 Tbsp	Vegetable Stock (page 364)
2 Tbsp	extra virgin olive oil

AGUADITO

2 cups	long-grain white rice
1	large Yukon gold potato, peeled and diced (about 2 cups)
1/2 lb	English peas, shelled and blanched (1/2 cup)
2	serrano chiles, roasted and peeled (see page 369), and finely diced

TO SERVE

	Pickled Red Pearl Onions (page 303)
8	slices baguette, toasted
1/4 cup	Red Chile Butter (recipe follows)

TO COOK THE DUCK, season the duck legs with the salt and pepper. Heat the vegetable oil in a stockpot or Dutch oven over medium-high heat, add the duck legs, and sear them for a couple of minutes on each side. Lift the duck legs out of the pot and set them aside. Lower the heat to medium and add the onion, garlic, jalapeños, and cumin and cook, stirring occasionally, until the onion is translucent and the cumin is fragrant, about 10 minutes. Stir in the ají amarillo paste and cook until very fragrant, 2 to 3 minutes. Pour in the beer and 2 quarts of the chicken stock and bring to a simmer over medium heat. Add the seared duck legs and cook until very tender, about 1 hour. (At this point you can store the soup for several days, see headnote.)

TO MAKE THE CILANTRO PURÉE, combine the cilantro and the vegetable stock in a blender and purée until very smooth. With the machine running, slowly add the olive oil in a thin stream and continue blending until the purée is emulsified.

TO FINISH THE STEW, add the remaining 1 quart chicken stock to the duck, add the rice and potato, and continue to simmer until all are tender, about 20 minutes. Stir in the cilantro purée, peas, and roasted serranos and cook for 5 additional minutes. Season to taste with salt and pepper. Garnish with pickled onions and baguette slices spread with red chile butter.

MANTEQUILLA DE ROCOTO
RED CHILE BUTTER

This versatile condiment will keep indefinitely in an airtight container in the refrigerator and can be used in any situation where spicy butter is in order, from spreading on toast or *pan de bono* to finishing roasted meats, vegetables, rice, noodles, and such. MAKES ABOUT 2/3 CUP

8 Tbsp	unsalted butter, at room temperature
2 Tbsp	ají rocoto chile paste (see Sources)
1	red Fresno chile, roasted (see page 369) and seeded
1 Tbsp	freshly squeezed lemon juice
	Kosher salt

Combine the butter, chile paste, roasted chile, and lemon juice in a food processor and purée until smooth. Season to taste with salt and store refrigerated until needed.

LIMA CON POLLO

Why Fernando, the debonair sixty-something gent who showed us around Lima, goes by the name Pollo, I do not know—*pollo* is Spanish for "chicken" and slang for "young guy." A lifelong Limeño and former restaurateur, the charismatic Pollo has boundless enthusiasm for the city's culinary scene. And the guy knows everyone—everywhere he goes, passersby call out to him, "Pollo!" He was a terrific leader for our expedition: five days and nights eating our way through Lima.

Of course there were plenty of sightseeing excursions as well. And Pollo, a pro surfer in another of his previous lives, was very keen to give us a taste of the waves that have made Lima, which is right on the Pacific, a surfing mecca. Now, I am a former lifeguard and spend as much time as I can in the ocean, but I have always had a strong inclination to keep my swimming and body surfing close to shore, where the bottom is never far out of reach. But Pollo was psyched to take us to his surf club, and our friends Joe and Roopa, being residents of Hawaii, were into the idea. Beatriz, ever the intrepid adventurer, was game. So I figured, what the hell.

Which is how I came to be packed into a wetsuit, belly-down on a great big board and paddling out into the ocean. The water was really choppy and really cold. We were smack dab in the middle of one the world's most seafood-rich stretches of ocean, and to me the presence of large marine animals was palpable. Churning waves relentlessly thumped the surfboard into my chest while the wetsuit tightened its rubbery grip on the entire length of my body, neck to ankles.

Not pleasant sensations in the best of circumstances, but combined with the previous few days and nights spent eating and drinking to excess with Pollo, this was torture. And while my body got battered, my mind went a little haywire—I couldn't stop thinking about how I'd heard people saying shark attacks happened around here sometimes. I paddled fast and furiously, certain that there were great whites circling just beneath me, and Pollo just kept looking back at me, grinning enthusiastically and flashing the thumbs-up sign . . . right up to the moment I barfed into the undulating waters.

Pollo somehow took this all in stride, ushering me back to shore and into the comforts of his surf club in no time. Before I knew it, all was once again right with the world, and Pollo had our whole group pleasantly absorbed in some local sightseeing. Then came another night out on the town, and by crack of dawn the next day, when Pollo handed us each a pair of tall rubber boots and piled us into a hired car, the whole surfing snafu was a distant memory. Now we were headed for the kind of marine experience that's more in my wheelhouse: the Terminal Pesquero, Lima's fish terminal.

The word "terminal" suggests airports and bus stations, and that's the scale we're talking here—several city blocks, easy. Pollo, who clearly enjoyed watching my jaw drop when I got my first look at the place, explained that the terminal is a major point of entry for the enormous amounts of fish and seafood consumed in the homes and restaurants of Lima; upwards of ten tons of harvest come through here daily, which is maybe half of the city's supply. And this is not only a wholesale-to-the-trade operation—home cooks are as much in the mix as food service pros.

The first area Pollo led us through was a vast open lot where commerce was being conducted in an aisle of sorts formed by two very long rows of backed-in trucks. Fishmongers called out their offerings to shoppers streaming past. Fish and seafood hauled in from the coast in the predawn hours were being sold essentially right out the rear cargo doors. Some of the vendors had tables set up with an umbrella or small canopy providing a little cover, but the majority of the product was offered up in the wide open, straight out of big plastic transport containers. Most everything was whole and unprocessed, all of it was sparkling fresh, and the quantities and variety were mind-boggling.

We saw sea creatures of all description: spiny green lobsters, shrimp in every conceivable size, piles of prickly sea urchins, and at least a dozen different kinds of live crab. There were endless shellfish—*concha negra* and all sorts of other clams, as well as assorted scallops, mussels, and sea snails—sometimes heaped between shimmering hills of *algas marinas*, edible seaweed. Waist-high cargo crates overflowed with glistening octopus, their sucker-covered tentacles draping over the sides and trailing along the puddled pavement. One truck specialized in giant squid clocking in at over 100 pounds and available both whole and butchered—sheets of snow-white flesh cut into three-foot squares and rolled into neat cylinders.

And the fish! We saw everything the algae-rich Humboldt Current serves up, from *corvina* (sea bass), mackerel, and shark to *merluza* (hake), pompano, and sole; and from shad and mounds of red pouches holding their roe to *anchoveta* and herring. One set of vendors specialized in prize specimens of deep-sea big-game fish like tuna, swordfish, sailfish, and marlin. Another set featured fish from the Amazon, including monstrous *arapaima* as long as I am tall and other prehistoric-looking jungle species formidably armed with thick scales, long whiskers, spiny barbs, and other evolutionary weaponry.

Handcarts loaded with fish and seafood zoomed past all around us, pushed by blue-aproned workers whistling a continuous, singsong alarm to part the crowd clogging their path. Pollo explained that they were headed for a huge open-sided hangar-like structure up ahead. We trooped over to check it out.

For a few extra *soles*, you could have your fish broken down into ready-to-cook fillets. This service was handled in a processing shed, which occupied a large area within the hangar. The only fully enclosed area in the terminal, it was as scrupulously clean as the rest of the place was ramshackle. Through the shed's enormous windows you could see dozens of workers, many of them women, using long thin blades to pull perfect fillets off whole fish in a few swift strokes. Each worker was ripping through I'd guess 100 or more fish per hour.

Another large section of the building was dedicated to prepped ceviche. At each stand, row upon row of trays held all manner of perfectly cut fish, and poaching stations were devoted to the various types of seafood requiring blanching, such as shrimp, octopus, and an encyclopedic range of shellfish. Everything was sold in a ceviche-ready state, needing only to be dressed and garnished to taste before serving.

Aside from a couple of stands selling Peruvian olives and a few others offering wild mushrooms, the entire terminal was strictly fish- and seafood-centric, with nary a snack in sight. Nothing like hours of meandering through a huge market ogling gorgeous food products to bring on a hearty appetite, so I was thankful to find that the sidewalk right outside the terminal was lined with street carts. A mighty appetizing char-grilled aroma drew us over to a row of flaming hibachis loaded with skewered meats—*anticuchos*, said to have originated with African slaves back in colonial times and traditionally made with chunks of marinated beef hearts and other offal. The moment to sample this hugely popular Peruvian street food had clearly arrived, and they were an earthy treat, chewy and gamey and infused with charcoal flavor.

As we polished off the *anticuchos*, a shrill voice called out "*Hue-VI-tos! Hue-VI-tos! Hue-VI-tos!*" ("TES-ticles! TES-ticles! TES-ticles!"). No way I was ingesting any more organs this early in the morning. Fortunately, Pollo quickly surmised that I was entirely mistaken in assuming the slang meaning of *huevitos*, when the addition of the -ito suffix to the word huevo can just as easily mean something to the effect of "eggs made with care." And here was a woman selling the loveliest of quail eggs, freshly boiled. She scooped about a dozen out of a tall steaming pot, whisked off the speckled shells, slid the tiny ivory orbs into a parchment cone, and sprinkled them with coarse sea salt and bright green olive oil before handing them over. Each tiny warm egg was a silky-smooth nugget, a bite-size dose of buttery rich goodness. A truly exquisite street snack—among the best I've ever had. *(Recipes follow.)*

HUEVOS DE CODORNIZ, HERVIDOS Y SALADOS

BOILED SALTED QUAIL EGGS

Peeling these little guys can be exasperating and time consuming. Here's my trick: boil and cool the eggs as instructed, let them sit for a little while at room temperature, then put them in a quart container with a lid. Put the top on and shake gently to crack the shells all over. Begin peeling from the loose spot over the air pocket in each shell. If you're gentle and careful, you should be able to wind the shell off the egg in a single continuous strip. SERVES 4

12	quail eggs (see Sources)
2 Tbsp	extra virgin olive oil
1 Tbsp	chopped fresh flat-leaf parsley
	Sea salt

Prepare an ice bath. Put the quail eggs in a small saucepan and add enough cold water to cover by about 1 inch. Bring to a boil, then lower to a simmer and cook for 3 minutes.

Use a slotted spoon to transfer the eggs to the ice bath to cool. Peel the eggs, rinse them to remove any clinging specks of shell, and pat them dry. Garnish with the oil, parsley, and sea salt.

ANTICUCHOS MIXTOS

GRILLED VEAL SWEETBREAD, BEEF SHORT RIB, AND MUSHROOM SKEWERS

Back in my days at Chicama in New York City, a chef named Ray Mohan took the fundamental concept of *anticuchos*—marinated protein, grilled over charcoal—and created sophisticated and incredibly delicious brochettes using choice ingredients like salmon belly and pork belly. I've enjoyed experimenting with various other takes on the premise ever since. Here I've put together a trio: sweetbreads (more delicate than the traditional beef hearts, but still earthy); Korean-style boneless beef short ribs (delicious and tender when prepared this way); and cremini mushrooms (offering their own distinct flavor and texture when marinated and char-grilled). Both *ají amarillo* and *ají mirasol* chile pastes are available at Latin groceries and online. Plan ahead when making these: the sweetbreads need 12 hours to soak and an additional 2 hours to marinate. SERVES 8

SWEETBREADS

1 lb	veal sweetbreads (thymus) (see Sources)
	Whole milk, for soaking

MARINADE

1/4 cup	extra virgin olive oil
1/4 cup	ají amarillo chile paste (see Sources)
1/4 cup	ají mirasol chile paste (see Sources)
1/4 cup	red wine vinegar
1/4 cup	minced garlic (12 to 16 cloves)
2 Tbsp	minced fresh oregano

BEEF AND MUSHROOMS

1 lb	boneless beef short ribs cut into 1/2 x1/2-inch cubes
1/4 lb	cremini mushrooms, stemmed and halved
	Kosher salt and freshly ground black pepper

TO SERVE

	Peruvian Chile Aïoli (recipe follows)
	Black Mint Sauce (recipe follows)

TO PREPARE THE SWEETBREADS, rinse them under cold water. Fully submerge them in milk and leave to soak in an airtight container in the refrigerator for 12 hours.

Drain the sweetbreads and discard the soaking milk. Bring a deep saucepan of lightly salted water to a gentle boil, add the sweetbreads, and poach, fully submerged, until just firm, 10 to 12 minutes. Transfer the sweetbreads to a plate and press gently while they to cool to room temperature.

Peel off and discard the outer membrane and any sinew. Cut the sweetbreads into 3/4-inch chunks.

TO MAKE THE MARINADE, combine the oil, chile pastes, vinegar, garlic, and oregano and mix well. Refrigerate the marinade in an airtight container until needed, up to 3 days.

In three separate containers, marinate the sweetbreads, short ribs, and mushrooms for 2 to 3 hours.

Soak 24 to 32 6-inch bamboo skewers in water for 30 minutes. Thread the sweetbreads, short ribs, and mushrooms onto separate skewers, 2 or 3 pieces per skewer, setting aside the marinade.

Heat a charcoal grill to medium, or a stovetop griddle over medium-high heat.

Meanwhile, bring the marinade to a boil in a small saucepan over medium heat. Simmer gently for at least 5 minutes. Remove from the heat and set aside.

Season the skewers with salt and pepper and grill 3 to 5 minutes until nicely browned and cooked through, brushing with the reserved marinade.

SERVE WITH aïoli and black mint sauce, for dipping.

ALLIOLI DE ROCOTO

PERUVIAN CHILE AÏOLI

This chunky, flavorful aïoli can be stored in an airtight container in the refrigerator for up to 3 days; use it anywhere you'd use mayonnaise.

MAKES ABOUT 1 CUP

2	large egg yolks
1/4 cup	(12 to 16 cloves) Roasted Garlic (page 366)
2 Tbsp	ají rocoto chile paste (see Sources)
2 Tbsp	freshly squeezed lemon juice
	Kosher salt
1/2 cup	vegetable oil

Combine the egg yolks, garlic, chile paste, lemon juice, and 1 tsp salt in a bowl and beat with a whisk until very smooth and frothy, 2 to 3 minutes. Continuing to whisk, drizzle in the oil very slowly; continue whisking until the aïoli is uniformly emulsified, about 1 minute more. (It should have the consistency of mayonnaise.) Season to taste with additional salt. Chill the aïoli in an airtight container in the refrigerator until needed, up to 3 days. Serve chilled.

SALSA DE HUACATAY

BLACK MINT SAUCE

Huacatay paste, made from an herb known as Andean or Peruvian black mint, can be found online and at well-stocked Latin groceries.

MAKES ABOUT 2 CUPS

1/4 cup	vegetable oil
1/4	small red onion, finely diced
1	jalapeño chile, seeds and ribs removed, finely diced
2 Tbsp	minced garlic (4 to 6 cloves)
1/2 cup	huacatay paste (see Sources)
1/2 cup	Vegetable Stock (page 364)
1/2 cup	(4 oz) cream cheese, at room temperature
1/4 cup	freshly squeezed lime juice (2 to 3 limes)
1/4 cup	chopped fresh mint
	Kosher salt

Combine the oil, onion, jalapeño, and garlic in a small sauté pan and set the pan over medium-low heat (do not preheat the oil). Cook, stirring often, until the onion is translucent, about 10 minutes. Stir in the huacatay paste and cook for 2 to 3 minutes more. Add the stock and continue cooking to reduce by half, 5 to 7 minutes. Take the pan off of the heat and allow the mixture to cool to room temperature.

Transfer the mixture to a blender, add the cream cheese and lime juice, and purée until smooth. Fold in the mint and season with salt to taste.

LIMA

Tiradito de Lubina | BLACK BASS CEVICHE WITH YUZU

Lomo Saltado con Arroz | SOY STIR-FRIED BEEF WITH RICE

The cuisine of Peru is at its core a 500-year *criollo* fusion of Indian and Spanish traditions intricately blended with African and mixed European influences. Adding another dimension, and setting Peruvian cuisine apart from any other, is a strong crosscurrent of Asian influences. The culinary intersection of Peruvian and Chinese is known as *chifa*, while the marriage of Peruvian and Japanese is called *nikkei*.

Chinese immigrants first arrived in Peru as contract workers in the mid-1800s, bringing with them soy sauce, gingerroot, and other flavorings as well as cooking methods, such as stir-frying. Improvising with the peculiar array of chiles and produce they found in Peru, the Chinese approximated dishes from back home—mainly from the southern provinces of Guangdong and Fujian. The resulting hybrid cuisine that evolved over the next century and a half is enormously popular all over Peru. Some dishes with *chifa* origins have been so fully integrated into the national cuisine that they are found on the home table as often as any creole staple; others are perennial favorites at Peruvian Chinese restaurants, known as *chifa*.

Japanese immigrants came to Peru as recruited laborers beginning in 1899. They brought with them a reverence for seafood and an artful approach to its preparation, both inherent to the cooking traditions of the Japanese archipelago. A remarkable fusion cuisine emerged when this culinary sensibility, characterized by precision and subtlety, encountered the distinctive seafood and produce—and the vibrant cooking style—of Peru. *Cevicherías* opened by Japanese arrivals were central to the evolution of this cuisine, *cocina nikkei*, which continued over the course of the twentieth century, bringing together Peruvian ingredients such as chiles, garlic, cilantro, and lemon and lime with an array of Japanese ingredients, techniques, and preparations. Ceviche, the iconic national dish of Peru, is the clearest illustration of how pervasive the effect of this fusion has been: decades ago, the fish was marinated for so long that it was firm and essentially "cooked" by the acidity of the marinade; now it is soaked much more briefly, if at all, and served basically raw, like sushi. Mind you, the chiles and the lime are still a strong presence, as are various garnishes. Anywhere ceviche is served, *nikkei* is in evidence—from beachfront *cevicherías* to high-end restaurants to humble *huariques*.

This menu, named for Lima, where the highest concentration of *nikkei* and *chifa* restaurants are found, pairs prime examples of first the Japanese and then the Chinese influence on Peruvian cuisine. The starter, a *tiradito*, is classic *nikkei*—ceviche sliced sashimi-thin instead of cut into cubes, then dressed in a kinder, gentler solution of lime juice and chiles and spiked with ginger rather than onion (ubiquitous in other Peruvian ceviche). The main dish, *lomo saltado*, is vintage *chifa*—a stir-fry of beef, peppers, tomatoes, and fried potatoes (in Peru, these are often actual French fries), all seasoned with chiles and soy. These are two of the most popular dishes in Peru and great additions to any home cook's repertoire.

P. 319 Tiradito de Lubina

P. 320 Lomo Saltado con Arroz

TIRADITO DE LUBINA
BLACK BASS CEVICHE WITH YUZU

Spicy red *ají rocoto*, an indigenous chile central to traditional Peruvian cooking, is hard to find outside of Peru. Though you would never, ever use dried chiles in a ceviche, *ají rocoto* chile paste, found in most Latin groceries, makes a good stand-in. Yuzu fruits look like golfball-size grapefruits. Both the juice and rind are used in Japanese cuisine to impart tart flavor and strong citrusy fragrance. The juice and packaged paste are typically found in the United States, usually stocked in Asian groceries. SERVES 4

CEVICHE

1/2 lb	fresh skinless black bass fillet, pin bones removed, sliced paper-thin on the diagonal
	Sea salt

TIRADITO SAUCE

1/4	small red onion, finely diced
1	Thai chile, seeds and ribs removed, finely diced
1 Tbsp	ají rocoto chile paste (see Sources)
3 Tbsp	yuzu juice (see Sources)
1 Tbsp	freshly squeezed lime juice
1 Tbsp	freshly squeezed orange juice
2 Tbsp	soy sauce
2 Tbsp	olive oil
1 Tbsp	agave nectar (see page 72)
2 Tbsp	chopped fresh cilantro
	Sea salt
	Granulated sugar

SESAME OIL

3 Tbsp	light sesame oil
2-inch	piece lemongrass (inner white part only), lightly crushed and minced (1 Tbsp)
1 tsp	minced garlic (1 clove)

TO SERVE

	Garlic Chips (page 242; optional)
	Fresh basil leaves (optional)

Chill four small plates.

TO MAKE THE CEVICHE, fan the fish slices on the chilled plates and lightly season with sea salt.

TO MAKE THE TIRADITO SAUCE, combine the onion, chile, chile paste, yuzu juice, lime juice, orange juice, soy sauce, olive oil, agave nectar, and cilantro in a small bowl. Mix well and season to taste with salt and sugar.

TO MAKE THE SESAME OIL, in a small sauté pan, combine the sesame oil, lemongrass, and garlic and cook over low heat just long enough to warm through, about 1 minute. Pour the hot sesame oil mixture over the fish slices.

TO SERVE, spoon the tiradito sauce over the fish. Garnish with garlic chips and basil leaves.

LOMO SALTADO CON ARROZ

SOY STIR-FRIED BEEF WITH RICE

When I was a kid, my mom picked up on *lomo saltado* from her Peruvian friend, Armida, and Ecuadorianized it (dialing down the chiles) into one of my family's favorite meat-and-potatoes dinners. I remember the sound of the potatoes hitting the frying oil, then the fantastic aroma that filled the house when my mom tossed the onions, peppers, and meat into her big cast-iron skillet, followed by a bunch of cilantro right at the end. I've switched up the order, frying up the meat first so that the beefy flavor in the pan infuses the potatoes. You can prepare the soy glaze in advance; it will keep in an airtight container in the refrigerator for up to 3 weeks and also works well as a marinade for chicken or vegetables, or a sauce for fried rice. *Xiao xing*, Chinese cooking wine, is readily available in most Asian groceries. If need be, you can substitute additional dry sherry (see photo, page 318). SERVES 4

SOY GLAZE

1 tsp	vegetable oil
1 Tbsp	thinly sliced peeled fresh ginger
3 Tbsp	thinly sliced garlic
1 tsp	crushed red pepper
2 Tbsp	dry sherry
1/4 cup	xiao xing wine
1/2 cup	light soy sauce
1/2 cup	water
2 Tbsp	honey
2 Tbsp	light sesame oil

STIR-FRIED BEEF

1/2 cup + 3 Tbsp	vegetable oil
2 lb	beef tenderloin, cut into thin strips
	Kosher salt and freshly ground pepper
1/2 lb	russet potatoes, peeled, cut into 1/4-inch sticks, boiled 5 to 7 minutes in lightly salted water, and drained
2	red bell peppers, cut into thin strips
1	large red onion, cut into thin strips
2	plum tomatoes, seeded and cut into thin strips
1/4 cup	fresh cilantro

TO SERVE

	White Rice (page 367)

TO MAKE THE SOY GLAZE, heat the vegetable oil in a small saucepan over medium heat and cook the ginger and garlic until translucent, 1 to 2 minutes. Add the red pepper and cook to lightly toast, stirring often, 15 to 20 seconds. Add the dry sherry and xiao xing, bring to a simmer, and reduce by about half, about 5 minutes. Add the soy sauce and water and bring to a boil. Remove from the heat and set it aside to steep for 30 minutes.

Strain the glaze through a fine-mesh sieve into a small bowl. Whisk in the honey and sesame oil. Store the soy glaze in an airtight container in the refrigerator until needed, up to 3 weeks.

TO COOK THE BEEF, heat 1/2 cup of the vegetable oil in a large cast-iron skillet over high heat. Season the beef with salt and pepper and quickly sear the beef strips until they are lightly browned, 2 to 3 minutes, stirring frequently. Remove the beef from the pan and set it aside.

Add the potatoes to the pan and fry until crispy on all sides, 2 to 3 minutes, turning once or twice. Remove the potatoes from the pan and set aside.

Pour off the frying oil without discarding the flavorful brown bits at the bottom of the pan. Set the pan over high heat and add the remaining 3 tablespoons vegetable oil. Sauté the bell pepper and onion, stirring often, just until wilted, 1 to 2 minutes. Add the soy glaze and return the beef and potatoes to the pan to warm through and coat with the glaze, about 1 minute. Add the tomatoes and cilantro and stir to incorporate.

SERVE IMMEDIATELY with rice.

ESSENTIALS

COSTAÑERA 700

The legendary restaurant Costañera 700 is not the discreet hideaway it used to be—the original location was a former garage on an unpaved street in Lima's shabby waterfront neighborhood of San Miguel, with no sign out front and a garbage dump up the block. A certain mystique remains, even in the much more conventionally upscale space the restaurant now occupies in the beachside suburb of Miraflores. For one thing, it is still a favorite power-lunch spot for Peru's highest-ranking *políticos* and business bigwigs (and, rumor has it, international spies and all sorts of other shadowy characters). But the main draw has always been chef-owner Humberto Sato's incredible food.

The son of Japanese immigrants, Sato was raised in Lima, where he trained to be a mechanic but instead became a culinary innovator and a leader in the modernization of Peru's *nikkei* cuisine (see page 316), further developing the use of Peruvian ingredients to create new takes on traditional Japanese flavors. For example, for a sushi and sashimi accompaniment, Sato replaced the searing horseradish heat of wasabi with a chile-fired blend of *ají rocoto*, soy, scallions, and juice from high-acid Peruvian lemons. Prominent chefs like Nobu Matsuhisa (who, before he built his international restaurant empire, worked with and learned from Sato in Peru) and Douglas Rodriguez, among others, have spread Sato's influence and inspiration around the world.

Back in Lima, Sato and his food are renowned, and his restaurant is one of the most highly regarded in the country. It is also the setting for many tales of intrigue. My favorite is one from back in the 1990s, when Costañera 700 was still in a rough part of town. At that time, clandestine peace talks were being held between Peru and Ecuador in an effort to end more than a century of border disputes. Discussions apparently went nowhere—until Peru's then-president Alberto Fujimori treated Ecuador's Abdalá Bucaram to a seventeen-course lunch at Costañera 700. A settlement between the two countries was eventually reached in 1998.

Having read about Sato's food for years and heard Douglas Rodriguez sing its praises many times, I eagerly anticipated experiencing it for myself. When I traveled to Peru, a visit to Costañera 700 was a key point on my itinerary. And I especially looked forward to his signature dish: *chita a la sal*, whole salt-baked fish.

Everything we ordered at Sato's restaurant—and there was a lot—was perfect, from the tempura prawns with garlic-ginger dipping sauce to the panko-crusted crab claws with yuzu mayo to the *tiradito* with yuzu and citrus. And the *chita a la sal* was a real showstopper. A big, steaming, golden-brown salt dome came toward us through the dining room, carried on a huge platter up on the shoulder of a server with a procession of two or three helpers trailing behind him. Once the tray was situated, the server and his helpers used square-ended spoons to go around the perimeter of the dome and crack through the thick salt shell. Lifting off the salt crust in big pieces released an aromatic steam and revealed a two- or three-pound fish, which they proceeded to deftly carve into chunks, set in serving bowls, and lightly dress with a sauce of grapeseed oil, ginger, scallion, and yuzu. Tasting the *chita*, I was stunned by the lavish texture and flavor—the salt had locked in and intensified all of the juices in the fish, making the flesh incredibly succulent and delicious. And the delicately flavored oil complemented the fish perfectly, making it even more luxurious in taste, texture, and aroma. I honestly cannot say I have ever had better fish. *(Recipes follow.)*

PESCADO EN SAL

SALT-BAKED FISH WITH GINGER OIL

A fish I've never encountered outside Peru, *chita* is a type of grunt with tender white flesh. This preparation is well suited to branzino, but you can use any white fish with firm but tender flesh, such as red snapper, black bass, or striped bass. SERVES 4

FISH

1 1/2 cups	kosher salt
1/3 cup	water
1/3 cup	egg whites (about 3 large egg whites)
1	whole fresh branzino (about 2 lb), cleaned and scaled
	Coarse sea salt
3 Tbsp	peeled fresh ginger cut into matchsticks
1 Tbsp	thinly sliced garlic (3 to 4 cloves)
8	cilantro leaves

TO SERVE

	Ginger Oil (recipe follows)
	White Rice (page 367)

Place a rack in the middle position and preheat the oven to 325°F.

TO PREPARE THE FISH, combine the kosher salt, water, and egg whites and mix until well combined.

Gently rinse the fish, inside and out, and pat dry. Season the cavity with sea salt and stuff with the ginger, garlic, and cilantro.

Line a baking sheet with parchment paper. Spread the paper with a quarter of the kosher salt mixture in an even layer. Lay the fish on the salt bed and mound the remaining

P. 325 Pescado en Sal

salt mixture on top of the fish to completely cover. Bake the fish for 30 minutes.

Remove the baking sheet from the oven and let the fish rest for 5 minutes at room temperature.

TO REMOVE THE SALT SHELL, hold a spoon perpendicular to the fish, and use another spoon to tap it gently—as you would a hammer and nail—working your way around the outer edge of the fish to carefully split open the crust. You should then be able to lift the crust away in big chunks. Discard the crust and use one of the spoons to delicately scrape the skin off the fish.

TO PORTION OUT THE FISH, use a dinner fork and a spoon to carefully remove the flesh—in chunks or as a whole fillet—from the top side of the fish. The skeleton will easily lift away from the bottom half of the fish, leaving a whole fillet that you can then lift away from its skin.

TO SERVE, drizzle the fish with 2 tablespoons of the ginger oil and serve with white rice and additional ginger oil on the side.

ESSENTIALS

ACEITE DE JENGIBRE
GINGER OIL

Leftover ginger oil is good for marinating or saucing chicken, fish, pork, or vegetables. You can store it in an airtight container in the refrigerator for up to 3 days. MAKES ABOUT 1 CUP

2 1/2 Tbsp	minced peeled fresh ginger
2 Tbsp	minced garlic (4 to 6 cloves)
1/2	scallion, thinly sliced on the diagonal
3/4 cup	grapeseed oil
2 Tbsp	chopped fresh cilantro

Combine all the ingredients and mix well.

CUZCO

Solterito | EDAMAME SALAD WITH GARLIC VINAIGRETTE

Parihuela | SEAFOOD CHOWDER

Pan Tostado de Ajo | GARLIC TOAST

When I put this menu together, I had in mind the whirlwind couple of days I spent in Cuzco and the Sacred Valley of the Incas with Beatriz and our friends Joe and Roopa. Being in that sky-high, ages-old, stunningly gorgeous place had an effect on me that I can only describe as profound. From the bright, thin air to the otherworldly landscape to the ubiquitous ancient ruins to the people themselves—everything had a mystical quality. I was utterly spellbound, and that was before we even got to Machu Picchu.

The best meal we had while we were up in the Andes was an extraordinary luncheon in the grand dining hall at Casa Hacienda Orihuela, a hilltop colonial estate near the archaeological sites of Pisac and Ollantaytambo. There must have been a dozen courses, all elegantly rendered traditional highland fare made with ingredients raised there on the estate, including mountain trout from the nearby rivers. Two highlights were dishes I would not necessarily have expected to enjoy, much less be blown away by: an alpaca carpaccio (maybe a play on traditional dried alpaca meat, aka *charqui*—the original jerky) and a confit and crisp-roasted *cuy* (guinea pig). Both of these were superb, and another stunner was a rich and complex *parihuela* that, being in essence a seafood stew, obviously translates a lot more readily than alpaca or *cuy* to North American ingredients.

To accompany my take on a *parihuela* is a *solterito* inspired by the light and refreshing lima-bean salads served at restaurants in Cuzco. Replacing the limas with edamame was an Asian spin I devised when developing the dish for the menu at Chifa.

P. 331 Parihuela

SOLTERITO
EDAMAME SALAD WITH GARLIC VINAIGRETTE

Use the leftover garlic vinaigrette as a dressing for any salad or simply prepared vegetable, or as a marinade for chicken. SERVES 4

GARLIC VINAIGRETTE

1/3 cup	vegetable oil
1/4 cup	minced garlic (12 to 16 cloves)
2 tsp	minced peeled fresh ginger
2 Tbsp	unseasoned rice vinegar
3/4 tsp	Dijon mustard
2 Tbsp	water
	Kosher salt and freshly ground black pepper

SALAD

1/2 lb	frozen shelled edamame (about 1 1/2 cups)
	Kosher salt
1/2 lb	Chinese long beans, haricots verts, or regular green beans
2	heads Boston or Bibb lettuce, separated into leaves, rinsed, and patted dry
4 oz	queso fresco, diced (1 cup)
2	plum tomatoes, seeded and diced
1 Tbsp	chopped fresh cilantro
	Freshly ground black pepper

TO MAKE THE VINAIGRETTE, heat the oil in a small sauté pan over very low heat, add the garlic and ginger, and cook for 1 minute, just until the garlic is fragrant and begins to take on a little color. Use a slotted spoon to transfer the toasted garlic and ginger to a blender, setting aside the oil. Add the vinegar, mustard, and water to the garlic and ginger and purée until very smooth. With the machine running, slowly drizzle in the reserved oil and continue blending until the vinaigrette is emulsified. Season to taste with salt and pepper. Refrigerate in an airtight container until needed, up to 3 days.

TO MAKE THE SALAD, bring a saucepan of well-salted water to a boil and prepare an ice bath. Boil the edamame for 2 to 3 minutes, then transfer them to the ice bath to cool for 2 to 3 minutes. Lift out of the ice bath and drain well.

Boil the long beans in the same water as the edamame for 2 to 3 minutes, cool them in the ice bath for 2 to 3 minutes, and cut crosswise into 1-inch pieces.

Combine the edamame and beans with the lettuce, cheese, tomatoes, and cilantro in a large bowl. Lightly dress the salad with 3 tablespoons of the garlic vinaigrette (reserve the remainder for another use) and season to taste with salt and pepper.

PARIHUELA

SEAFOOD CHOWDER

It is fine to use just mussels (ask your fishmonger to debeard them) or just clams rather than a combination of the two. *Chicha de jora*, a fermented corn brew with a cider-like taste, is an acquired taste as a beverage but adds a balancing acidity and a subtle hint of fermented flavor to the *parihuela*. SERVES 4

CHOWDER

2 Tbsp	extra virgin olive oil
1/2	Spanish onion, finely diced
2 Tbsp	minced garlic (4 to 6 cloves)
1 Tbsp	minced peeled fresh ginger
1 Tbsp	ají rocoto chile paste (see Sources)
1 Tbsp	ají panca chile paste (see Sources)
1/4 cup	diced plum tomato
1/2 cup	chicha de jora (see Sources)
1 1/2 qts	Fish Stock (page 365)
1	large (1 lb) russet potato, peeled and diced
12	fresh clams (preferably Spanish cockles or littlenecks), scrubbed and rinsed under cold water
12	fresh mussels (preferably PEI Blue Bay), scrubbed and rinsed under cold water
1/4 lb	fresh skinless red snapper fillet, pin bones removed, cut into 1-inch chunks
12	large fresh shrimp, peeled and deveined
1/4 lb	fresh jumbo lump crabmeat
	Kosher salt

TO SERVE

1 Tbsp	chopped fresh oregano
2 Tbsp	chopped chives
8 to 10	grape tomatoes, quartered
	Lime wedges
	Garlic Toast (recipe follows)

TO **MAKE THE CHOWDER**, heat the oil in a large saucepan over medium heat. Add the onion and cook until translucent, about 10 minutes. Add the garlic and ginger and cook for 2 to 3 minutes more. Add the chile pastes and plum tomato and cook until the juices have evaporated, 5 to 7 minutes. Add the chicha de jora and cook to reduce by half, 5 to 7 minutes. Stir in the stock and bring to a low boil. Lower the heat to a simmer, add the potatoes, and cook, uncovered, for 30 minutes.

Add the clams and mussels and cook just until their shells open, about 2 minutes. Discard any that don't open. Add the snapper and shrimp and cook just until opaque, about 2 minutes more. Fold in the crabmeat and season to taste with salt.

TO **SERVE**, divide the chowder among 4 warmed bowls and garnish with oregano, chives, tomatoes, lime wedges, and garlic toast.

PAN TOSTADO DE AJO
GARLIC TOAST

SERVES 4

8	baguette slices, cut on a long diagonal
1	clove garlic, crushed
2 Tbsp	extra virgin olive oil
1 Tbsp	minced fresh thyme
	Freshly grated zest of 1 lemon

Place a rack in the middle position and preheat the oven to 350°F.

Rub the baguette slices with the garlic and brush with the oil. Garnish each slice with thyme and lemon zest and toast in the oven until just golden, about 5 minutes.

CUZCO MARKET

A colonial metropolis overlaid on an Inca capital, Cuzco is the oldest inhabited city in the Americas, full of ancient ruins, Baroque churches, treasure-filled museums, Andean street vendors, and throngs of tourists from all over the world. For most visitors, it's standard practice to spend a day or two in Cuzco acclimating to the 11,000-foot elevation before making the trip to the area's main attraction: Machu Picchu.

Our contingent (Beatriz and I and our friends Joe and Roopa) flew in from Lima and spent much of the first day contending with *soroche*, aka altitude sickness. This meant lying low, swilling coca tea, and keeping a coca leaf parked between the cheek and gum. Come next morning, the rest and folk remedies had us more or less back on our feet, still bleary and easily winded, but ready to see more of this amazing city than the inside of our hotel and a couple of nearby restaurants. So we wended our way through the cobbled streets of Cuzco, arriving at the sprawling central market out of breath and very punchy. This is, it turns out, a common effect of altitude: the thin air means the brain's coming up short on oxygen. In any case, it made for a pretty hilarious trip through certain parts of the market.

Assorted entrails, headless chickens, and other basic carnage weren't terribly unusual sights for any of us. Yes, the *cuys* (guinea pigs) were gruesome—skinned, skewered, and oh-so-scrawny—but we'd expected those. Things only really took a turn for the macabre with the severed calves' heads, casually strewn on a bloodstained wooden shelf, each one's eyes and mouth slightly agape, mortal wound midforehead, plain as day, and the heap of whiskery, loose-lipped cow snouts. But the shaman's shop was really something. A huge glass jug of fat, pickled-looking snakes? Now, that's hard to look at. A bundle of desiccated llama fetuses dangling at face level from a string tied around their wizened necks? Okay! Time to move on to the produce!

There was a large open area devoted to vegetables farmed all over the surrounding fertile valley: corn, beans, quinoa, squash, cucumbers, carrots, onions, sweet potatoes, and yuca, as well as tomatoes, avocados, and more. Here and there was a basket of tropical fruit from the lush cloud forest at the edge of the valley or the jungle just beyond. The vendors were native women in brightly embroidered garments and dark felt fedoras, and most were selling small amounts of just one or two types of produce, laid out on the ground on woven textiles—the same cloths they'd bundled and carried their wares in, slung over their backs, from their patch of farmland somewhere in the surrounding Urubamba Valley.

Most plentiful and diverse by far were the potatoes (*papas*). I'd known full well that potatoes originated in this part of the world (domesticated by indigenous Andean farmers more than 7,000 years ago) and that countless varieties are still grown all over Peru, from sea level to high altitude. Even so, I was amazed by the kaleidoscopic array on display here. Every vendor seemed to offer a different selection in little color-coded piles, a spectrum of colors and shades from deep purple to cobalt blue, dark red to dusky pink, Tang orange to saffron yellow, even some bicolored, striped and spotted varieties. In shape and luster they called to mind everything from lumpy stones to shiny eggs to waxy fingers to knobby twigs. Strolling amid all this beauty and bounty was a great way to recover both our composure and our appetites. Maybe there was time to duck back into the market, head over to the stands serving up various local specialties, and grab some *papas rellenas* to tide me over until lunchtime. *(Recipes follow.)*

PAPAS RELLENAS
POTATO FRITTERS FILLED WITH BEEF PICADILLO

There are variations on this filled, fried potato-shaped cake in any Latin cuisine. Once you get a feel for the basic recipe provided here, you can easily create your own rendition with whatever filling you like—cheese, chicken, etc. Note that a ricer or food mill is essential for getting the potatoes silky smooth and developing their starches properly (see photo, page 339). SERVES 8

POTATO DOUGH

3 lb	russet potatoes, peeled and chopped into 1-inch chunks
1	large egg
4 Tbsp	unsalted butter, melted and cooled
2 Tbsp	all-purpose flour
1 Tbsp	kosher salt

PICADILLO

1/2 cup	golden raisins
2 Tbsp	extra virgin olive oil
1	Spanish onion, diced
2 Tbsp	minced garlic (4 to 6 cloves)
1 Tbsp	Spanish smoked sweet paprika
1 1/2 tsp	whole cumin seeds, toasted (see page 368) and ground
1/2 lb	top sirloin, ground
	Kosher salt and freshly ground black pepper
2 Tbsp	Beef Stock (page 363)
2 Tbsp	unsalted butter
2 Tbsp	minced fresh flat-leaf parsley

1 1/2 qts	vegetable oil, for frying
3 Tbsp	all-purpose flour, for dusting

TO MAKE THE POTATO DOUGH, boil the potatoes in a large saucepan of lightly salted water until fork-tender, about 20 minutes. Drain the potatoes and while they are still hot, pass them through a potato ricer or food mill into a large bowl. Mix in the egg and melted butter, then the flour, with your hands, kneading to form a smooth dough. Knead in the salt. Cover with plastic wrap and refrigerate until needed, up to 3 days.

TO MAKE THE PICADILLO FILLING, cover the raisins with hot water to soak for about 30 minutes. Meanwhile, heat the olive oil in a large skillet over medium heat. Add the onion and cook, stirring often, until translucent, about 10 minutes. Add the garlic, paprika, and cumin and cook, stirring frequently, until very fragrant and lightly toasted, about 2 minutes. Add the sirloin and cook, stirring occasionally, until the meat is just browned, 8 to 10 minutes. Season with salt and pepper. Add the stock and butter, stirring until the butter is melted and the mixture is saucy. Remove from the heat. Drain and chop the raisins and stir them in with the parsley. Allow the picadillo to cool to room temperature before filling the potato cakes. (At this point, the picadillo can be kept in the refrigerator in an airtight container for up to 2 days.)

TO FORM THE CAKES, divide the potato dough into 8 equal portions, about 1/2 cup each. Use your hands to form each portion into an oval about the shape and size of an egg. Spoon 2 to 3 tablespoons picadillo onto the center of each cake. Fold the dough over the filling, joining the edges of the dough together to fully enclose the filling and gently molding the cake into an oval.

Heat the vegetable oil to 375°F in a deep heavy skillet, using a candy or deep-fry thermometer to monitor the temperature. Line a baking sheet with parchment paper. If you won't be serving the cakes right away, preheat the oven to 200°F.

TO COOK THE CAKES, lightly dust each with flour, gently shaking off excess. Fry the cakes in batches, 2 or 3 at a time, until golden brown and crispy on both sides, flipping once, 3 to 4 minutes. Drain them on the baking sheet.

Season the cakes to taste with salt and serve them immediately, or keep them warm in the oven for up to 1 hour.

CAUSA DE ATÚN

CHILLED MASHED POTATOES WITH TUNA, LIME, AND CHILES

Causa is a cold mashed potato dish that is popular all over Peru. The potatoes are typically mixed with oil, chiles, and lime juice; the filling is usually tuna or another seafood and avocado. *Causas* can be dumpling- or pie-like, with the filling in the center, or more like a terrine or layered salad, with alternating layers of filling and potato. Garnishes often include avocados, hard-boiled egg, and olives. Traditional *causa* is a hefty portion commonly eaten for lunch. This recipe is a much lighter version with an elegant single-bite presentation—great for entertaining. SERVES 8

POTATO MIXTURE

2 lb	Yukon gold potatoes, peeled and chopped
1/4 cup	extra virgin olive oil
2 Tbsp	freshly squeezed lime juice
2 Tbsp	ají amarillo chile paste (see Sources)
	Kosher salt and freshly ground black pepper

TOPPING

2	(8.5-oz) jars bonito del norte (Spanish white tuna packed in oil, see page 117), drained well
1/2 cup	quartered grape tomatoes
2 Tbsp	minced fresh Italian flat-leaf parsley

TO SERVE

2 Tbsp	ají amarillo chile paste (see Sources)
1/4 cup	slivered green olives

TO MAKE THE POTATO MIXTURE, boil the potatoes in a large saucepan of salted water until tender, about 20 minutes. Thoroughly drain the potatoes and, while they are still hot, mash them until smooth. Add the oil, lime juice, and chile paste and mix to incorporate. Season with salt and pepper. Transfer the potato mixture to a large zip-top plastic bag. (At this point the potato mixture can be refrigerated for up to 2 days.)

TO MAKE THE TOPPING, combine the bonito, tomatoes, and parsley and mix well. Season to taste with salt and pepper.

TO SERVE, cut one corner off of the bag holding the mashed potatoes and pipe the mixture into eight Asian soup spoons or appetizer plates. Top each portion with a dot of the ají amarillo paste, a bit of the tuna mixture, and a sliver of green olive.

P. 336 Papas Rellenas

P. 338 Causa de Atún

HUANCAYO

Chicha Morada | PURPLE CORN PUNCH

Yuquitas | FRIED YUCA

Ceviche de Pargo con Salsa de Maracuyá | PINK SNAPPER CEVICHE WITH PASSION FRUIT

Pachamanca | ROASTED MEATS IN BANANA LEAVES

Salsa Chimichurri | ROSEMARY-MINT CHIMICHURRI

Salsa de Huancaina | SPICY CHEESE SAUCE

Picarones con Miel | PERUVIAN DOUGHNUTS

This fun and festive menu gets going with a boozy punch, essentially a Peruvian soft drink (*chicha morada*) that you home-brew from purple corn kernels and then corrupt into a cocktail with *pisco* (Peruvian brandy) and Demerara rum. One sip of the sweet-tart punch infused with aromatic spices will all but bring on a balmy Pacific breeze like the one that drifts through any beachfront bar in Lima.

For an appetizer, there is crispy *yuquitas* (fried yuca), a ubiquitous snack and side dish in Peru, and terrifically delicious whether you serve it straight up with just a sprinkling of salt and cilantro, or bust out a little chile-spiked ketchup or some *salsa de huancaina*.

The first course is a lush, sophisticated pink snapper ceviche. Along with the chile heat and citrusy acidity typical of a Peruvian ceviche, this dish incorporates the extraordinary aroma and sweet-tart fruitiness of *maracuyá* (passion fruit) for a decidedly tropical effect.

The main event of the evening leaves the coast behind and heads into the Andes: a savory banquet-like spread of roasted meats and vegetables inspired by *pachamanca*, an iconic ritual feast of the Peruvian highlands. Traditional *pachamanca* is a big production: dig a pit in the ground and line it with glowing hot volcanic stones; layer in potatoes and sweet potatoes and marinated meats such as beef, pork, lamb, chicken, and *cuy* (guinea pig); add more hot stones and a blanket of fragrant herbs and banana leaves; top that off with corn and maybe some beans, cheese, and *humitas* (corn cakes); pile everything with damp sacks plus another stratum of hot stones; and then seal up the whole thing with a thick layer of earth and leave it to slow-cook for hours in the steamy aromatic underground chamber. Hence the name *pachamanca*—Quechua for "earth pot"—which not only describes the cooking method but evokes the symbolic significance of taking all of these ingredients born of the earth and returning them to the earth to be cooked.

In a way, *pachamanca* is really another great take on barbecue. Many if not all cultures have a favored approach to the celebratory cooking of meat outdoors; it's certainly true of the Latin cuisines I'm familiar with. This distinctly Andean mode also happens to adapt well to methods that don't require an earthen pit and incandescent volcanic stones. All over Peru, chefs and home cooks serve up various oven-based and stovetop renditions of *pachamanca*, layering assorted combinations of meat and vegetables and herbs into ceramic pots and other cooking vessels. I find that a dual-method cooking process—first roasting everything in the oven under a snug wrapping of banana leaves and aluminum foil, then finishing the meats on the grill—does an excellent job of imparting some of the steamy smokiness and earthy depth of flavor that characterizes a true pit-roasted *pachamanca*. For me, retaining this hint of earth-pot essence evokes a sense of the dish's origins in ancient Andean cultures.

Though nothing can convey the profound feeling of standing upon Machu Picchu, beholding natural and archaeological wonders that defy description and banish any doubt that the Earth is sacred, this quasi *pachamanca* does capture a uniquely Andean harmony with its combination of savory marinated meats, tender roasted potatoes, yams, and corn, and aromatic herbs. It's a really special meal, no question. A duo of brilliant sauces—herbaceous *chimichurri* and creamy *huancaina*—rounds things out nicely.

And then there are the *picarones*, which may well bring down the house. In Peru, airy, delicately spiced squash fritters like these are served at celebrations, but they are too damn good to have only on special occasions. A good *picaronera* does quite the brisk business on the streets of Peru; with a swift one-handed maneuver she whips pieces of the stretchy dough into loops and flings them into a vat of hot oil, then uses a wooden stick to spin the fritters around in the bubbling oil to perfect their round shape and cook them evenly, and finally threads the entire batch of golden brown rings onto the stick to lift them out of the oil, sliding them onto paper plates in little stacks and drizzling them with a rich syrup. A long line of hopeful patrons snakes down the block, eventually dispersing when, inevitably, the *picaronera* has once again sold out for the day. In short, expect these treats to disappear as soon as you serve them.

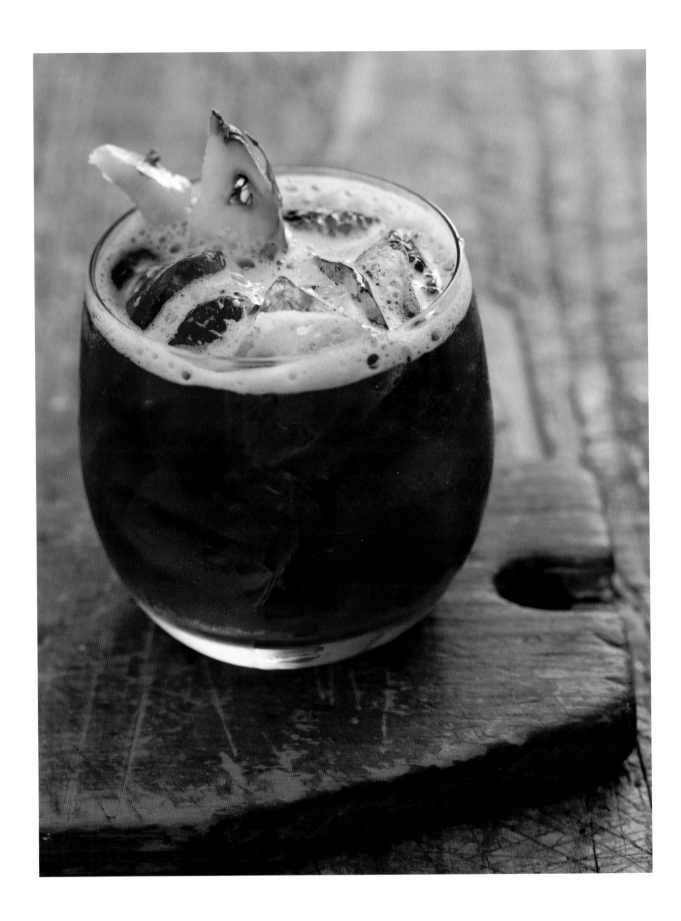

CHICHA MORADA
PURPLE CORN PUNCH

To turn a soft drink into a sangría-like cocktail, master mixologist Keith Raimondi first devised a *chicha morada* base prepared in a fairly traditional manner—a little labor intensive but well worth it for the extraordinary purple color and earthy flavor. For the alcohol component, Keith combined Peruvian brandy (*pisco*) and South American rum. (Note: Demerara rum, from Guyana, has a deep, distinctive flavor. You can substitute dark Jamaican rum, but it will change the taste of the drink a little.) The *chicha morada* base makes about 1 quart, approximately 1 1/2 cups more than you will need to make a round of cocktails for eight people. This leaves enough for a smaller second round or a batch of nonalcoholic chicha soda (just add seltzer and fruit). Or you can set aside the extra for another time—it will keep just fine in the fridge for up to 2 weeks. SERVES 8

CHICHA MORADA BASE

3	ears dried purple corn (about 1 1/2 cups; see Sources)
1 1/2 qts	water
	Skin of 1 pineapple
	Rind of 1 lemon
	Rind of 1 lime
3	cinnamon sticks
10	whole cloves

COCKTAIL

	Ice
1 cup	pisco (Peruvian brandy)
1/2 cup	Demerara rum
1/2 cup + 2 Tbsp	Simple Syrup (page 367)
1/2 cup	freshly squeezed lime juice (about 5 limes)

TO SERVE

	Ice
	Sliced fresh pineapple
	Cinnamon sticks

TO MAKE THE CHICHA MORADA BASE, strip the corn kernels off of the cobs with your hands. Combine the corn kernels, water, fruit skins, cinnamon sticks, and cloves in a large nonreactive saucepan and simmer for 1 hour.

Strain the chicha morada base and chill before use. (It can be kept in an airtight container in the refrigerator for up to 2 weeks.)

TO MAKE THE COCKTAIL, fill a large pitcher with ice. Measure out 2 1/2 cups of the chicha morada base. Combine it with the pisco, rum, simple syrup, and lime juice in the pitcher and stir vigorously.

SERVE OVER FRESH ICE and garnish each glass with a pineapple slice threaded onto a cinnamon stick.

YUQUITAS

FRIED YUCA

The boiled yuca may come out of the water looking messy. No worries: cool and drain thoroughly, then proceed with frying, and the *yuquitas* will become crispy and golden. They are delicious simply tossed with salt and cilantro, as directed here. I also like to serve them with ketchup spiked with a little *rocoto* chile paste, or with *salsa de huancaina* (page 352). SERVES 4

	Kosher salt
2 lb	yuca, peeled and cut into sticks about 1/2-inch thick and 3 inches long (the size of steak fries)
1 1/2 qts	vegetable oil
2 Tbsp	chopped fresh cilantro

Bring a large saucepan of lightly salted water to a boil. Line a large baking sheet with parchment paper.

Boil the yuca until tender, about 25 minutes. Transfer the yuca with a slotted spoon or skimmer to the baking sheet to drain and cool.

Heat the oil to 375°F in a stockpot, using a candy or deep-fry thermometer to monitor the temperature.

Fry the yuca until crispy, stirring frequently, 3 to 4 minutes.

While the yuca is frying, discard the wet parchment, wipe the baking sheet dry, and line it with fresh paper.

Transfer the yuquitas to the baking sheet with a slotted spoon or skimmer to drain briefly, then toss with salt and cilantro and serve immediately.

CEVICHE DE PARGO CON SALSA DE MARACUYÁ

PINK SNAPPER CEVICHE WITH PASSION FRUIT

This ceviche is derived from one that my team and I created for an Iron Chef America battle in which the secret ingredient was passion fruit and I relied on my knowledge of Peruvian-style ceviche preparation to pull out a winning dish. You can use any firm-fleshed white fish as long as it's supremely fresh. The sauce needs at least an hour to chill, but can be made 3 days in advance, stored in the refrigerator. SERVES 8

PASSION FRUIT SAUCE

2 tsp	minced garlic (2 cloves)
1	small shallot, finely diced
2	red Fresno chiles, seeded and minced
1/4 cup	grapeseed oil
1 qt	store-bought passion fruit juice
1/4 cup	freshly squeezed orange juice
1/4 cup	freshly squeezed lime juice
	Agave nectar (see page 72)
	Kosher salt

CEVICHE

1 lb	fresh skinless pink snapper, red snapper, or black bass fillet, pin bones removed, diced small
1/4 cup	extra virgin olive oil
2	small shallots, finely diced
2	red Fresno chiles, thinly slivered
1/4 cup	chopped fresh cilantro
	Kosher salt
2	fresh passion fruits, halved, seeds and pulp scooped out with a spoon and reserved, skin discarded
2 Tbsp	black sesame seeds
2	scallions (white and green parts), thinly sliced
	Coarse sea salt

TO MAKE THE PASSION FRUIT SAUCE, combine the garlic, shallot, chiles, and grapeseed oil in a small saucepan over low heat and cook, stirring often, until the shallots are translucent, about 10 minutes. Add the passion fruit juice and cook until reduced to 1 1/2 cups, 12 to 15 minutes. Transfer the mixture to a blender and purée until smooth. Add the orange and lime juices and pulse to combine. Season to taste with 1 Tbsp agave nectar and 1 Tbsp salt. Chill thoroughly before using, at least 1 to 2 hours and up to 3 days (keep in an airtight container).

TO MAKE THE CEVICHE, measure out 1/4 cup of the passion fruit sauce and combine it in a small bowl with the fish, olive oil, shallots, chiles, and cilantro. Season to taste with kosher salt. Divide the ceviche among eight chilled glass bowls and garnish each portion with some passion fruit seeds and pulp, black sesame seeds, scallion, and sea salt. Pass the remaining passion fruit sauce at the table.

PACHAMANCA
ROASTED MEATS IN BANANA LEAVES

Using the banana leaves approximates the steaming effect and consequent juiciness of the traditional pit method for *pachamanca*, while the grilling step at the end brings in some of the smokiness you'd get from cooking the *pachamanca* in an underground pit with hot stones, leaves, and so forth. The two sauces, highly acidic *chimichurri* and creamy *huancaina*, are delicious accompaniments to the hearty, rustic flavors of the meats and starches.

Although *huacatay* is also known as Peruvian or Andean black mint, it is not in the same plant family as any mint and no other herb really duplicates its earthy-minty flavor. It is sometimes found fresh or frozen in Latin groceries catering to a South American clientele. *Huacatay* paste is much easier to come by and makes a decent stand-in.

Start this dish a day in advance: the meats need 24 hours to marinate (see photo, page 351). SERVES 8

MARINADE

1	bunch huacatay, or 3 Tbsp huacatay paste (see Sources)
1	bunch flat-leaf parsley
2	bunches cilantro
1/2 cup	crushed garlic (about 1 head)
1/2 cup	ají rocoto chile paste (see Sources)
1 cup	chicha de jora (see Sources)

MEATS

2	racks pork spare ribs (7 to 8 lb)
1	boneless lamb shoulder (about 6 lb)
6 lb	whole skin-on, bone-in chicken legs
	Kosher salt and freshly ground black pepper

BANANA LEAVES AND VEGETABLES

1	(16-oz) package frozen banana leaves, thawed (see Sources)
8	small sweet potatoes (3 to 4 lb)
8	Yukon gold potatoes (3 to 4 lb)
8	small purple potatoes (3 to 4 lb)
4	sprigs rosemary
6 Tbsp	extra virgin olive oil
8	ears fresh sweet corn, husked

TO SERVE

1/4 cup	chopped fresh cilantro
1/4 cup	chopped fresh flat-leaf parsley
	Rosemary Mint Chimichurri (recipe follows)
	Spicy Cheese Sauce (recipe follows)

TO MAKE THE MARINADE, combine the huacatay, parsley, cilantro, garlic, and chile paste in a food processor and pulse to finely chop the herbs. Continue pulsing until the mixture forms a rough paste. With the machine running, slowly drizzle in the chicha de jora. Pulse until the marinade becomes smooth.

TO MARINATE THE MEATS, set the pork, lamb, and chicken in separate large containers, brush each with generous amounts of the marinade, cover, and marinate for 24 hours in the refrigerator.

Remove the meats from the marinade, setting aside 2 cups of the marinade, and season the meats with salt and pepper.

Place a rack in the middle position and preheat the oven to 350°F. Line a large roasting pan with heavy-duty aluminum foil. Layer in the banana leaves, overlapping the leaves, with the leaves overhanging the edge of the roasting pan by about 1 foot on all sides.

TO PREPARE THE VEGETABLES, in a large bowl, combine the sweet potatoes, Yukon gold potatoes, purple potatoes, rosemary, and oil. Toss the vegetables to lightly coat, season them with salt and pepper, and transfer them to the roasting pan, spreading them out to cover the entire bottom of the pan. Next layer in the marinated pork, lamb, and chicken, in that order, followed by the corn. Fold the banana leaves over to enclose the meat and vegetables, cover the pan tightly with two layers of foil, and cook for 3 1/2 hours.

Take the pan out of the oven and allow the pachamanca to rest for 20 minutes before opening the foil and leaves. Meanwhile, heat a charcoal grill to high. Bring the reserved marinade to a boil and simmer for 5 minutes.

Lift the meats and vegetables out of the roasting pan and set aside any juices that have accumulated in the bottom of the pan. Brush the meats with the reserved marinade and grill over direct heat until nicely charred, 4 to 5 minutes per side.

TO SERVE, carve the lamb shoulder into thin slices; separate the chicken legs and thighs; cut the pork ribs into 2-bone sections. Arrange the meats together on a large serving platter or separately on smaller serving dishes. Toss the potatoes with the reserved pan juices, cilantro, and parsley; season to taste with salt and serve in a large bowl or alongside the meats and corn. Pass small bowls of the chimichurri and cheese sauce at the table.

P. 348 Pachamanca

SALSA CHIMICHURRI

ROSEMARY-MINT CHIMICHURRI

Chimichurri is a classic accompaniment to any grilled meat or vegetable. It can be stored in an airtight container in the refrigerator for up to 3 days. MAKES 2 CUPS

3 to 4	small shallots, finely diced
1/4 cup	minced garlic (12 to 16 cloves)
1/2 cup	extra virgin olive oil
2 Tbsp	dried oregano
1/2 cup	red wine vinegar
1/4 cup	minced fresh rosemary
2 Tbsp	granulated sugar
1/4 cup	minced fresh mint leaves
2 Tbsp	chopped fresh parsley
1 tsp	ancho powder
	Kosher salt

In a small nonreactive saucepan over medium heat, combine the shallots, garlic, oil, and oregano and cook, stirring often, until the shallots are translucent, about 10 minutes.

Take the pan off of the heat, stir in the vinegar, rosemary, and sugar, and allow to cool to room temperature. Fold in the mint, parsley, and ancho powder and season to taste with salt just before serving.

SALSA DE HUANCAINA

SPICY CHEESE SAUCE

My mom used to make a very basic, blender-mixed version of *huancaina*, which she served alongside boiled potatoes—an adaptation of her Peruvian friend Armida's traditional *papas a la huancaina*. Creamy, with bits of cheese and a touch of heat, this sauce is the perfect companion to starchy root vegetables of any kind. Store leftover sauce in an airtight container in the refrigerator for up to 3 days.

MAKES ABOUT 3 1/2 CUPS

2 Tbsp	vegetable oil
1	Spanish onion, finely diced
2 Tbsp	chopped garlic (4 to 6 cloves)
1/4 cup	ají amarillo chile paste (see Sources)
2 cups	canned evaporated milk
1/4 lb	queso fresco, grated (1 cup)
6	saltine crackers
	Kosher salt and freshly ground black pepper

Heat the oil in a small skillet over medium heat. Add the onion and garlic and cook, stirring often, until translucent, about 10 minutes. Stir in the chile paste and cook until very fragrant, about 3 minutes.

Transfer the mixture to a food processor. Add the milk, cheese, and crackers and purée until smooth. Strain through a medium-mesh sieve and season to taste with salt and pepper.

P. 348 Pachamanca

P. 352 Salsa Chimichurri

P. 352 Salsa de Huancaina

PICARONES CON MIEL
PERUVIAN DOUGHNUTS

These doughnuts were inspired by the ones at Bolivar, the restaurant in New York City where I got my first professional experience cooking Peruvian food. The *picarones* at Bolivar were made with sweet potato and served with an anise-scented syrup; at Chifa we use pumpkin purée and serve them with a fragrant infused honey that features star anise as well as bay leaf and cinnamon. Any leftover honey can be used anywhere you would use regular honey; store it in an airtight container at room temperature. SERVES 8

INFUSED HONEY

1	navel orange
2 cups	acacia honey (see Sources)
2	bay leaves (preferably fresh)
1	cinnamon stick
1	star anise

PICARONES

2	(1/4-oz) packets instant yeast
1/4 cup	warm milk
2 Tbsp	granulated sugar
1	large egg
2 cups	canned pumpkin purée
1 tsp	kosher salt
3 cups	all-purpose flour
1 1/2 qts	vegetable oil, for frying
	Confectioners' sugar, for serving (optional)

TO MAKE THE INFUSED HONEY, use a vegetable peeler to remove the zest (with no pith) from the orange in wide strips; set aside the fruit for another use. Combine the orange zest with the honey, bay leaves, cinnamon stick, and star anise in a small saucepan and bring to a simmer over medium heat. Take the pan off the heat and allow the honey to steep for 1 hour. Strain the honey, cover, and store at room temperature until needed.

TO MAKE THE PICARONES, combine the yeast with the warm water in a small bowl and leave at room temperature for 10 minutes until foamy. Transfer the mixture to the bowl of a stand mixer fitted with a dough hook. Add the sugar, egg, pumpkin purée, and salt and mix on medium speed until well combined. Slowly add the flour, about one-half cup at a time. Continue to mix at medium speed until the dough is smooth and elastic, about 8 minutes. Turn the dough out onto a clean, dry work surface, cover it with a clean, dry kitchen towel, and leave it to rise at room temperature until doubled in size, about 1 hour.

Heat the oil to 350°F in a stockpot, using a candy or deep-fry thermometer to monitor the temperature. Line a baking sheet with parchment paper.

Punch down the dough with your fists, deflating it enough to handle and portion it into 16 equal balls. Roll each ball into a 6-inch rope (3 inches in diameter) and press the ends together to form a ring. Let the rings rest for 10 minutes.

Fry the rings in batches, turning once, until crispy and golden brown, about 2 minutes per side. Drain on the baking sheet.

Sprinkle the picarones with confectioners' sugar and serve hot, with the infused honey drizzled over the top or in a bowl for dipping.

CHIFA

Peru has its very own version of Cantonese cuisine, evolved over 150-some years and hugely popular in Lima, where Chinese restaurants are said to number in the thousands, many of them hole-in-the-wall joints along the Calle Capón, the city's Chinatown.

Both the food served in these places and the establishments themselves are known as *chifa*. In characteristic Peruvian fashion, *chifa* dishes are bold and generously spiced with *ají* (chiles). In some cases, not much has been altered in the translation, as with pork spareribs and cabbage-filled egg rolls; in other instances, the hybrid has produced unique dishes like *lomo saltado* (page 320) and *chaufa* rice. The combination of these two seemingly different food cultures—the way their common elements, such as fresh seafood, liberal seasoning, and rice-based dishes come together—is endlessly fascinating to me, simultaneously new and comfortingly familiar. *Chaufa* rice perfectly illustrates this aspect; it's a distinctly Peruvian take on Cantonese shrimp fried rice, and it's one of my favorite menu items from my very own *chifa*-inspired restaurant, Chifa. *(Recipe follows.)*

ARROZ CHAUFA

SHRIMP, CHORIZO, AND MANGO FRIED RICE

Sushi rice isn't Chinese, but works well here because it's soft and sticky, binding together especially well with the other ingredients and crisping up nicely. Mango brings some natural sweetness and tartness that balances out the overall richness of the dish. Be sure to make the sushi rice ahead of time and give it time to chill. SERVES 4

1/4 cup	vegetable oil
1 cup	peeled finely diced Spanish chorizo (about 4 oz)
3 Tbsp	minced peeled fresh ginger
3 Tbsp	minced garlic (8 to 10 cloves)
8	fresh large shrimp, peeled and deveined, tails removed
1/2 lb	Chinese long beans, haricots verts, or green beans, cut crosswise into 1/2-inch pieces (1 cup)
1 cup	shelled cooked edamame
3 1/2 cups	cooked sushi rice, cold
1 1/2 cups	Soy Glaze (page 320)
1/2 cup	finely diced mango
3 or 4	scallions (white and green parts), thinly sliced on the diagonal
4	large eggs, scrambled
2 Tbsp	chopped fresh cilantro
	Kosher salt and freshly ground black pepper

Heat the oil in a wok or a large cast-iron skillet over high heat. Add the chorizo and stir-fry until just rendered and crispy, about 2 minutes.

Add the ginger, garlic, shrimp, long beans, and edamame and stir-fry until the vegetables are slightly charred at the edges, about 1 minute.

Add the rice and continue stir-frying until the rice is warmed through and slightly crispy, about 2 minutes.

Add the soy glaze and toss to lightly coat the rice. Transfer the rice mixture to a bowl and stir in the mango, scallion, scrambled eggs, and cilantro. Season the chaufa with salt and pepper to taste and portion into four warm bowls.

SUISIN
Hi Quality & Sharp
Kitchen Knife
白二鋼
RICHCRAFT STAINLESS MADE IN LOS ANGELES USA
CDN

APPENDIX

BASICS

CHICKEN STOCK

MAKES 1 1/2 GALLONS

2 gallons	cold water
5 lb	chicken wings
2	large Spanish onions, diced small
2	large celery stalks, diced small
1	large carrot, peeled and diced small
1	leek (white and light green part only), cleaned and diced small
1	plum tomato, quartered
10	sprigs thyme
2	bay leaves (preferably fresh)
10	whole black peppercorns
3	juniper berries

Combine everything in a stockpot and bring to a low boil. Reduce the heat and simmer for 2 hours, periodically skimming off any foam that forms on the surface as the stock cooks.

Remove the pot from the heat. Prepare a deep ice bath in the kitchen sink. Strain the stock through a fine-mesh sieve into a nonreactive container and chill in the ice bath. Skim the fat off the surface of the cooled stock.

Transfer the stock to smaller containers and store in the refrigerator, covered, for up to 3 days, or freeze for up to 3 months.

ROASTED CHICKEN STOCK

MAKES 2 GALLONS

2 Tbsp	vegetable oil
5 lb	chicken wings
2	large Spanish onions, diced small
2	large celery stalks, diced small
1	large carrot, peeled and diced small
1	leek (white and light green part only), cleaned and diced small
1	plum tomato, quartered
1/2 cup	tomato paste
2 cups	dry red wine
2	sprigs rosemary
10	sprigs thyme
2	bay leaves (preferably fresh)
10	whole black peppercorns
3	juniper berries
3 gallons	cold water

Place a large roasting pan in the oven and preheat to 450°F.

Pour the oil into the hot pan, then add the chicken wings in a single layer. Roast until browned on all sides, 20 to 25 minutes. Transfer the wings to a stockpot and set aside.

Spread the onions, celery, carrot, and leeks evenly in the roasting pan, return to it to the oven, and roast the vegetables, stirring frequently, until very tender and lightly caramelized, about 15 minutes. Add the plum tomato and tomato paste and stir to incorporate; roast until the tomato is lightly caramelized, about 10 minutes. Add the red wine, rosemary, thyme, bay leaves, peppercorns, and juniper berries and roast until the wine is reduced by three-quarters, about 10 minutes.

Remove the pan from the oven and transfer the vegetables to the stockpot. Add the water and bring to a low boil, then reduce to a simmer and cook until the stock is slightly reduced, about 3 hours, periodically skimming off any foam that forms on the surface as the stock cooks.

Remove the pot from the heat. Prepare a deep ice bath in the kitchen sink. Strain the stock through a fine-mesh sieve into a nonreactive container, and chill in the ice bath. Skim the fat off the surface of the cooled stock.

Transfer the stock to smaller containers and store in the refrigerator, covered, for up to 3 days, or freeze for up to 3 months.

BEEF STOCK

MAKES 2 GALLONS

3 gallons	cold water
2 Tbsp	vegetable oil
8 lb	beef stock bones (available at most butcher shops)
2	large Spanish onions, diced small
2	large celery stalks, diced small
1	jumbo carrot, peeled and diced small
1	leek (white and light green part only), cleaned and diced small
1	plum tomato, quartered
1/2 cup	tomato paste
2 cups	dry red wine
2	sprigs rosemary
10	sprigs thyme
2	bay leaves (preferably fresh)
10	whole black peppercorns
3	juniper berries

Place a large roasting pan in the oven and preheat to 450°F.

Pour the oil into the hot pan and arrange the beef bones in a single layer. Roast until browned on all sides, 20 to 25 minutes. Transfer the bones from the roasting pan to a stockpot and set aside.

Spread the onion, celery, carrot, and leek in the roasting pan, return it to the oven, and roast the vegetables, stirring frequently, until very tender and lightly caramelized, about 15 minutes. Add the plum tomato and tomato paste and stir to incorporate; roast until the tomato paste is lightly caramelized, about 10 minutes. Add the red wine, rosemary, thyme, bay leaves, peppercorns, and juniper berries and roast until the wine is reduced by three-quarters, about 10 minutes.

Remove the pan from the oven and transfer the cooked vegetables to the stockpot. Add the water and bring to a low boil, then reduce the heat to a simmer and cook until the stock is slightly reduced, about 3 hours, periodically skimming off any foam that forms on the surface as the stock cooks.

Remove the pot from the heat. Prepare a deep ice bath in the kitchen sink. Strain the stock through a fine-mesh sieve into a nonreactive container, and chill in the ice bath. Skim the fat off the surface of the cooled stock.

Transfer the stock to smaller containers and store in the refrigerator, covered, for up to 3 days, or freeze for up to 3 months.

VEGETABLE STOCK

MAKES 2 GALLONS

3 gallons	cold water
3	Spanish onions, coarsely chopped
3	celery stalks, coarsely chopped
1	large carrot, peeled and coarsely chopped
2	beefsteak tomatoes, quartered
2	Granny Smith apples, cored, coarsely chopped
1	small fennel bulb, with green tops, coarsely chopped
2	bay leaves (preferably fresh)
10	sprigs thyme
10	whole black peppercorns
2	juniper berries

Combine everything in a stockpot and bring to a simmer over medium heat. Gently cook for 1 hour, periodically skimming off any foam that forms on the surface as the stock cooks.

Remove the pot from the heat. Prepare a deep ice bath in the kitchen sink. Strain the stock through a fine-mesh sieve into a nonreactive container, and chill in the ice bath.

Transfer the stock to smaller containers and store in the refrigerator, covered, for up to 3 days, or freeze for up to 3 months.

MUSHROOM STOCK

MAKES 1 1/2 GALLONS

1/4 cup	vegetable oil
1 lb	cremini mushrooms with stems, brushed clean and coarsely chopped (about 3 cups)
1	Spanish onion, diced small (about 1 cup)
1	celery stalk, diced small (about 1/2 cup)
4	cloves garlic, crushed
1 cup	dry sherry
10	sprigs thyme
1	sprig rosemary
10	whole black peppercorns
2	juniper berries
2 gallons	cold water

Heat the oil in a stockpot over high heat. Add the mushrooms and cook until well browned, 10 to 12 minutes, stirring frequently. Add onions, celery, and garlic and cook until translucent, about 10 minutes more. Add the sherry and cook, scraping up the browned bits, until the liquid has completely evaporated.

Add the thyme, rosemary, black peppercorns, juniper berries, and water and bring to a simmer over medium heat. Gently cook the stock for 1 hour, periodically skimming off any foam that forms on the surface as the stock cooks.

Remove the pot from the heat. Prepare a deep ice bath in the kitchen sink. Strain the stock through a fine-mesh sieve into a nonreactive container, and chill in the ice bath.

Transfer the stock to smaller containers and store in the refrigerator, covered, for up to 3 days, or freeze for up to 3 months.

FISH STOCK

MAKES 1 1/2 GALLONS

2 gallons + 2 gallons	cold water
2 cups	kosher salt
3 lb	whole cleaned flatfish, such as flounder or sole
4 cups	ice cubes
1	large Spanish onion, diced small
2	large celery stalks, diced small
	Zest of 2 navel oranges, in strips
2	bay leaves (preferably fresh)
10	whole white peppercorns
10	coriander seeds
	Pinch of Spanish saffron threads

In a stockpot, stir together 2 gallons of the cold water with the kosher salt until the salt is completely dissolved. Add the fish bodies and ice cubes and let sit for 30 minutes. (This purges the blood from the fish.) Drain the fish and rinse them under cold running water. Discard the soaking water, which will be very murky.

Wash out the stockpot and combine the remaining 2 gallons of cold water with the purged fish bodies and the onion, celery, orange zest, bay leaves, white peppercorns, coriander seeds, and saffron. Bring to a simmer over medium heat and gently cook for 1 hour, periodically skimming off any foam that forms on the surface as the stock cooks.

Remove the pot from the heat. Prepare a deep ice bath in the kitchen sink. Strain the stock through a fine-mesh sieve into a nonreactive container, and chill in the ice bath.

Transfer the stock to smaller containers and store in the refrigerator, covered, for up to 3 days, or freeze for up to 3 months.

ROASTED GARLIC

MAKES ABOUT 3/4 CUP

A quick note about roasted garlic as I have used it throughout this book: I have found that a much more versatile and easy method for roasting garlic is to cook it gently in oil, similar to the manner in which you would confit a protein or dense vegetable. Not only does the garlic cook evenly, but it can be stored for up to two weeks, submerged in its cooking oil. Also, the oil is extremely useful in marinades and is great for dressing vegetables before roasting or grilling.

1 cup	peeled garlic cloves
2 cups	vegetable oil

Preheat the oven to 325°F.

Combine the garlic and oil in a shallow baking dish made of glass or other nonreactive material. The garlic cloves must be completely submerged, or they will not cook evenly. Cover the baking dish tightly with aluminum foil and bake until the garlic is very tender and lightly caramelized, 45 minutes to 1 hour.

Take the baking dish out of the oven and allow the garlic and oil to cool to room temperature before transferring them to a sealed container. Keep refrigerated until needed, up to 2 weeks.

CARAMELIZED ONIONS

MAKES 1 CUP

3 Tbsp	vegetable oil
1	large Spanish onion, sliced very thin
1 tsp	kosher salt

Heat the oil in a large sauté pan over medium-high heat. Add the onion and salt and cook, stirring frequently, until the onions are soft and deeply browned, 15 to 18 minutes. Transfer the onions to a dinner plate to cool before using. Store the caramelized onions in a sealed container in the refrigerator for up to 4 days.

ROASTED PLUM TOMATOES

MAKES 4 CUPS

12	plum tomatoes, cut lengthwise into 8 equal wedges
1/3 cup	extra virgin olive oil
6	sprigs thyme, leaves finely chopped
	Kosher salt and freshly ground black pepper

Preheat the oven to 325°F.

Combine the tomatoes, oil, and thyme leaves in a large bowl, toss gently to coat the tomatoes with the oil and herbs, and season with salt and pepper. Transfer the tomatoes to a baking sheet lined with a perforated rack and spread into a single layer. Roast until the tomatoes are well wilted and slightly dried out, 20 to 25 minutes. Keep a close eye on the tomatoes as they are cooking; you want them gently cooked, not browned. The finished tomatoes will have an intense red color and full, concentrated tomato flavor. The tomatoes can be stored in an airtight, nonreactive container in the refrigerator for up to 1 week.

PICKLED JALAPEÑOS

MAKES ABOUT 1 CUP

1/2 cup	water
1/4 cup	cider vinegar
2 Tbsp	granulated sugar
1 tsp	kosher salt
1 tsp	dried Mexican oregano
5 or 6	jalapeños, sliced crosswise into rings

Combine the water, vinegar, sugar, salt, and oregano in a small saucepan and bring to boil over high heat. Remove from the heat and allow to cool to room temperature.

Transfer to a jar or other container with a tight-fitting lid and add the jalapeño slices. The pickles can be used after 2 hours. They will keep in the refrigerator for up to 1 week.

WHITE RICE

MAKE ABOUT 5 CUPS COOKED RICE

2 cups	long-grain white rice
3 cups	water
2 Tbsp	vegetable oil
	Pinch of kosher salt

Combine the rice, water, oil, and salt in a medium saucepan and bring to a gentle boil. Reduce the heat to low, cover, and cook until all of the water is absorbed, 16 to 18 minutes. Fluff with a fork before serving.

SIMPLE SYRUP

MAKES ABOUT 2 1/2 CUPS

Basic simple syrup, just sugar and water, will keep indefinitely in your refrigerator as long as it is kept in an airtight container. Use it to sweeten iced tea, iced coffee, and aguas frescas; or steep citrus peels, herbs, and spices in the hot syrup (strain before storing) to add another dimension to your favorite cocktails.

2 cups	granulated sugar
2 cups	water

Combine the sugar and water in a medium saucepan and stir to dissolve the sugar. Bring to a boil, then reduce the heat and simmer until it thickens slightly. Use the syrup right away if steeping or cool thoroughly before using in iced drinks.

DRY-TOASTING NUTS AND SEEDS

It's generally preferable to toast nuts and seeds whole, so that they cook evenly. Crushed nuts and ground seeds tend to burn easily. Depending on how well your oven is calibrated, the actual time the toasting takes may vary from the typical range of 5 to 7 minutes, less for small seeds, more for large nuts—so it's best to stay close to the oven and check for doneness from time to time. While you watch and wait, note how the nuts or seeds look and smell as they toast. If you happen to burn a small batch, don't fret, just remember the associated aroma; this will help you learn to use your senses in the kitchen.

Preheat the oven to 325°F.

Spread the nuts or seeds in an even layer on a flat, unlined, rimmed baking sheet. Put the sheet in the oven and toast the nuts or seeds, checking frequently, until they are light golden and very fragrant. You may need to rotate the baking sheet to ensure even cooking. Remove pan from oven and allow the nuts to cool to room temperature before using. Nuts can be stored in an airtight container at room temperature for up to 1 week.

TOASTING SPICES

Toasting spices, just like toasting nuts and seeds, is a delicate process that requires your full attention— toasted becomes burnt in just a few moments' time. When toasting an assortment of spices, be sure to keep them separate, as differences in their size and density will affect how they toast. It's very helpful to have several rimmed baking sheets on hand to speed up the process. Always use whole seeds, berries, pods, and so forth; ground spices will just burn.

Preheat the oven to 325°F.

Spread the spice in a single even layer on a flat, rimmed baking sheet and toast until fragrant, 2 to 5 minutes, depending on size and density. Cool completely before grinding in a dedicated coffee grinder. Store the ground spices in a sealed container until needed, up to 1 week.

CHARRING VEGETABLES

Place a rack in the top position of the oven and heat the broiler to high. Set the vegetables on a clean, dry baking sheet (with no oil or seasoning of any kind) and broil until heavily browned, turning once halfway through, 10 to 12 minutes. Store the vegetables in a sealed container in the refrigerator for up to 3 days.

ROASTING FRESH CHILES

To roast fresh chiles one by one on a gas stove, turn on one of the burners to high and set a chile directly over the flame, turning it with tongs until the skin is charred all over, 5 to 7 minutes per chile.

Alternatively, dry-roast chiles in a sauté pan over high heat (do not put oil or anything else in the pan other than the chiles), turning them with tongs until charred, 8 to 10 minutes.

Transfer the charred chiles to a bowl and cover the bowl with plastic wrap. (This will allow the skins to steam off.) Once the chiles have cooled, use a damp kitchen towel to wipe the charred skins away from the flesh. Discard the skins and stems, and cut open the chiles, scraping the seeds out with a knife. Be sure to wash your hands immediately.

CHILE PASTE

This method can be used to make a paste out of any type of dried chile.

	Dried chiles, dry-toasted
	Hot water

Put the chiles in a heatproof container and cover with hot water. Weigh down the chiles with a small salad plate or saucer and leave them to steep until very soft, 10 to 12 minutes.

Drain the chiles over a bowl to catch the soaking liquid. Transfer the chiles to a blender and purée until very smooth, adding enough of the soaking liquid to form a paste. Strain the purée through fine-mesh sieve to remove any remaining tough bits, pressing on the purée with the back of a spoon. Keep the chile paste refrigerated in an airtight container until needed; it keeps well for several weeks.

TOASTING DRIED CHILES

There are dozens of varieties of dried chiles throughout Mexico and Latin America, most of which benefit from a quick toasting in a warm oven (or briefly—and very carefully—flashed over an open flame) to heighten their flavors, some sweet and fruity, some nutty, some floral, and some just plain hot. As with nuts, seeds, and spices, it's important to pay close attention when toasting chiles; they need only a minute or so to bring out their oils and will proceed to burnt—and bitter tasting—very easily.

I recommend wearing a pair of latex or vinyl surgical gloves when handling chiles. You can find them easily at most drug stores or online in a small, easy-to-manage quantity.

	Dried Mexican chiles (such as guajillo, ancho, or pasilla)

Preheat oven to 250°F.

Remove and discard the stems, cut open the chile, and scrape out the seeds and internal ribs with a knife. Lay the chiles in a single layer on a baking sheet. Transfer the sheet to the oven and toast until the chiles are pliable and very fragrant, no more than 1 minute. Use the chiles while still warm.

APPENDIX

SOURCES

I am willing to bet that you will find most of what you need right in your own neighborhood, or reasonably close by, if you look. There may be a Mexican or Cuban flag dominating the front window of local groceries, but in most cases they are not nationally exclusive and seek to cater to the needs of the smaller Latin-American communities as a whole. And it's not uncommon these days for most big box grocery stores, or even your local farmers' markets, to carry some of these items, usually at very reasonable prices. So I encourage you to explore the unfamiliar, as you have already begun to do as you read this book, and see what you discover right around you.

As I mentioned earlier, my father and I would venture into a Mexican grocery to find nearly everything we needed, and we weren't cooking Mexican food at home. This was my early lesson, and one of my first and fondest experiences with culinary exploration and travel, before I was even allowed to leave my own street without permission. Go find what you are looking for.

Acacia Honey

WHAT IT IS: A clear, delicate honey with vanilla and floral aromas and a liquid, even runny, texture

WHERE TO FIND IT: L'Epicerie (lepicerie.com), amazon.com

WHAT TO USE INSTEAD: Any raw honey

Achiote

WHAT IT IS: A brick-red paste originally from the Yucatán with a mild flavor; made from the seeds of the annatto tree and other spices

WHERE TO FIND IT: Local Latin grocer, amazon.com

Ají Amarillo Pepper Paste

WHAT IT IS: A paste made from fruity, pungent yellow-orange chiles, common in Peru

WHERE TO FIND IT: Local Latin grocer, amazon.com, La Tienda (tienda.com)

WHAT TO USE INSTEAD: Anaheim chiles, which are similar in flavor but lack the vibrant color

Ají Panca Pepper Paste

WHAT IT IS: A paste made from the mild, fruity, dark red Peruvian pepper

WHERE TO FIND IT: Local Latin grocer, amazon.com, La Tienda (tienda.com)

WHAT TO USE INSTEAD: Guajillo chile paste

Ají Rocoto Pepper Paste

WHAT IT IS: A paste made from the slightly fruity yet very spicy red ají rocoto pepper, one of the indigenous chiles central to traditional Peruvian cooking

WHERE TO FIND IT: Local Latin grocer, amazon.com, La Tienda (tienda.com)

WHAT TO USE INSTEAD: Habanero chile paste

Amarena Fabbri Cherries

WHAT THEY ARE: Small, deep red, slightly sour Italian cherries packaged in a sugar syrup

WHERE TO FIND THEM: Di Bruno Bros (dibruno.com), amazon.com

WHAT TO USE INSTEAD: Fresh, pitted black cherries soaked in brandy and simple syrup (equal parts) for 24 hours

Arbequina Olive Oil

WHAT IT IS: Sweet, fruity, creamy oil pressed from the small, greenish-brown arbequina olive, native to Spain

WHERE TO FIND IT: Despaña Brand Foods (despanabrandfoods.com), La Tienda (tienda.com), Olé Olé (oleolefoods.com), amazon.com

WHAT TO USE INSTEAD: Any high-quality extra virgin olive oil that's light-bodied, with a lightly fruity/olive flavor

Avocado Oil

WHAT IT IS: Oil pressed from the pulp of the avocado, comparable to extra virgin olive oil

WHERE TO FIND IT: Amazon.com

WHAT TO USE INSTEAD: Extra virgin olive oil

Baby Whitebait

WHAT IT IS: Tiny, immature fish of various species—in Spanish cuisine often including anchovies or sardines—eaten whole, as the head, tail, and bones all break down when they're cooked

WHERE TO FIND IT: Local Asian grocers and fish markets

Banana Leaves

WHAT THEY ARE: The fibrous leaves of the banana tree; used for wrapping food but not typically eaten

WHERE TO FIND THEM: Local Latin grocer (frozen section), amazon.com

Cachucha Chiles

WHAT THEY ARE: Mild, sweet Cuban chiles similar in shape to habaneros, but without the heat

WHERE TO FIND THEM: Local Latin grocer

Caperberries

WHAT THEY ARE: From the same plant (the caper bush) as capers, but whereas capers are the immature buds of the bush, caperberries are the actual flowers—much bigger than capers (about the size of a grape) and with more pronounced flavor

WHERE TO FIND THEM: Amazon.com

Chipotle Chile in Adobo

WHAT THEY ARE: Smoke-dried jalapeños canned in a marinade usually containing tomatoes, salt, garlic, spices, and vinegar; pronounced smoky flavor and a tendency to be spicy

WHERE TO FIND THEM: Latin aisle of any supermarket, local Latin grocer, amazon.com

WHAT TO USE INSTEAD: Ancho chiles

Choclo

WHAT IT IS: Oversized, chewy South American corn kernels

WHERE TO FIND IT: Often sold frozen at local Latin grocers, amazon.com (canned)

WHAT TO USE INSTEAD: Fresh white corn

Corn Nuts

WHAT THEY ARE: Corn kernels that have been soaked in water, then roasted or deep-fried

WHERE TO FIND THEM: Local Latin grocer, amazon.com

Dried Fava Beans

WHAT THEY ARE: Broad, flattish beans also known as broad beans

WHERE TO FIND THEM: Amazon.com

Duck Legs, Confit

WHAT IT IS: A typically French preparation for duck, in which it is salt-cured for up to 36 hours, then poached in its own fat

WHERE TO FIND THEM: D'Artagnan (dartagnan.com)

Guindilla Peppers, Dried

WHAT THEY ARE: Long dried red chiles with a medium-hot flavor

WHERE TO FIND THEM: Local Latin grocer

WHAT TO USE INSTEAD: Other dried chiles, such as milder Mexican guajillo and pasilla chiles; crushed red pepper

Guindilla Peppers, Pickled

WHAT THEY ARE: Young guindillas picked while thin and green, pickled in vinegar, and often enjoyed with tapas for their spicy-sweet, tangy flavor

WHERE TO FIND THEM: La Tienda (tienda.com), amazon.com

WHAT TO USE INSTEAD: Pepperoncini

Hominy, Dried and Canned

WHAT IT IS: Dried corn kernels that have undergone nixtamalization, an ancient Mesoamerican process of soaking and cooking in limewater

WHERE TO FIND IT: Latin aisle of major supermarkets; local Latin grocer, amazon.com

WHAT TO USE INSTEAD: Fresh white corn

Huacatay

WHAT IT IS: An herb known as Peruvian black mint, with a strong fragrance; available fresh, dried, and as a paste

WHERE TO FIND IT: Latin Merchant (latinmerchant.com), amazon.com

Ibarra Chocolate

WHAT IT IS: A brand of Mexican dark chocolate flavored with cinnamon and sugar; often sold in thick disks

WHERE TO FIND IT: Local Latin grocer, amazon.com

WHAT TO USE INSTEAD: Any dark, almost bitter, chocolate

La Peral

WHAT IT IS: A blue-veined, slightly crumbly, buttery cheese from Asturias in northern Spain; made from pasteurized cow's and sheep's milk

WHERE TO FIND IT: Amazon.com, Artisanal Premium Cheese (artisanalcheese.com), Di Bruno Bros (dibruno.com)

WHAT TO USE INSTEAD: Gorgonzola, Cabrales

Malanga

WHAT IT IS: A staple root vegetable throughout much of the Caribbean; brown and a bit hairy on the outside and creamy white, yellow, or even pinkish on the inside, depending on the variety; related to the taro root
WHERE TO FIND IT: local Latin grocer
WHAT TO USE INSTEAD: Taro root

Masa Harina

WHAT IT IS: Dried corn flour; a staple in Mexican cooking; Maseca is the most recognizable brand.
WHERE TO FIND IT: Local Latin grocer, amazon.com

Pequín Chile Powder

WHAT IT IS: Powder ground from the very spicy pequín chile; popular in Mexican cuisine
WHERE TO FIND IT: Local Latin grocer, amazon.com
WHAT TO USE INSTEAD: Cayenne powder, chile de árbol powder, ground Aleppo pepper

Purple Corn, Dried

WHAT IT IS: A strain of corn cultivated in Peru that is instantly recognizable by its deep purple hue
WHERE TO FIND IT: Amazon.com (kernels), La Tienda (tienda.com) (whole cobs)

Rabbit Legs

WHAT THEY ARE: Comparable in flavor to chicken, a very lean meat; have been hunted as game but also bred for their meat
WHERE TO FIND THEM: D'Artagnan (dartagnan.com)
WHAT TO USE INSTEAD: Chicken legs

Seville Oranges

WHAT THEY ARE: The variety of orange used to make orange marmalade; also known as bitter or sour oranges
WHERE TO FIND THEM: Local Latin grocer, some supermarkets and specialty produce markets (often available on request or by special order)
WHAT TO USE INSTEAD: Cara cara oranges, any good quality orange

Sweetbreads

WHAT THEY ARE: The thymus glands of veal, lamb, or pork (usually from animals less than a year old, as the gland shrinks and disappears as the animal grows); earthy flavor
WHERE TO FIND THEM: D'Artagnan (dartagnan.com)

Tahitian Vanilla Bean

WHAT IT IS: A variety of vanilla bean prized by many pastry chefs as the best in the world
WHERE TO FIND THEM: Amazon.com
WHAT TO USE INSTEAD: Any variety of vanilla bean

White Anchovy Fillets, Marinated in Olive Oil

WHERE TO FIND THEM: Amazon.com
WHAT TO USE INSTEAD: Fresh sardine fillets, packed in salt and marinated in olive oil

White Arepa Flour

WHAT IT IS: Instant white corn flour; Doñarepa is a good brand
WHERE TO FIND IT: Local Latin grocer, amazon.com

Yuca Flour

WHAT IT IS: Flour made from yuca, a starchy vegetable, also known as manioc and cassava; common throughout Latin America
WHERE TO FIND IT: Local Latin grocer, amazon.com, Whole Foods

Yuzu Juice

WHAT IT IS: Juice that comes from the yuzu fruit, a golfball-size grapefruit, and is frequently used in Japanese cuisine to impart tart flavor and strong citrusy fragrance
WHERE TO FIND IT: Local Asian grocer, amazon.com
WHAT TO USE INSTEAD: A mixture of equal parts of freshly squeezed lime, grapefruit, and orange juices

INDEX

Page numbers in italics refer to maps.

Sources for Quick Info

Aguilera Pleguezuelo, José. Las cocinas árabe y judía y la cocina española. Editorial Arguval.

Benavides-Barajas, L. Al-Andalus, la cocina y su historia: Los Reinos de Taifas, Norte de África, Judíos, Mudéjares y Moriscos. Dulcinea.

Bruhns, Karen Olsen. Ancient South America. New York: Cambridge University Press, 1994.

Coe, Sophie D. America's First Cuisines. Austin: University of Texas Press, 1994.

Gjelten, Tom. Bacardi and the Long Fight for Cuba. New York: Penguin Books, 2008.

Moseley, Michael E. The Incas and Their Ancestors: The Archaeology of Peru. New York: Thames and Hudson, 1992.

Palazuelos, Susanna. México: The Beautiful Cookbook. New York: HarperCollins Publishers, 1996.

Pilcher, Jeffrey M. ¡Que vivan los tamales! Food and the Making of Mexican Identity.

Albuquerque: University of New Mexico Press, 1998.

Trutter, Marion (Ed.). Culinaria Spain. Culinaria Könemann, 2004.

https://www.cia.gov/library/publications/the-world-factbook/geos/ec.html

https://www.cia.gov/library/publications/the-world-factbook/geos/cu.html

https://www.cia.gov/library/publications/the-world-factbook/geos/mx.html

https://www.cia.gov/library/publications/the-world-factbook/geos/pe.html

https://www.cia.gov/library/publications/the-world-factbook/geos/sp.html